The Stones of Athens

The Stones of Athens

R. E. Wycherley

Princeton University Press
Princeton, New Jersey
1978

Library of Congress Cataloging-in-Publication Data

Wycherley, Richard Ernest.
The stones of Athens.

Bibliography: p.
1. Athens—Antiquities.   2. Excavations (Archaeology)—Greece,
Modern—Athens.   I. Title.
DF275.W92   938'.5   77-72142
ISBN 0-691-03553-9
ISBN 0-691-10059-4 pbk.

This book has been composed in Linotype Granjon

Princeton University Press books are printed on acid-free paper
and meet the guidelines for permanence and durability of the
Committee on Production Guidelines for Book Longevity of the
Council on Library Resources

Printed in the United States of America

9   8   7   6   5

To Homer and Dorothy Thompson

Preface

"His eye mostly resting on stone, the quarries of ruins in the Eternal City reminded him of the quarries of maiden rock at home." When I thought of giving the whole book the title originally used for the appendix, I had these words from *The Well Beloved* of Thomas Hardy in mind and the great quarries of Penmaenmawr in view. But the title is taken without apology from Ruskin. He would, I believe, have approved at least of the idea behind the book, and of the title. We have something in common in that *The Stones of Venice* includes a section on the cries of the gondoliers.

This book is composed of a number of *Athenaioi logoi*, essays on Athenian subjects, based on a study of the monuments interpreted in the light of the literature. Several of the sections have appeared as independent articles over a number of years. These have been revised and coordinated, and others have been added to give a representative if not exhaustive account of the ancient city; but each section remains complete in itself and may be read separately or in almost any order. The first section, on the walls, attempts a historical synopsis or recapitulation, emphasizing the main epochs and the outstanding events which mark them. I assume that most readers will know something of Greek history, but many will appreciate a few reminders. The book is primarily concerned with "classical" Athens—the city of Perikles and Demosthenes, Sophokles and Aristophanes, Thucydides and Plato—which for several generations was one of the centers of the earth, and which we need to know if we are to appreciate the greatest Attic writers and artists; but from this viewpoint, as occasion arises, we shall look backward and forward over more than three millennia of Athenian history.

I have kept in mind both the general reader and, in the provision of bibliographies and notes, the student who wishes to pursue particular subjects further. Full documentation would have produced a much bulkier volume. I have tried to give key references, "blanket" references, and important new items—enough, I hope, to set the feet of the student on the right path. Sometimes he will find himself in a tangle of paths or a maze. The very nature of the evidence, even though it is much fuller than a few years ago, means that the subject teems with difficult problems and lively controversies. Having said this, and having given plenty of examples in the text below, I can make no pretence of dealing with many of these questions in detail, still less of producing "definitive" answers. One learns to say with as good a grace as possible, "I don't know." It would be treason to add "I don't care"; but in fact one can now understand the character of this most remarkable city and of the elements which composed it without solving every archaeological and topographical problem. Though there are still many gaps, the time is perhaps opportune for a synthesis of our knowledge. Since investigation was resumed after the War, notable advances have been made on many fronts. Surprisingly, even the rash of high-rise buildings, which has transformed the face of Athens yet again, has helped at various points. Lofty buildings mean deep digging for foundations, and this may penetrate the Turkish and Byzantine accretions to the Roman and Greek strata, and even the Mycenean.

One intractable problem which I make no claim to have solved is the spelling of Greek names in English. Usually I keep the ancient Greek spelling, but, as is already clear, there are names which I cannot bear to see in this form. Complete consistency is impossible. Let him who is without sin—and who writes "Aiskhulos"—cast the first stone.

My many debts can be seen in the bibliographies and notes. If the general bibliography begins with the names of Wachsmuth and Wilamowitz, Jane Harrison and James Frazer, this is not merely a pious gesture. The works of such scholars do not lose their interest and value. Judeich after nearly half a century is still indispensable; Hill after nearly a quarter still provides a very useful summary. In recent years the work of John Travlos has been of unique importance, on the sites, at the drawing board, and in his two superb books; one should constantly turn to the *Pictorial Dictionary* for a great wealth of fine illustrations. He has generously given me permission to make any use I wish of his plans and drawings; and he has taken me over the sites and answered many queries. Two other scholars whose knowledge of Athens is unsurpassed have for many years been ready to help me in every possible way—Homer Thompson and Eugene Vanderpool. Here at Bangor I have had the benefit of frequent discussions with my colleague John Ellis Jones; he has helped me greatly in the matter of illustrations, and his own lively drawings make an important contribution to the book.

For permission to adapt material from earlier articles I should like to thank the Editor of *Phoenix* (chapter 7), the Editor of *Greek Roman and Byzantine Studies* (6), the Editor of *Greece and Rome* and the Oxford University Press (3,9, Postscript), and the Editor of the *Journal of the Royal Institute of British Architects* (10).

The American School of Classical Studies at Athens and the authorities of the Agora Excavations have allowed me to use many plans, drawings and photos, mostly published in the volumes of *The Athenian Agora* and in *Hesperia*, and I should like to thank Mrs. Marian McAllister at Princeton and Mrs. Effie Sakellarakis at Athens for their helpfulness. Many of these photos are by Miss Alison Frantz, who has also allowed me to draw freely on her own magnificent collection. Mr. Manolis Vernardos of Athens has taken several photos specially for me. The German Archaeological Institute has generously provided me with a number of drawings and photos. The plan of the Kerameikos cemetery (Fig. 74), though based on the Institute's drawings, is taken from *Greek Burial Customs*, by Donna C. Kurtz and John Boardman, with the authors' permission. Professor H. Mussche has provided material on Thorikos, and passed on to me a number of drawings by J. E. Jones, originally made for a colloquium at Ghent. I am indebted to Dr. Ingeborg Scheibler for the section through the archaic cemetery (Fig. 73) and to Professor Walter Graham for the plan of an *andron* with mosaic floor (Fig. 69). Professor J. S. Boersma has not only allowed me to use several plans from *Athenian Building Policy*, but has lent me the original drawings of these. Professor Frank Brommer has sent me several photos of details of the Parthenon; I owe the photo of the column drums of the Olympieion to Mr. Travlos and that of the Boundary of the Garden of the Muses to Professor Vanderpool; the title page shows, with Professor Homer Thompson's permission, a water color in his possession. I should like to thank all these, and also the publishers who have freely concurred in the use of this material, Verlag Ernst Wasmuth, Tübingen (Travlos, *Pictorial Dictionary*), H. D. Tjeenk Willink, Groningen (Boersma, *Athenian Building Policy*), Thames and Hudson, London (Kurtz and Boardman, *Greek Burial Customs*), Esperos, Athens (Scheibler, *The Archaic Cemetery*).

I am much indebted to Mrs. Margaret Roberts and Miss Nerys Williams who prepared a difficult typescript; my wife who worked over the whole book at each stage and devoted much hard labor to the index; and to Princeton University Press, and in particular Miss Harriet Anderson, who have handled the book with meticulous care and patience. This, I should mention finally, is not the only Princeton connection. I could hardly have completed this work if I had not had the benefit of several periods at the Institute for Advanced Study, and the help and encouragement of many members, in particular Professor Homer Thompson and Mrs. Dorothy Thompson, and Professor B. D. Meritt and Mrs. Lucy Shoe Meritt.

October 1, 1976   R. E. WYCHERLEY
University College of North Wales

Contents

Illustrations

List of Illustrations

List of Illustrations

Abbreviations

Other shortened but recognizable titles are used in the notes when the full title has been given immediately before or appears in the chapter bibliography.

AA: *Archäologischer Anzeiger* (with *Jahrbuch*)

AAA: *Athens Annals of Archaeology*

Agora: *The Athenian Agora*, American School of Classical Studies at Athens, Princeton
> III R. E. Wycherley, *Literary and Epigraphical Testimonia*, 1957.
> XIV H. A. Thompson and R. E. Wycherley, *The Agora of Athens, the History, Shape and Uses of an Ancient City Center*, 1972

AJA: *American Journal of Archaeology*

AJP: *American Journal of Philology*

ArchEph: *Archaiologike Ephemeris*

AthMitt: *Mitteilungen des Deutschen Archäologischen Instituts, Athenische Abteilung*

BCH: *Bulletin de correspondance hellénique*

BSA: *Annual of the British School at Athens*

CQ: *Classical Quarterly*

Deltion: *Archaiologikon Deltion* (date given is year of publication, not year covered by reports)

Dinsmoor, *Architecture*: W. B. Dinsmoor, *The Architecture of Ancient Greece*, London and New York 1950

Edmonds *FAC*: J. M. Edmonds, *Fragments of Attic Comedy*, Leiden 1957–1961

Ergon: *Ergon of the Archaeological Society* (Greek)

GRBS: *Greek, Roman and Byzantine Studies*

Hill: I. T. Hill, *The Ancient City of Athens*, London 1953

IG: *Inscriptiones Graecae*

Jacoby, *FGH*: F. Jacoby, *Die Fragmente der griechischen Historiker*, Berlin and Leiden, 1923–1958

Jahrbuch: *Jahrbuch des Deutschen Archäologischen Instituts*

JHS: *Journal of Hellenic Studies*

Abbreviations

Judeich: W. Judeich, *Topographie von Athen*, 2d edn. München 1931

Richter, *Sculpture and Sculptors*: G.M.A. Richter, *Sculpture and Sculptors of the Greeks*, 4th edn. New Haven 1970

SEG: *Supplementum Epigraphicum Graecum*

Travlos, *PDA*:   J. Travlos, *Pictorial Dictionary of Ancient Athens*, New York 1971; German version Tübingen 1971

Travlos, *PEA*:   J. Travlos, *Poleodomike Exelixis ton Athenon* (in Greek; *Architectural Development of Athens*) Athens 1960

The Stones of Athens

Introduction

"There is no end to it in this city—wherever we walk, we set foot upon some history" (Lucius Cicero to Marcus and friends in 79 B.C., *de Finibus* 5.1.)

To what Cicero says we can add that wherever one digs a hole in this city, one digs up some history. Fifty or sixty such items appear annually in *Deltion*. A trench dug for a drain reveals a bit of the ancient city wall or a group of graves; the foundation trench of a house reveals a bit of an ancient house or a small shrine. Nothing escapes the watchful eyes of the Greek archaeologists; and these chance finds help greatly to fill the gaps between the extensive official excavations, and to give a picture which, though still far from complete, is much more representative of the ancient city than what we had thirty or forty years ago.

In some things we have an advantage over the Ciceros. They walked from the Gymnasium of Ptolemy, in the center of the city north of the Acropolis, past the agora, out through the main city gate, the Dipylon, past the tombs of the great men of Athens, to the "justly famous walks" of the Academy, the gymnasium and school of Plato. Around them were the monuments of classical Athens, the city of Perikles and Lycurgus, and the later buildings which were owed to the generosity of Hellenistic kings. Some of these had very recently, in 86 B.C., suffered badly when the city was violently assaulted by Sulla in the course of the Mithridatic War. The benefactions of philathenian emperors, especially Augustus and Hadrian, shown in reconstructions and splendid new buildings, were yet to come. The remains of archaic, pre-Persian Athens, the city of Peisistratos, were literally underfoot, not to be brought to light till modern times; and the same is even more true of prehistoric, Mycenean Athens.

Archaeological investigation, with the resuscitation of the ancient city, was inaugurated amid great enthusiasm soon after the liberation of Athens from the Turks. Wolfensberger's vivid painting epitomizes the situation in 1834, showing the northern part of the site of the agora, the very heart of the city. The Temple of Hephaistos stands miraculously preserved on the hill above to the west. A headless ancient giant is emerging from the ruins of Turkish houses, as if shaking himself free. The new Greece is "riding triumphantly forward."

(3)

Of the ancient buildings which still stood above ground most important of course were the great temples. On the Acropolis much of the main structure of the Parthenon, the Erechtheion, and the Propylaia had survived the damage and attrition of the centuries, though severely battered and embedded in Turkish buildings. Of the temple of Olympian Zeus in southeastern Athens sixteen of the ninety-six great columns were erect. Of other surviving structures the most impressive were certain massive sections of the walls of Hellenistic and Roman buildings, incorporated in later fortifications—the Stoa of Eumenes and the Odeion of Herodes on the south side of the Acropolis, and the Stoa of Attalos and the Library of Hadrian to the north. There were freakish survivals such as the choregic monument of Lysikrates, preserved almost intact incorporated in the structure of a monastery. Very little of the ancient city wall was standing, but its line could be traced from slight remains at various points. The agora had been repeatedly pillaged and built over; the pitiful remains lay deeply buried.

Athens was naturally designated as capital of the new Greek kingdom; and ambitious plans were put forward for combining old and new by reserving the whole of the central parts of the ancient city—the Acropolis and its slopes, and an extensive area to the north, including the agora—as an archaeological zone, to be cleared of debris and excavated. Such plans however proved to be far too ambitious. In the early phases work was concentrated on clearing the Acropolis and its southern slope, including the theaters. One very fortunate result of the clearance of the top of the hill was the revelation of the architectural and sculptural glories of the archaic Acropolis, the foundations of the great temple of Athena, and the mass of exquisite sculpture hidden away after the Persian Wars.

The work of the Greek authorities was supplemented by the foreign archaeological schools, most notably by the Germans in the region of the Dipylon and the cemetery of the Kerameikos outside. For a century the city center, the agora, still lay hidden, except for a little on the western fringe. Even to Judeich in 1930 most of this area was unknown. In 1931 the American School began what proved to be an archaeological task as formidable and as complicated as any ever undertaken, the clearance of the whole area of the agora, much of it heavily built up. After more than forty years the great work is near completion, except for a strip on the north side which is still not accessible. The remains of the very numerous monuments found *in situ* are exiguous in the extreme; but supplemented by innumerable finds of all sorts, from the finest sculpture (usually very battered) to household utensils, and interpreted in the light (often dim) of ancient literature and the thousands of inscriptions, they add to our knowledge of every part of Athenian life, besides clarifying the history and form of the center of Athens.

Meanwhile on a smaller scale much has been done in other parts of Athens too. In quite recent times much of the region around the Olympieion in the southeast, peculiarly important for its ancient cults, has been cleared. It is only in the last quarter of a century that satisfactory evidence has been found for the ordinary domestic and industrial quarters of Athens, mainly on the fringes of the agora, but also at other scattered points. Many more sections of the city wall have come to light, and its whole line can now be traced with great accuracy. Excavation at the Dipylon and in the Kerameikos has been extended. One can look forward to a time when an archaeological zone will reach out from the agora to the Dipylon and eventually on to the Academy. At present, in spite of extensive but inconclusive excavations at the Academy before and after the War, the principal deficiency in our picture of the city is due to lack of precise knowledge of any of the three great suburban gymnasia which played such an important part in Athenian life. The district immediately north of the Acropolis and east of the agora still holds important secrets, including the Prytaneion, the Theseion, and other important shrines, and the urban gymnasium of Ptolemy. One can only hope that in time the dreams of the 1830s come true.

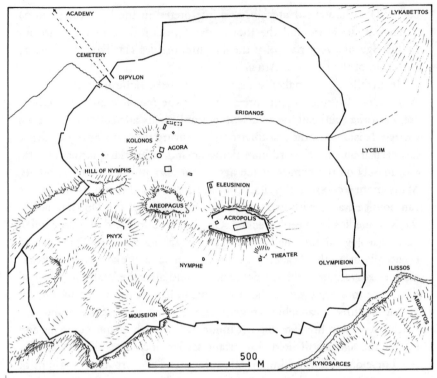

I. Athens, ca. 460 B.C., showing Themistoklean Wall (J. E. Jones, after Judeich, Travlos, and Boersma)

CHAPTER I

The Walls

The history of the walls of Athens is the history of the expansion and contraction of the city in its successive phases of growth and decline, in victory, disaster, and recovery.[1] Construction and destruction mark the great epochs; and an account of the walls will incidentally provide a general historical introduction. What follows is mainly a study of the great Themistoklean circuit of classical Athens, built immediately after the glorious defeat of the Persian invasion of 480 B.C. This was a dominant feature of the city in her greatest days, an object of immense expenditure of effort and resources by the Athenian Demos, a symbol of the power of Athens, and a notable example of Greek military architecture; and, with repeated repair and reconstruction of course, it remained more or less in being for sixteen centuries of varying fortunes, rising again and again after severe dilapidation. At the same time, in the light of modern archaeological investigation, one can put this wall in its place in a series which extends over three thousand years.

In prehistoric Athens, when the Acropolis with its immediate adjuncts was the *polis*, as Thucydides tells us (2.15.3), the fortification of the Acropolis with its outworks was the city wall. The hill was surrounded by a powerful wall in the Mycenean period, with additional fortifications, of which only slight traces have been found, to protect the main approach on the west. This fortress is probably what was known as the Pelasgikon or Pelargikon, though in certain contexts (notably Thucydides, 2.17.1) the name seems to be used of the western outwork in particular.[2] Naturally the alternative names gave rise to confusion in the minds of the ancients and of the writers of manuscripts. Pelasgikon means "building of the Pelasgi," the very obscure early inhabitants of Attica; Pelargikon means "stork-building." The origin of the name is not known; the stork seems to

[1] Maier, *Mauerbauinschriften* II 114, brings this out very clearly.

[2] Judeich 113ff; A. W. Gomme, *A Historical Commentary on Thucydides* II, Oxford 1956, 63ff; S. Iakovides, *The Mycenean Acropolis of Athens* (in Greek), Athens 1962; Travlos *PEA* 21ff; *PDA* 52, 55; R. J. Hopper, *The Acropolis*, London 1971, 22, 28. The "wooden wall" (Herodotus 8.51) presumably supplemented the old stones.

have been a bird of some significance on the early Acropolis—it is found in the decoration of the cornice of the old temple of Athena. The structure known as Enneapylon, Nine-gated, is commonly thought to be the western approach to the fortress, but this is uncertain.

In modern times the evidence of the massive walls has been supplemented increasingly by other finds; and we can see that Mycenean Athens, though not one of the major centers, was a place of moderate importance.[3]

The Pelasgic wall continued to guard the Acropolis, for seven centuries or more, that is, through the "sub-Mycenean" dark ages, the geometric period (9th and 8th centuries) when the pottery and other finds show that Athens enjoyed a certain degree of culture and prosperity even though as in the rest of Greece architecture had reverted to primitive forms, the archaic period (7th and 6th centuries) when the city made great progress commercially, politically, and artistically, and indeed up to the time of the Persian invasion (480 B.C.). On the northern side little trace of this wall has been found, and it is assumed that it has been obliterated by the post-Persian wall, built by Kimon, which took the same irregular

2. Cyclopean Wall near Propylaia (Photo: Alison Frantz)

[3] See also p. 143 below.

course; there are indications of successive posterngates east and west of the Erechtheion. On the south side, where the straight lines of the wall of Kimon thrust farther outwards, forming a great terrace, massive sections have been preserved, notably south of the Propylaia, southwest of the Parthenon (deep in the terrace fill, forming a kind of intermediate retaining wall) and at the extreme eastern end of the hill, near the modern Museum. At the southwest corner a bastion was constructed to threaten a flank of attackers who advanced as far as the principal gate. The main wall nearby abuts somewhat awkwardly on the south wing of the Propylaia. At this crucial point it is over 5m broad (elsewhere it is somewhat less). The style of the masonry is fine Cyclopean, with huge blocks of the native limestone, roughly worked on the outer face, small blocks filling the interstices, and originally with some use of clay bedding. The inner part was of less careful construction. The old wall now stands here to a height of nearly 4m; but the working of the wall of the Propylaia shows that in the fifth century it was no less than 10m high—an impressive monument to Athens' legendary past. By this time the western extension, farther down the slope, hardly served as a fortification of any kind; but its line still marked a traditionally sacred area. The old tag quoted by Thucydides said, "The Pelargikon is better unworked."

The Cyclopean wall of the Acropolis is solid enough. The very existence of a pre-Persian wall around the whole city, not to speak of its date and its course, is still a matter of dispute.[4] Literary sources are ambiguous and tell us nothing definite and positive. Even more surprising, if there was indeed a wall, is the fact that no certain trace of it has been found, whereas enough is known of the Themistoklean circuit and its gates to determine most of its course. The earlier wall may have been of simple construction, rough stone socle with crude brick superstructure; but even walls of this kind seldom vanish without trace; and some at least of its course must have run through known archaeological areas.

On general grounds, one would not expect Athens to be still unfortified at the beginning of the fifth century; as Travlos points out, walls had already been built at Eleusis. Thucydides' evidence is crucial but interpreted

---

[4] Judeich accepted it, 120ff, and so do most more recent writers—Travlos *PEA* 33f, 40f; R. Young, *Hesperia* 20, 1951, 133; Winter, *Greek Fortifications* 61; E. Vanderpool, *Phoros, Tribute to B. D. Meritt*, New York 1974, 156–60; H. Lauter, *AA* 1975, 1–9. Maier, *Mauerbauinschriften* 1 19ff, thinks it on the whole improbable.

Besides Thucydides, Herodotus 9.13.2 and Andokides 1.108 also seem to imply an early wall.

in different ways. After the Persian invasion, he says, "The Athenians set about rebuilding the city and the walls; for only short sections of the circuit (*peribolos*) were still standing" (1.89.3); and again (93. 2) "the *peribolos* of the city was extended on all sides." It is somewhat perverse to take the view that Thucydides has in mind the primitive fortifications of the Acropolis and its immediate appendages, and not an outer circuit. Of course he may simply be mistaken; but it is reasonable to assume that he knew what he was talking about, and to let him turn the scale in favor of an early wall.

Another passage (Thuc. 6.57.1–3) is relevant not only to the existence but also to the position of this wall. Finding the tyrant Hippias "outside in the Kerameikos" marshaling the Panathenaic procession, Harmodios and Aristogeiton rushed inside the gates, where they met and killed his brother Hipparchos near the shrine called the Leokorion (in 514 B.C.). This probably implies that the wall ran past the northwest corner of the classical agora; and at this point many centuries later Pausanias (1.15.1) saw a gateway which, like such structures in modern cities, e.g., Paris, may have marked the site of a primitive town gate. It has been suggested that the Arch of Hadrian, diagonally opposite in southeast Athens, may also have been the successor of the early gate; but this is even more highly conjectural—the Arch may be explained simply as an ornamental approach to the region of the Olympieion, with its fine Hadrianic buildings, the orientation being due to the line of an ancient street leading in this direction.

When so much is uncertain it is perhaps rash to attempt to trace the line of the early wall even approximately. One can assume that it formed a rough circle or ellipse around the Acropolis—this shape may have helped to suggest the adjective "wheel-shaped" which is applied to Athens in an oracle quoted by Herodotus (7.140.2)—and that on the north it stopped short of the Eridanos stream. Judeich would take it over the crest of the southwestern hills, the Mouseion, the Pnyx, and the Hill of the Nymphs. Travlos confines it more closely to the slopes of the Acropolis and the Areopagus, with a total length of about 2600m; he assumes gates on the principal arteries of communication, corresponding to the most important gates, placed farther out of course, in the Themistoklean wall.

When such a wall can have been first constructed is entirely conjectural, and dates from the late seventh century to the late sixth have been suggested. Early in the sixth century, in the time of Solon, the city expanded northwards and the spacious agora was established northwest of the

Acropolis. This quarter needed protection; the idea of enclosing the whole city was to some extent bound up with the emergence of more broadly based democratic institutions. On the other hand the tyrant Peisistratos (561–527 B.C.) was much concerned with giving visible expression to the growing power of Athens, and he may have constructed or completed the circuit.

The restored democracy had to face the might of the Persian invader; and in 480 B.C. whatever fortification the city had was quite inadequate, and victory depended on the fleet at Salamis. After the defeat of the Persians defense works took precedence over temples and public buildings.

Thucydides (1.90) describes how in 479 B.C., while Themistokles talked evasively to the Spartans, who, suspicious and jealous as ever, wished to discourage their allies from building powerful fortifications, his fellow-citizens back home threw up their new wall to a defensible height in an incredibly short time. Everyone joined in the work, and all kinds of material, including funeral monuments, were flung in. One might have expected that a wall built in such haste and in such an apparently makeshift and amateurish fashion would before long be discarded and superseded by something more deliberately planned and more carefully constructed. In fact the defenses of Athens remained for centuries essentially the Themistoklean wall.

Perhaps Thucydides exaggerates somewhat the impromptu character of the work. Though a certain amount of odd material was indeed incorporated in places, as the remains at the Dipylon and elsewhere show, the stone socle was built solidly enough. The greater part of the wall was of course of unbaked brick. "With such a method of construction," says I. T. Hill,[5] "it would certainly have been possible to complete it in the short space of a month or so"; but one doubts whether the wall reached its full height in so short a time. In fact the method was not essentially different from what was in general use. The main difference lay in the great numbers at work on the job, supplemented by a saving of time in the working of some of the stones.

It may well be that Themistokles, who with a view to developing Athenian naval power had planned and begun the massive fortifications of Peiraeus in his archonship in 493/2 B.C., had also given some thought to the planning of the wall of the upper city. In a purely makeshift job, one might have expected that the old wall would be repaired, if it existed; or if it did not, that a less extensive and ambitious circuit would be attempt-

[5] *Ancient City of Athens* 32.

ed. The line chosen allowed for a great extension of the city, and defensively it could not be greatly bettered. Where possible, i.e. mainly on the hills in the west and southwest, natural features were skillfully used. Even though remains are very scanty, the line can now be traced with great accuracy. Few continuous stretches have been thoroughly investigated, but odd bits are constantly coming to light, often in chance excavations;[6] a number of towers and gates are known—they were more solidly built than most of the rest. A few sections no longer visible were noted by early topographers such as Stuart and Revett.

The position of the cemeteries helps—it can be assumed that from the fifth century onwards all graves except those of very young children are outside the city. All this evidence leaves little to be deduced from a general consideration of the contours. In his plan of forty years ago Judeich was able to indicate the line of the wall with remarkable accuracy, and with the help of more recent finds and researches Travlos has now given it greater precision, especially on the east and south; there are more deviations from a simple continuous line, more kinks and reentrants, than was formerly imagined.[7]

From the region of the Dipylon and the Sacred Gate on the northwest the wall ran southwest to the Peiraeus Gate (excavated a few years ago) and then swung southeast to climb the Hill of the Nymphs, on the slope of which a section is still conspicuous. From here, instead of cutting across southeastwards to the Mouseion Hill, as did the later *diateichisma* or cross-wall, the Themistoklean wall made a large outward loop round the southwestern spurs of the Pnyx Hill. The course of this section, from which ran the Long Walls to Peiraeus, is not very clear, but it eventually attained the summit of the Mouseion. Descending the hill it ran almost due east, and after making several salients it turned northwards past the Olympieion. Little of the wall has been found on the eastern side; but its course can now be plotted with considerable accuracy, since at several points lucky finds have produced unmistakable traces of the ditch which was later dug outside the wall in the fourth century. Broken pottery and other rubbish was later tipped into the ditch, and this has come to light in great quantities. Remains of the Acharnian Gate and several sections of the wall give the line on the north. On this side as on the east there was little possibility of natural defense, and the wall took a fairly regular course.

[6] One finds examples in most years of *Deltion*; see Travlos *PDA* 162–63; further *Deltion* 25B, 1972, 77f.

[7] Travlos makes the total length 6450m, *PEA* 50, justifying the figure of Thucydides 2.13.7.

The Walls

The city wall was built largely in the technique which remained common in Greece even after more elegant and solid masonry had become frequent—unbaked brick on a stone socle, composed of several courses of massive well-shaped blocks on either face of a core of rougher stone. The material was poros or harder limestone, with increasing use of conglomerate in later phases. This is not the place to go into details of style and technique.[8] The masonry of Greek walls is notoriously difficult to date in default of some chance piece of archaeological evidence. Walls needed repeated reconstruction or repair, and it is often hard to say to which phase a surviving piece of masonry belongs. There is not as in other arts any clear and consistent development or sequence of styles.

The mode of construction can best be seen and studied in the neighborhood of the Dipylon and the Sacred Gate. The well-preserved section adjacent to the Sacred Gate conveniently fell apart in bad weather several years ago, and the German archaeologists were able to examine its structure before making good the damage.[9] The outer face consists of three successive layers of masonry superimposed on each other, distinguished by material and style. The lowest is assigned to the original Themistoklean wall; the second, of larger polygonal blocks, to the repairs of Konon early in the fourth century (perhaps much of the original socle was below the ground level of that time); the uppermost layer belongs to the reconstruction in the latter part of the fourth century. The filling between the massive blocks of the two faces was stone in the earlier and lower stages, but in the third phase brickwork of the Kononian wall was retained as a core and has thus been unusually well preserved. The full height is entirely conjectural. The width of the curtain wall at this point is about 3.5m. In other sections a width of 3m or somewhat more is commonly found. Clearly, construction varied in different places and times. An exceptionally well-preserved and strongly built stretch of wall socle, of the end of the fourth century, was found several years ago in the northeastern sector, with solid conglomerate masonry about 5m thick standing to a height of eight courses, and with an even greater width at the base to support a stair.[10] As the arts of war advanced, stronger defenses were necessary in the Greek cities. The Athenians made great efforts to keep abreast of the besiegers, but the effect must have been somewhat patchy and hardly equal to the finest fortifications of the period.

[8] A little more is said in the Appendix below; the subject may be studied in Wrede, *Attische Mauern*; Scranton, *Greek Walls*; R. Martin, *Manuel d'Architecture Grecque* I, Paris 1965; Winter, *Greek Fortifications*.

[9] *AA* 1965, 360–68.   [10] *AJA* 62, 1958, 321; Travlos *PDA* 177.

3. City Wall near Sacred Gate (Photo: German Archaeological Institute)

4. City Wall near Sacred Gate (Photo: German Archaeological Institute)

According to Thucydides the Themistoklean walls of Peiraeus were of finer construction than those of the upper city, being of solid masonry throughout, but when we examine the remains of the harbor town we find reason to doubt his statement and to believe that it is true only of limited sections.[11] However this may be, together with the walls of the upper city and the connecting Long Walls they formed a single great system of fortification. The Long Walls were not built in the time of Themistokles, as Pausanias says (1.2.2), but some years later.[12] Towards

[11] See p. 263 below.

[12] Judeich 155ff; R. L. Scranton, "The Fortifications of Athens at the Opening of the Peloponnesian War," *AJA* 42, 1938, 525–36; Travlos *PEA* 48–50; *PDA* 160, 163. *AAA* 5, 1972, 339–46, gives a good recently discovered section.

the middle of the century two walls were built, one running straight to Peiraeus, the other to Phaleron, 5 km farther east. After several years, on Perikles' suggestion, as Plato tells us (*Gorgias* 455e), a third wall was added, running parallel to the original wall to Peiraeus at a distance of about 167m. The line of the two parallel walls has been well-established

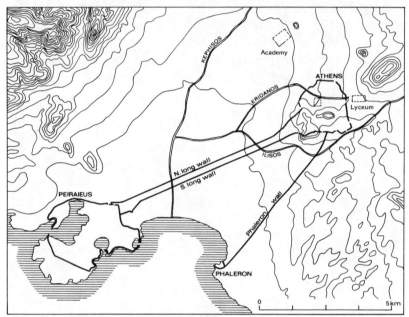

5. Athens, Peiraeus, and Long Walls (Boersma, *Athenian Building Policy* 157, after Travlos)

by remains found here and there; the line of the Phaleric Wall, which was not restored after its destruction in 404 B.C., cannot be so precisely fixed. It was not till the whole scheme was near completion, after the middle of the century, that the Athenians were able to turn their thoughts and devote their resources wholeheartedly to embellishing their city with the splendid new temples and other buildings of Perikles' time.

One should bear in mind that Athens' first line of defense was not the city walls but the great mountain barriers, supplemented by walls such as the so-called "Dema" between Mt. Aigaleos and Mt. Parnes,[13] and by the border forts, some of which provide finer examples both of military architecture and of the stonemason's art than anything at Athens itself, for example at Panakton and Phyle.

[13] J. E. Jones et al., *BSA* 52, 1957, 152–89.

We have evidence—literary, archaeological, or both—for about fifteen gates in the walls of the upper city,[14] besides small posterns or sally ports, simple apertures in the wall closed by doors, of which several are known. The gates were distributed around the whole circumference, in accordance with the lay of the land and the needs of communication, with a concentration of four in the northwestern sector: from northeast to southwest 1) the gate called Eriai, leading out through a cemetery to Kolonos Hippios, 2) the great Dipylon, 3) the Sacred Gate, on the Road to Eleusis, and 4) the Peiraeus Gate. The Gate of Diochares on the east probably has its position fixed by a road and an interruption in the later moat. Of particular interest is a double gate found just north of the Olympieion. Like the socle of the adjacent wall it was built, no doubt in the time of Themistokles himself, of sawn-up column drums from the unfinished Peisistratid temple of Olympian Zeus.[15] The Diomeian and Itonian Gates led southeastwards. The position of the southward "Gate to the Sea" is fixed by traces of an ancient road leading to Phaleron. It was through this that the celebrants of the Mysteries went out to perform their ablutions, crying "Halade Mystai," "Mystai to the sea." Remains of yet another southern gate have been found farther west, at the foot of the Mouseion Hill.

The gates were defended by towers, and there were numerous towers at other strategic points. Most of them were square, normally about 5m or 6m, but considerably larger where great strength was required; the half-round form too was used in the later phases. A number of important gates had both an inner and an outer entrance, with an enclosed court between. The Peiraeus Gate shows the simple basic form; the Sacred Gate was larger and more elaborate. The principal entrance to the city, on the northwest, the Thriasian Gate, later usually called the Dipylon (a name first found in an inscription of 288/7 B.C.) was given an exceptionally monumental form.[16] The structure formed a court measuring about 41m deep from northwest to southeast, and 22m across. A massive square tower stood at each corner; the pair flanking the outer opening stood in the line of the main city wall; beyond the inner towers the wall of the courtyard made a short return at right angles on either side to form the inner gateway. The outer entrance, originally left open to entrap the enemy, was later closed by two gates, roofed over, probably early in the first century

---

[14] For a full list, with identifications, see Travlos *PDA* 159–63; cf. L. H. Jeffery, *BSA* 57, 1962, 116–33; Y. Garlan, *BCH* 93, 1969, 153ff (Hippades Gate and others).

[15] See p. 157 below.

[16] G. Gruben, *AA* 1964, 385–419; 1969, 38; Travlos *PDA* 159, 300f.

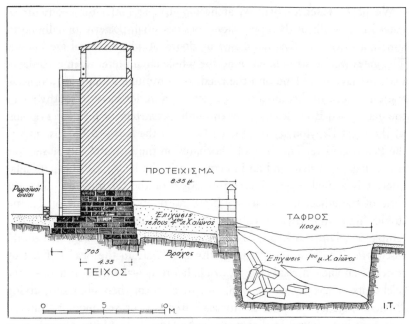

6. City Wall, end of 4th c. B.C. (Section, Travlos *PEA* 77 fig. 38)

B.C. The remains which one sees, consisting chiefly of great conglomerate blocks, belong for the most part to a reconstruction of the late fourth or early third century; but careful examination of earlier traces shows that the original Themistoklean gate was similar in form, though not so powerfully built.

On the city side of the pier which stands in the middle of the inner gateway is a round marble altar on a poros base, inscribed in letters of the third century with a dedication to Zeus Herkeios (god of the courtyard), Hermes (god of gates), and Akamas, eponymous hero of the tribe to which belonged the deme Kerameis, in which the gate is situated.[17] Fortifications in the Greek cities were not intrinsically sacred objects, but cults and shrines frequently attached themselves. At Athens we hear of the altar of Zeus Astrapaios, presumably where lightning had struck, on the wall.[18] The Dipylon had a sacred and processional character, curiously duplicating its close neighbor to the south, the Sacred Gate. In addition,

[17] *IG* II² 4983.

[18] The Greek *en* can well mean this, or "built into," rather than "within" the wall; see p. 167 below.

(18)

besides being a deathtrap to attackers, for the peaceful visitor arriving at Athens it was a symbol of the power and impregnability of the city. At the same time a welcoming hand was extended to him; in the corner formed by the inner cross wall and an inward extension of the northern side wall was neatly fitted an elegant fountain house, with a columnar facade in front of an L-shaped basin, where he might pause and slake his thirst. The fountain as one sees it was built after the later Dipylon, but there are pipes which seem to belong to an earlier building.[19]

To go back and resume the history of the walls—in the Peloponnesian War the great fortifications for many years proved an adequate defense of the city, even though the land of Attica was ravaged. After the final defeat of Athens by Sparta and her allies with Persian aid in 404 B.C., the peace terms demanded that the Long Walls and the Peiraeus fortifications should be taken down, and the demolition was carried out to the sound of flutes.[20] We are not told that the circuit of the upper city was included in the order, but we can imagine that the Themistoklean wall had suffered some dilapidation and stood in need of repair. Athens made a remarkable recovery after her humiliation, and only a few years later, thanks to the efforts of the admiral Konon—and, sadly, with Persian help again—the walls were rebuilt.

In the fourth century we learn something from inscriptions about the construction, repair, and maintenance. One group is concerned with rebuilding in the time of Konon, 395/4–392/1 B.C.[21] The inscriptions are cut on actual wall blocks or on marble slabs which were probably built into the wall. The work, as was usual with major building projects, was let out to numerous private contractors in small sections, such as a stretch of the curtain and perhaps an adjoining tower. One of the contractors, curiously, was a Boeotian. We read of the transport of stones on waggons; the cleaning up of the stone socle (presumably the old socle where it was usable); the construction of towers, curtains, and steps; and the application of plaster which would protect the unbaked bricks. These bricks were used in vast quantities, reckoned by the thousand. The officials called *teichopoioi* or wall makers are mentioned for the first time.

In 338 B.C. Greek resistance to the growing power of Philip of Macedonia, an opponent politically and strategically more formidable than the Persian King, was finally crushed at Chaironeia, and henceforth the Greek

[19] Note also the bathing establishment just outside the gate, p. 252 below.
[20] Xenophon *Hellenica* 2. 2. 20–23.
[21] *IG* II² 1656–64; Maier, *Mauerbauinschriften* 1 21–36.

city states no longer enjoyed full and true autonomy. Inevitably they became involved in the wars of the Hellenistic kingdoms, into which the vast empire of Philip's son Alexander the Great fell apart. Two long inscriptions from the latter part of the fourth century show how their fortifications were a source of recurrent care to the Athenians in these troubled times, when the art of warfare and in particular siege craft was constantly advancing. The first, of which the probable date is 337/6 B.C., is concerned with Peiraeus and the Long Walls only, but it shows in general what great trouble and expense was devoted to these matters, and what an elaborate organization was involved.[22] The officials concerned include *teichopoioi*, treasurers, *epimeletai* or overseers, architects, and a clerk. The Council devotes special sessions to the subject. When the work is completed and approved, dedications are to be made. The general decree about finance and organization is followed by detailed specifications. The operations were to extend over several years. They included, where stone was concerned, cutting and rough-shaping (*pelekesis*) in the quarry, then transport and final working. A round tower was to have its rubble filling removed and replaced by solid masonry. Solid stone walls are mentioned but apparently only in one particular section, probably at Peiraeus. No doubt unbaked brick was still used for most of the upper structure.

The second inscription, which may be dated most probably in 307/6 B.C., records another thorough overhaul and an attempt to modernize the walls.[23] After the decree and the specifications, part of the contracts for the various sections of wall is preserved. The architect chosen by the Demos is to divide the walls of the upper city, the walls of the Peiraeus, and the Long Walls into ten sections each. Reconstruction involves all parts of the wall—the stone socle, stairs, roofs of towers (which are apparently gabled), and the main body of the wall, which is to have its brickwork strengthened and its plaster renewed where necessary. The work is to be spread over four years; and the contractors are given exemption from the military services.

The most interesting feature is new—a covered way on top of the wall, in place of the usual open walk with simple breastwork. This provision was to be made on the walls of Athens itself (except the cross wall near the Pnyx) and the Long Walls, not at Peiraeus. Highly detailed specifications are given, and their interpretation has been much disputed. It has even been suggested that elaborate as they are they refer merely to the

[22] *IG* ii² 244; Maier 1 36–48; cf. F. Winter, *AJA* 67, 1963, 376.
[23] *IG* ii² 463; Maier 1 48–67.

treatment of the parapet walk and the top of the outer breastwork, but this is highly unlikely. Maier's account seems acceptable in all essentials.[24] On the outer edge of the main wall, the top of which was paved, was set a brick wall pierced with shuttered openings; on the inner side were brick pillars through which ran wooden rails. The roof had as its basis a complex timber structure on which were placed reeds, a bed of "fortified" clay, and finally the tiles. One wonders whether this construction was actually carried out over the whole length of the walls.[25]

Inscriptions tell of occasional work on the walls in the Hellenistic period. Public-spirited persons liked to provide a tower with which their names might be associated. The wealthy and energetic Eurykleides instigated general repair of the Themistoklean wall, as is recorded in an honorary decree dated shortly after 229 B.C.;[26] it is notable that his program is confined to the city and Peiraeus. By now the Long Walls had been abandoned, which meant that the *diateichisma* or cross wall on the Pnyx became part of the main fortification. As Maier remarks, it was beyond the power of the Athenians ever to replan and rebuild their walls fundamentally.

An inscription (see Fig. 59.1) of quite a different character, dated late in the fifth century, probably throws some further light on the defenses of Athens. It was found a few years ago just outside the Dipylon gate, and it reads "Boundary of the pool [*telma*] of Athena."[27] The circumstances of finding suggest that the pool was in fact a moat outside the wall.

When Athens was looking to her defenses in the latter part of the fourth century, the outworks were strengthened; a *proteichisma* or first line of defense, in the form of a lighter wall, was built at a distance of about 10m around a considerable part of the circuit, in fact where the ground was level and natural contours gave the defenders little help. Outside the *proteichisma* a ditch was dug, about 10m or 11m wide; no doubt at points where water flowed this would form a veritable moat. Traces of the outer wall have been found at various points, traces of the ditch at many more. It was in this phase too that a strong *diateichisma* was built over the south-

[24] See however L. B. Holland, *Phoenix* 13, 1959, 161ff; R. Martin, *Manuel d'Architecture Grecque* I, Paris 1965, 5.

[25] Winter, *Greek Fortifications*, 141, suggests that it was built in limited sections to protect torsion guns from the weather; it would hardly protect the defenders from heavy artillery.

[26] *IG* II² 834; Maier I 76–80.

[27] *Deltion* 16B, 1962, 26–27; 25B, 1972, 38; *AA* 1964, 413–15; 1969, 33–36. Travlos *PDA* 158, 176, 301.

7. Post-Herulian Wall,
western face (Photo: Agora
Excavations)

8. Post-Herulian Wall,
inner structure (Photo:
Agora Excavations)

(22)

western ridges, with numerous towers, and gates on the saddles between the hills.[28] The new wall cut out the large salient which had extended in this direction to join the Long Walls. Its construction was unusual, the great conglomerate blocks being laid at intervals as headers, meeting in the middle and dividing the socle into compartments. The fortification which made a kind of separate castle of the summit of the Mouseion Hill was due to the Macedonians and Demetrios Poliorketes early in the third century.[29]

Athens unwisely supported King Mithridates of Pontus in his war against Rome. In consequence the fortifications were severely damaged by the Roman general Sulla in 86 B.C., and the Long Walls and the Walls of Peiraeus never rose again. The wall of the upper city lay neglected and dilapidated for several centuries. Under the peace of Augustus and even more under the patronage of Hadrian Athens enjoyed happier times, in which there was no need for powerful defenses; but in the middle of the third century A.D. in the reign of the Emperor Valerian the wall was repaired to face the threat of barbarian invasions. It still followed the Themistoklean line, except that it extended far out to the east to include the new quarter which had sprung up in the time of Hadrian. This eastward extension, formerly attributed to Hadrian, has now been shown by Travlos to belong to the time of Valerian.[30] The new wall failed to withstand the Herulians, the barbarian invaders who sacked the city in 267 A.D. For a time Athens suffered a violent contraction, and a wall was hastily built enclosing a small area immediately north of the Acropolis, leaving even the old agora outside. This post-Herulian Wall has proved a godsend to the archaeologist, a veritable museum of the earlier glories of the city. Not only were sections of standing walls of the Hellenistic Stoa of Attalos and of the Library of Hadrian incorporated, but countless architectural members of ruined monuments were used as building material; and, carefully extracted, these have made possible the reconstruction (on paper) of many famous buildings of which almost nothing has survived *in situ*.[31] In the fourth century there was a partial revival and renewed expansion, and by the end of the century the outer wall seems to have been made

[28] H. A. Thompson and R. L. Scranton, *Stoas and City Walls on the Pnyx*, *Hesperia* 12, 1943, 301–83.

[29] Judeich 91f, 162; *Hesperia* 12, 1943, 331; Hill 202; Travlos *PDA* 178.

[30] *PEA* 122; *PDA* 161; *Deltion* 17B, 1963, 12–13.

[31] Travlos *PEA* 125–29; *PDA* 161, 163, 179. For later phases see Travlos *PEA* 144f, 149, 156, 161, 163, 172, 173f, 193ff, 254, 281.

defensible again and manned to face the onslaught of Alaric the Goth. With further repairs by Justinian in the middle of the sixth century, the Themistoklean circuit, with its eastward extension, continued to be the basis of the city's defense. It was to be many centuries before Athens received a new city wall built quite independently of the ancient structures.

Through the Byzantine period, the distribution of the churches and of the remains of houses shows that the area between the outer and inner walls was fairly well populated, and that Athens, though no longer one of the centers of the earth, was a considerable city. But troubled times were to follow. Probably in the middle of the eleventh century, though the date is disputed, it was found necessary to build an inner fortification close under the slopes of the Acropolis (hence its name Rizokastro), again incorporating, on the south side, the standing walls of famous ancient buildings. Thus for a time the Athenians had three lines of defense, though one may doubt whether they could fully maintain and defend the old outer wall. In the period of "Frankokratia" (1204–1456), invaded, occupied, and fought over by French, Catalans, Florentines and Venetians, the city shrank within its narrower confines. The outer wall, still after many repairs and rebuilding essentially the wall of Themistokles, was abandoned forever; but, says Travlos, "For many centuries yet the scanty but impressive remains of the wall made a vivid impression on visitors to Athens, revealing the great extent of the ancient city and at the same time emphasizing the smallness of its Frankish successor." Naturally the Acropolis resumed its importance, and much work was done there, especially on the western defenses. The tall "Frankish Tower" seen in pictures made before 1875, when it was dismantled, was built as a watch post. It was towards the end of this period that the antiquarian Cyriacus of Ancona visited Athens and described what he saw, copying inscriptions, many of which he found incorporated in the walls.[32]

After the Turkish conquest, the little town expanded considerably again, but it was still confined to the north side of the Acropolis and even here fell far short of the limits of the ancient city. For many years there was no outer fortification, though some provision for defense was made by linking house walls to form a circuit of a kind. Meanwhile the Acropolis became a detached fortress again.

In 1687–88 the city suffered a devastating incursion by the Venetians. After this the Turks greatly strengthened the fortifications of the Acrop-

[32] E. W. Bodnar, *Cyriacus of Ancona and Athens*, Brussels 1960.

olis, using much ancient material, and adding western outworks as their Mycenean forerunners had done nearly 3000 years earlier.

Finally a wall, Athens' last, was built around the whole city. It was completed in 1778, under the direction of Hadji Ali Khasseki, the most cruel and rapacious of the Turkish governors. It was a poor thing compared with the ancient walls, 3m high and less than 1m wide, poorly constructed, incorporating much ancient material, including the stones of the beautiful little Ionic temple on the farther bank of the River Ilissos, which had somehow survived till this period. A large area of northern and eastern Athens was enclosed; indeed on the north and northeast Hadji Ali followed the same line as Themistokles.

Naturally this wall did not survive the War of Liberation in the 1830s, but traces of it have been uncovered at many points. Chosen inevitably as the capital of Free Greece, Athens rose from her ruins and developed in spectacular manner, and in the present century the city has burst all bonds with a great explosion, and spilled and sprawled all over the Attic plain, far beyond the widest extent of the ancient city, engulfing what were pleasant suburbs such as the Academy, vast olive groves, and outlying demes, with no wall or limit other than the great mountain barrier of Aigaleos, Parnes, Pentelikon, and Hymettos, and the sea.

BIBLIOGRAPHY

Judeich 113–65
W. Wrede, *Attische Mauern*, Athens 1933
R. L. Scranton, *Greek Walls*, Harvard 1941
F. G. Maier, *Griechische Mauerbauinschriften*, Heidelberg 1959–61
F. E. Winter, *Greek Fortifications*, London 1971
Travlos *PDA* 158ff, 301

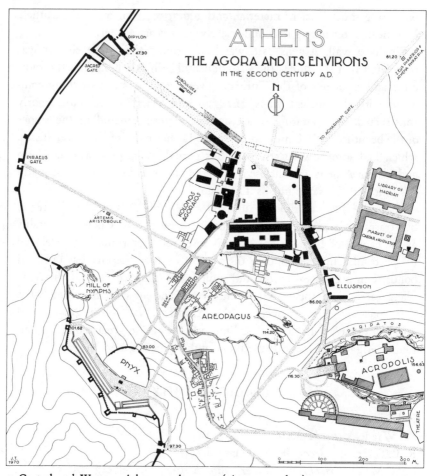

9. Central and Western Athens, 2nd c. A.D. (*Agora* XIV pl. 1)

CHAPTER II

The Agora: Political and Religious Center

ARCHAIC AGORA

From the sixth century B.C. till A.D. 267 the center of the city of Athens was the area north of the Areopagus and east of the low hill which came to be called Kolonos Agoraios or Market Hill. Though in religion it was overshadowed by the Acropolis, and though there were subsidiary political and social centers, the predominance of the agora as focus of the life of the city was unquestionable.

The site occupied the inner part of the region called Kerameikos or Potters' Quarter, which also extended far to the northwest; the ground sloped gently downwards to the bed of the Eridanos stream on the north. In prehistoric and early archaic times the area was occupied by dwellings and tombs; the archaeological evidence would seem to indicate that early in the sixth century, perhaps in the time of Solon, much of it was cleared and surfaced and made available for public use.[1] One may naturally assume that before this time Athens had a primitive agora, perhaps with a few simple shrines and public buildings; a likely site is at the western approach to the Propylaia, on the saddle between the Acropolis and the Areopagus, but positive evidence for the location or even the existence of an early agora is extremely slight.[2]

In the development of the agora which we know an important part was played by several already existing streets.[3] One of these approached from the northwest, and traversed the agora diagonally towards the Acropolis; this was to be the great Panathenaic processional way or *dromos*. A second

[1] *Agora* XIV 16, 19. *Hesperia* 44, 1975, 370ff reports still more burials, in the northwestern sector.

[2] *Agora* XIV 19; I find it difficult to accept an old agora southwest or northwest of the Acropolis, as proposed respectively by A. N. Oikonomides, *The Two Agoras of Ancient Athens*, Chicago 1964, and Travlos *PEA* 24, 28, 34 and *PDA* 2; see *Phoenix* 20, 1966, 285–93.

[3] *Agora* XIV 17f, 20, 192f.

(27)

diverged from it at the northwest corner, ran down the west side, and continued southwards. A third formed the southern border and crossed both the other two.

Both in the original development of the agora and in its developed form the southwestern sector seems to have been a focal point. This region was what the Athenians later called the *archeia* or "public offices";[4] and here in the course of the sixth century was built a series of buildings which were very probably the archaic predecessors of the Bouleuterion (Council House), the Tholos, and other offices which occupied the site in post-Persian times.[5] They were of simple construction, with irregular socles of Acropolis limestone and upper walls of unbaked brick; but they were too substantial and, in the case of the main building, too elaborate in plan to be mere houses. A terrace was created at the southeastern foot of the Kolonos, supported by a retaining wall built on the west side of the western street. On the north side of an extensive open area, early in the sixth century, a rectangular building (C) was placed, measuring 15m east to west and 6.7m north to south, divided into two rooms opening southwards. About the middle of the century a large building (F: 27m east to west and 18.5m north to south in its greatest dimensions), highly irregular in shape and highly complex in plan, was built on the south side of the area. Its principal feature was a courtyard extending east and west, with colonnades on the north and south sides, and rooms of various sizes behind them. Adjoining this on the west were still more rooms built round a much smaller court. The site was occupied in the following centuries by the Tholos and its adjuncts, and it is reasonable to conjecture that here we have a principal element in the *archeia* of the sixth-century Athens, that the complex provided accommodation for the Prytaneis, the committee of Councillors, and for various officials. The western annex may have served for culinary and menial purposes—broiling pits have been found on its north side—leaving the more spacious eastern part free for more dignified use. Eating and drinking together in *syssitia* was to remain a feature of Athenian official life. One can imagine that the Boule[6] met in

[4] *Agora* III 126; XIV 20.

[5] H. A. Thompson, *Hesperia* Suppl. 4, 1940, 3–44; *Agora* XIV 25–29.

[6] In spite of the skepticism of C. Hignett, *A History of the Athenian Constitution*, Oxford 1952, 92ff, a popular Council of 400, created by Solon, is generally accepted for this period; see P. J. Rhodes, *The Athenian Boule*, Oxford 1972, 208–9 (Rhodes, however, does not accept a prytany system for this time, see below n. 50); L. H. Jeffery, *Archaic Greece*, London 1976, 93, 107. E. S. Staveley, *Greek and Roman Voting and Elections*, London 1972, 52, rejects the Solonian Council.

10. Athens from Hill of Nymphs; Mt. Pentelikon in far distance on left (Photo: Agora Excavations)

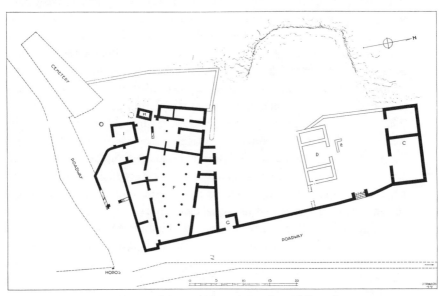

11. Early Buildings Southwest of Agora (*Hesperia* Suppl. 4, 16 fig. 13)

the open space between Building F and Building C, a site which coincides partly with that of the later Bouleuterion; Building C was far from adequate to put a roof over their heads (and indeed one would not expect a roofed chamber for so many so early), but it would provide a useful annex.

A short distance to the north of this group of buildings are slight traces of a temple of apsidal plan, built about the middle of the sixth century, to judge from the archaeological evidence.[7] Within the apse is a poros block, no doubt the base of the cult statue, and this may well have been made in a bronze-casting pit which has been discovered nearby, containing parts of the clay mold. The figure cast in this mold was appropriate for an archaic Apollo; and since the temple built on the site in the fourth century was undoubtedly sacred to Apollo Patroos, ancestral deity of the Athenians, this deity no doubt occupied the apsidal building too. Farther north are slight traces of another shrine, with a statue base enclosed on the east, north, and south by a wall, and an altar to the east; this is the site on which the statue and stoa of Zeus later stood.[8]

At the north end of the west side, near the lowest point of the agora, a small stoa was built, a simple, even primitive example of its type, the first of the Athenian stoas.[9] Its remains were not unearthed until 1970, when at last it proved possible to push the excavations beyond the railway cutting which slices off a segment of the agora on this side. At once it was recognized, through its place in Pausanias and other evidence, as the Stoa Basileios, where the archon called Basileus, King, conducted his affairs; the belief which had previously prevailed, that the Basileios and the Stoa of Zeus were one and the same building, had to be abandoned. The stoa was unexpectedly small, not more than about 7.5m by 17.7m. The material is mainly poros. There were eight columns on the facade, facing the agora; and interior columns to support the ridgepole, at first only two, later four. The remains are very confusing and difficult to date since there was obviously much reconstruction and much re-use of old material. The Doric columns with their spreading capitals and shafts with only sixteen flutes seem to belong to the middle of the sixth century, but other evidence points to construction of the building as we have it

---

[7] *Hesperia* 6, 1937, 79ff; *Agora* XIV 136f.

[8] *Hesperia* 6, 8ff; *Agora* XIV 96.

[9] T. L. Shear, *AAA* 3, 1970, 297–301; *Agora* XIV 83ff; *Hesperia* 40, 1971, 243ff; 44, 1975, 365ff. For the terracotta figures see also *Hesperia* 6, 1937, 37–39, 66f; R. Nicholls, *Hesperia*, 39, 1970, 115–38; cf. 42, 1973, 402.

early in the fifth. At the end of the fifth century small columnar wings were somewhat awkwardly added projecting from the facade at either end. Pausanias saw terracotta figures on the roof, representing Theseus throwing Skiron into the sea and Eos carrying off Kephalos. Bits which probably belong to these have been found and can be dated not earlier than the middle of the fifth century.

Many fragments of Herms and Herm bases have been found in and near the stoa. Several of them were dedicated by men who had served as Basileus, a fact which clinches the identification of the building. We shall be looking at the Herms in the northwestern part of the agora in another context.

Immediately in front of the stylobate, just north of center, still lies a large slab of hard brown poros, roughly shaped and worn smooth on top. It seems to have been in place from an early date, and there can be little doubt that it was the "archons' stone," on which, according to Aristotle's *Constitution* (7.1) they took oath to maintain the laws. The area in front of the stoa was treated as a kind of forecourt or precinct, and here have been found a number of "thrones," seats of honor presumably for dignitaries at the civic ceremonies; some are of poros, others, no doubt later replacements, are of marble.[10]

The kingly functions which the democratically appointed Basileus inherited from the old kings were concerned with religious matters, and he also presided over lawsuits in which these were involved. Plato shows us Sokrates going along to the Basileios for the preliminary of his trial.[11] The little stoa was very convenient for such purposes, but it cannot have held the jury of many hundreds before which Sokrates was eventually tried. On the other hand there was just about room for the Court of the Areopagus, which, Demosthenes tells us (25.23) sometimes met there, with a rope barrier to keep unauthorized persons away.

The stoa was used as a repository for copies of the laws. We are told by Aristotle (7.1) that the laws of Solon were set up here, but this cannot have been in the time of the legislator if the dating of the building is correct.[12] The tradition was continued in the great revision of the law

---

[10] See p. 205 below for the *theatron* in this area. H. A. Thompson is studying further the building and the whole area.

[11] *Euthyphron* 2a; *Theaitetos* 210d.

[12] This is not the place to do more than draw attention to the problems of the *axones* and *kurbeis*, on which the laws were inscribed, what they were and where they stood; they have been most recently discussed by A. Andrewes, *Phoros, Tribute*

codes which was carried out in the closing years of the fifth century. Andokides tells us (1.82, 84, 85) that the revised laws were inscribed in the stoa "on the wall"; and we need not doubt that this means the Basileios. One special stele, inscribed with Drakon's law on homicide, was placed, according to its own text, "in front of the Basileia" (an unusual spelling).[13] Many fragments of the code have been found in the agora excavations, and they belong to stelai which were placed continuously to form a kind of wall, or indeed several walls.[14] The columnar wings may well have been added to provide a place for some of the stelai, and suitable beddings have been found in them; yet other stelai may have been placed in front of the back wall of the main building which was thickened at the bottom as though to provide a ledge. The total inscribed surface must have been enormous; we have here one of the most remarkable examples of the determination of the Athenians to get everything down on stone.

The Athenians loved this curious little building. It became a symbol, like the Tholos, of their way of life, democratic but rooted in age-old tradition. They could not bear to pull it down and build a greater; so they built the handsome Stoa of Zeus alongside it, with only a very narrow alley in between. Functionally the two may have been regarded as parts of a single whole. Even the ground level of the forecourt of the Basileios was maintained, against the general rise of level in this low-lying part of the agora, by means of steps and retaining walls. Patched and repatched, the little stoa continued to stand, among its ever grander companions, throughout antiquity. It has provided a glimpse down the vista which faces us.

To resume our general account of the archaic agora, the west side was now occupied by a row of public buildings and shrines. On other sides architectural development seems to have been more sporadic. At the southeast corner, as part of the plan of the tyrant Peisistratos to improve the city's water supply, a fountain house was built, fed by a pipeline coming from the east.[15] In the middle of the northern part of the agora the

---

to B. D. Meritt, New York 1974; cf. H. Hansen, *HSCP* 75, 1971, 201, and *Philologus* 119, 1975, 39–45; R. S. Stroud, "Athenian Kyrbeis," *AJA* 79, 1975, 151; the works cited in nn. 13 and 14 below are relevant.

[13] *IG* I² 115; R. S. Stroud, *Drakon's Law on Homicide*, Univ. of California 1968.

[14] The "Walls" have been much discussed and still await full publication; see S. Dow, *Proceedings of Massachusetts Historical Society*, 71, 1953–57, 3–36; most recently A. Fingarette, *Hesperia* 40, 1971, 330ff; cf. *Agora* III 22; XIV 88f.

[15] See p. 248 below.

younger Peisistratos, son of the tyrant, in his archonship in 521 B.C., established the Altar of the Twelve Gods, within a square fenced enclosure constructed of stone posts with thin slabs between them (the form of the monument will be studied more carefully below in connection with the later reconstruction).[16] The remains have been identified beyond doubt by the discovery of a statue base set against the outer face of the western side of the poros sill which carried the fence; the stone bears an inscription of the early fifth century, "Leagros son of Glaukon dedicated this to the Twelve Gods."[17] The establishment of the altar marked this precise spot as the very center of Athens; it served as a central milestone from which distances were measured,[18] and it was almost certainly what Pindar called in his dithyramb in honor of the Athenians "the *omphalos* (navel) of the city, much-trodden, fragrant with incense."[19]

At the very end of the archaic period, probably not long before the Persian invasion (one cannot give more precise dates) more ambitious schemes were taken in hand for the southwestern sector, and more monumental buildings were planned. A series of stone markers (*horoi*), inscribed "I am the boundary of the agora," belong to this phase.[20] Two have been found still in position, one at a point where the western street forks, just opposite Building F and the later Tholos, the other about 21m farther south. They consist of upright marble slabs, with the inscription running along the top and down one side of one face; on the southern stone the inscription is retrograde. Fragments of two more *horoi* of the agora, one of marble, one of poros, have been found out of context.

These markers were probably distributed around the periphery of the agora, at important points and especially where streets entered; they designated the central square as in some sense sacred ground. To the same period belongs the great stone-built drain on the west side of the agora, which was to be the principal artery of drainage for the region for many centuries.[21] The most important building in the program was a large square hall a little to the north of Building F; it can be identified as a Bouleuterion, no doubt intended to house the Council of 500 instituted by Kleisthenes.[22] Its overall dimensions were 23.3m east to west by 23.8m

[16] See p. 64 below.

[17] *Hesperia* 5, 1936, 358; *Agora* III 122.

[18] Herodotus 2.7.1; cf. *IG* II² 2640.

[19] See p. 205 below.

[20] *Agora* III 218; XIV 117f.

[21] See p. 250 below.

[22] *Hesperia* 6, 1937, 127–35; *Agora* XIV 29f.

12. Boundary Stone of Agora (Photo: Agora Excavations)

north to south, at foundation level. A cross wall cut off a section 6.2m deep on the south to form an anteroom. The principal foundations were of large irregular blocks of Acropolis limestone, incorporating much re-used material; almost nothing of the superstructure survives. The roof of the main chamber was supported by columns; part of the foundations of three are in place, and there were no doubt five in all, disposed as shown in the plan. One can imagine that the seating would consist of wooden benches in tiers along the north, east, and west sides. A little to the north, and south of the shrine of Apollo, are the foundations (again of limestone) of a temple measuring 6.9m by about 18m, consisting of a cella and a deep porch with perhaps two columns. This temple has the same orientation as the Bouleuterion and is probably contemporary. It can be identified confidently as the Metroon;[23] from this time onwards there was a very close association between the cult of the Mother of the Gods and the Bouleuterion.

Another notable structure of approximately the same period was a large rectangular walled enclosure at the western end of the south side of the agora, some distance to the southeast of the public buildings which we have been examining. Its interior dimensions were about 26.5m north to south by 31m east to west, and it had its main entrance in the middle of the north side and a door on the east. The height of the wall is conjectural; it was well built of squared blocks of Aiginetan stone, and the crowning course had a markedly projecting cornice. When one looks for a purpose for this spacious enclosure in the region of the *archeia*, the most probable is as a law court. We shall see more of the character of these elusive buildings in the next section. The present example could have ac-commodated as many as 1500 jurymen; it may indeed have been the Heliaia itself, the major or parent court of the peculiar Athenian system.[24]

Thus, if our identifications are correct, by the early years of the fifth century most of the principal instruments of government were con-centrated in the agora and accommodated modestly in its western part. The supreme authority however, the Ekklesia or general assembly, met on the slope of the Pnyx Hill to the southwest, which may be regarded as an appendage of the agora. The first signs of planning and construction in this political theater are dated somewhere near 500 B.C. It is natural to assume that through most of the sixth century the agora was the meeting place of the Ekklesia; there is no clear proof, but on certain particular

[23] *Hesperia* 6, 1937, 135–40; *Agora* XIV 30f.
[24] See p. 54 below.

occasions Solon and in turn Peisistratos are said to have harangued the people in the agora.[25] Ostracism, the process instituted probably by Kleisthenes to get rid of dangerous or awkward politicians, was conducted in the agora and continued through the fifth century—the citizens entered a fenced enclosure to hand in their *ostraka*, the potsherds on which each inscribed the name of the man he wished to ostracize.

Finally, the agora provided a simple theater in which to see sacred dances and perhaps dramatic performances; indeed on some festal occasions the whole agora may have been a veritable *theatron*. In early times, before the stadium was developed, athletic games may have been held on the *dromos* in the agora, and certain equestrian events took place there even later. [26]

AGORA OF PERIKLES AND LYCURGUS

The Persians left the agora in ruins, and after 480 B.C. the planners and architects had to make a fresh beginning, slowly and tentatively at first. Between the archaic agora and the agora of the time of Kimon and Perikles there are notable differences, but there is also a certain continuity both in particular features and in general character. The most important public building, the Bouleuterion, must have been patched up, and it continued in use. The adjacent Tholos, with its round chamber, was something quite new, but it stood in a precinct which curiously preserved the irregular outlines of the old buildings on the site. This was the age in which the stoa attained great importance in city planning, and several were built in the agora in the course of the fifth century. The old shrines were refurbished and new ones were added, but no temple was built in the agora itself for many years after the Persian invasion; however, from

---

[25] Plutarch *Solon* 8.2, 30.4. On ostracism see E. Vanderpool, *Ostracism at Athens*, University of Cincinnati (Louise Taft Semple Lectures) 1970; cf. R. Meiggs and D. Lewis, *Greek Historical Inscriptions*, Oxford 1969, 40–47; *Agora* III 164f; XIV 50f; J. J. Keaney and A. E. Raubitschek, *AJP* 93, 1972, 87–91.

R. Thomsen, *The Origin of Ostracism*, Copenhagen 1972, maintains, against those who would date it later, that ostracism was indeed introduced by Kleisthenes; cf. L. H. Jeffery, *Archaic Greece*, London 1976, 103, 247f. In *Hesperia* 44, 1975, 189–93, Vanderpool gives yet more *ostraka* from the agora.

[26] *Agora* XIV 121. Recently a row of stone bases, with sockets for posts, as if for a starting-line, dated about the middle of the fifth century B.C., has been found near the northwest corner, *Hesperia* 44, 1975, 363–65; *The Athenian Agora: A Short Guide*, 1976 (Excavations of the Athenian Agora, Picture Book No. 16), fig. 15.

13. Agora from Northwest (Photo: Agora Excavations)

the middle of the fifth century the Hephaisteion on the hill to the west dominated the scene and added a touch of grandeur. Kimon manifested love of beauty with economy by planting plane-trees in the square.[27] In general, the agora in the days of Athens' greatest political and cultural glory remained simple and informal in plan, and, although it contained several buildings of distinction and a number of great works of art in both sculpture and painting, modest and unpretentious in aesthetic character.

It will probably be most helpful to take a look at the stoas before dealing with buildings designed for a more specialized purpose. The stoa was a peculiarly Hellenic type of building.[28] Essentially it was a long narrow structure with a solid wall on one long side and an open colonnade on the other. This basic form was capable of many variations, of which we shall see some examples. Colonnades were of course attached to various buildings; in particular when placed on all sides of the cella they gave

[27] Plutarch *Kimon* 13.8; *Agora* III 219.
[28] R. Martin, *Recherches sur l'Agora Grecque*, Paris 1951, 449ff; R. E. Wycherley, *How the Greeks Built Cities*, 2d edn. London 1962, 110–19; on this subject I owe much to unpublished work by J. J. Coulton (see now p. 279 below).

the temple its most impressive form. The type of stoa with which we are now concerned was not attached to any other structure, but rather formed the edge of an open space. It was not an architectural unit complete in itself, but rather an adjunct. For many purposes nothing more than a bit of open ground was absolutely necessary. But complete openness and lack of protection has obvious disadvantages. The stoa mitigated these in an impressive and yet economical way; it provided a kind of compromise between an open area and a covered building, offering some protection from hot sun and cold winds and rain. It was useful in many contexts, most particularly in the agora.

Two stoas on the north side were among the earliest post-Persian buildings. A southward aspect was favored for stoas wherever possible; it enabled them to catch the winter sun and to exclude the north wind. After defeating the Persians at Eion in Thrace in 476/5 B.C., Kimon and his fellow generals commemorated their victory by setting up three stone figures of Hermes in what came to be called "the Stoa of the Herms."[29] This building can be approximately located at the west end of the north side of the agora not far from the place where an inscription relating to it was found several years ago. The northwestern corner of the agora was in fact known as "the Herms," since it was a favorite spot for setting up monuments of this kind. Apart from the dedication by Kimon, we hear nothing further of the Stoa of the Herms; apparently it did not play a very important part in public life.

Its neighbor the Poikile or Painted Stoa was one of the most celebrated monuments of Athens. There can now be no doubt that it stood on the north side. It was built not long before 460 B.C.; this dating depends on the character of architectural fragments which can be assigned to it, on our knowledge of the artists who painted the pictures on the walls, and more particularly of Peisianax, a relative of Kimon, who was in some sense responsible for its erection and provided the building with its first name, Stoa Peisianakteios.

[29] Aischines 3.183–85; Menekles-Kallikrates, Jacoby *FGH* IIIB 232; *Agora* III 103ff; J. Threpsiades and E. Vanderpool, *Deltion* 18, 1964, 103ff; *Agora* XIV 94ff. Vanderpool has drawn my attention to a reference to the Herms in Menander, ed. Sandbach, Oxford 1972, 160, *Kitharistes* line 65. A. D. Trendall and T.B.L. Webster, *Illustrations of Greek Drama*, London 1971, I, 18–20, illustrate certain vases which may be relevant. On the Herms, and the cavalry and their contest (the Anthippasia), and the base of a victory monument signed by the sculptor Bryaxis, see now Vanderpool, *Hesperia* 43, 1974, 311–13.

14. a) Head of Herm,
possibly from Stoa of Herms
(Photo: Agora Excavations)

b) Head of Nike from Stoa
of Zeus (Photo: Agora
Excavations)

(39)

The fragments, mostly of brown Aiginetan poros, though some are of the harder poros of Peiraeus, were found in the northeastern part of the excavation (the building itself must have stood still farther north, beyond the railway and the excavated area).[30] Both Doric and Ionic elements were introduced, the latter presumably in the interior order. Some of the stones bear traces of painted decoration. An anta capital appears to belong not to a side wall but to a wall which made a return along the front. Presumably this arrangement was employed at both ends, limiting the open colonnade to the middle section and thus giving the paintings greater protection. Most interesting are wall blocks in which are holes containing remains of iron pins; these must have supported a wooden frame to which were attached the boards on which the pictures were painted. References to boards in certain late authors had already suggested that the pictures were not painted directly on the walls, and this is now confirmed.

Pausanias describes the paintings in sequence (1.15). The first which he saw showed "the Athenians arrayed at Oinoe in the Argive territory against the Lacedaemonians" (possibly in 457 B.C., but we do not know for sure).[31] "On the middle of the walls," whatever that means, were shown Theseus and the Athenians fighting the Amazons. Next followed the scene after the capture of Troy. "The last part of the painting" depicted the battle of Marathon.[32] The disposition of the pictures in the stoa is purely conjectural. Possibly the Amazons, Troy, and Marathon were on the back wall, Oinoe on one end wall, the captured shields on the other.

This adornment gave the stoa the character of a hall of victories. One of the bronze shields taken from the Spartans at Sphakteria has been found, not in the region of the stoa but in a cistern on the Kolonos, to which it was transferred (possibly, after being damaged, to serve as a lid) long before the time of Pausanias. It bears an inscription in punched let-

[30] *Hesperia* 19, 1950, 327–29; *Phoenix* 7, 1953, 20–35; Lucy Shoe Meritt, *Hesperia* 39, 1970, 233–64.

[31] L. H. Jeffery, *BSA* 60, 1965, 41–57; R. Meiggs, *The Athenian Empire*, Oxford 1972, 469ff.

[32] In *Proceedings of the Cambridge Philological Society*, NS 18, 1972, 78, I have raised objections to the view of J. H. Schreiner, *PCPS*, NS 16, 1970, 97–112, that there were *two* paintings showing two successive phases of the battle of Marathon. T. Hölscher, *Griechische Historienbilder des 5 und 4 Jahrhunderts*, Wurzburg 1973, 50ff, 259, discusses the paintings, especially Marathon, and rejects the view that the south frieze of the temple of Athena Nike was an adaptation of the Marathon painting, as suggested by E. B. Harrison, *AJA* 76, 1972, 353–78.

ters saying, "The Athenians from the Lacedaemonians from Pylos."[33]

Some of the finest artists of the day were employed. We have it on good authority that Mikon of Athens painted the Amazons, and Polygnotos of Thasos the Trojan scene. Marathon is variously attributed to Panainos, Mikon, or, improbably, Polygnotos.[34] The painter of the battle of Oinoe is not mentioned.

The most extraordinary thing about these paintings is that they stood not in a secluded gallery where they could be examined by interested visitors at leisure but in an open colonnade facing the busiest spot in Athens, where they were seen by people of all kinds going about their varied business. Plentiful evidence shows that the Poikile had the character of a *lesche* or lounge (of which there were many at Athens, mostly of course much smaller and simpler) where people could sit, stand, or stroll around and talk; and that it was frequented by all types of men from poets and philosophers to parasites and beggars.[35]

That it was occasionally used for official purposes is shown by two inscriptions of the middle of the fourth century, which mention lawsuits tried in the Poikile before a jury of 500.[36] Demosthenes (45.17) mentions an arbitration in the stoa. Like most public buildings at Athens, it had religious associations and functions too; we hear of a proclamation made from it on the occasion of the Eleusinian mysteries.[37]

The Cynic philosopher Krates, according to gossip, being a homeless person like many of his sect, took his beautiful young bride Hipparchia to the Poikile. More respectably, Zeno and the Stoics made it their favorite meeting place in the early days of the school, and took their name from it; but of course they cannot have monopolized it to the exclusion of ordinary citizens.[38] Lucian gives a lively account of the more informal and popular kind of philosophical discussion which often took place there; a Stoic and an Epicurean engage in a heated theological debate before a crowd of enthusiastic listeners.[39] One need not doubt that St. Paul, "picking up seeds" in the Athenian agora, found them liberally scattered in the stoa.

---

[33] *Hesperia* 6, 1937, 346–48; *Agora* XIV 92.

[34] *Agora* III 31, 45.　　　　　[35] *Agora* III 31ff; XIV 92ff.

[36] *IG* II² 1641; 1670.

[37] Schol. Aristophanes *Frogs* 369; Diogenes Laertius 7.1.14 mentions an altar in the stoa.

[38] Apuleius *Florida* 14; cf. *Agora* III 33; Diogenes 7.1.5.

[39] *Iuppiter Tragoedus* 15,16,32; Acts 17:18.

The Agora: Political and Religious Center

Some thirty years after the building of the Poikile—years during which architectural efforts were concentrated on the Acropolis—probably about 430 B.C. according to the archaeological evidence, another stoa was added, towards the north end of the west side, facing eastwards, immediately south of the Basileios, which was refurbished after the Persian destruction. The new building, dedicated to Zeus under the title of Soter or Eleutherios, because he had saved the freedom of Athens from the Persian threat, represented a more sophisticated conception in stoa design. Gabled,

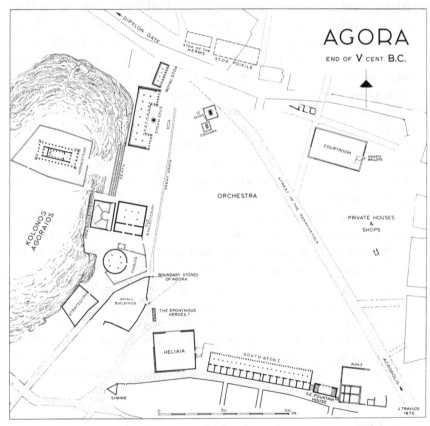

15. Agora, end of 5th c. B.C. (*Agora* XIV pl. 5)

temple-like wings were thrust forward at either end of the facade. The columns of these were more closely spaced than those of the central portion in between. The length of the building was 46.55m, its depth about 18m in the wings and 12m in the middle. The plan is clear enough from the surviving foundations and cuttings; the elevation can be reconstructed from fragments of the various members, scanty though these are. The outer order was Doric; interior Ionic columns supported the roofbeam. The floor was originally of clay but was flagged with marble in Roman times. The walls were lined with stone benches, for which much of the bedding survives.[40]

The materials show an interesting variety and a certain degree of economy. The foundations were of two kinds of poros, a softer and a harder; the steps were of marble, including a darker Hymettian which may have been confined to the lowest step. The walls were of Aiginetan poros. Columns, both Doric and Ionic, architrave, probably metopes, and cornice were of Pentelic marble; but the triglyphs were of the Aiginetan stone.

Decorative sculpture consisted of akroteria only. Parts of two flying Nikai have been found nearby, of Pentelic marble and exquisite late fifth-century style; these no doubt stood on outer angles of the gables. In front of the stoa Pausanias (1.3.2) saw statues of Konon and Timotheos, Zeus Eleutherios himself, and Hadrian.[41] Three appropriate bases have been found in the space between the wings, and the god no doubt occupied the one in the middle, which was circular and 4.2m in diameter. In the fourth century the walls of this stoa too were adorned with pictures, by the sculptor-painter Euphranor. The Twelve Gods were shown, according to Pausanias, and, on "the wall opposite" Theseus, Democracy, and Demos; a third subject was a cavalry engagement at the battle of Mantinea (362 B.C.), with the Athenians assisting the Lacedaemonians.

The stoa was a notable addition to the civic architecture of Athens. Though we do not hear of its being used for official or forensic purposes,

---

[40] *Hesperia* 2, 1933, 110–30; 6, 1937, 5–77, 225–26; *Agora* xiv 96ff; newly found fragments—*Hesperia* 40, 1971, 276ff.

[41] *Hesperia* 6, 1937, 56ff, 68; *Agora* xiv 101. The torso of Hadrian has been found, *Hesperia* 2, 1933, 178ff; E. B. Harrison, *Agora* i: *Portrait Sculpture*, Princeton 1953, 71–74. An impressive draped female torso, of the 4th century B.C., was found recently farther north near a base in front of the Stoa Basileios, on which it probably stood; it is suggested that the figure represents Agathe Tyche (Good Fortune), Demokratia, or some such abstraction; *Agora* xiv 84; *Hesperia* 40, 1971, 270f. On the Mantinea painting, see now T. Hölscher (n. 32 above) 116–19.

(43)

one can well imagine that in some way it supplemented the modest resources of the adjacent Basileios. Otherwise it was available as another
lesche for the general public. In the Platonic dialogues we find Sokrates
there, talking with his friends.[42] Diogenes the Cynic said that in the Stoa
of Zeus, as in the Pompeion, the Athenians had provided him with somewhere to live.[43]

Towards the end of the fifth century a building of quite a different
type, though it can still be called a stoa, was placed on the south side of
the agora.[44] Its double colonnade extended for more than 80m between
the old courthouse on the west and the fountain on the east, from both
of which it was separated by a narrow stepped ramp. Behind were fifteen
rooms, and there are slight indications that a second story was superimposed on these, perhaps in the form of a continuous gallery opening
on the southern street, which lay behind at a higher level than the square.

The new stoa was not such a handsome building as the Stoa of Zeus;
it was more severely practical, less impressive in design, and less costly
in construction. The principal material was poros; except for the back
wall, which had to support the street behind, the upper parts of the walls
were of unbaked brick, of which a little survives. The outer columns
were Doric, with unfluted shafts, as is shown by a poros fragment of a
capital and a curved bit of white stucco. The inner order is not known
but the spacing, presumably twice that of the outer columns, is given by
several foundation blocks still in position at the east end.

The rooms were a little less than 5m square inside. Most of them
were entered from the colonnade through doors placed not exactly in the
middle but towards one side, an arrangement commonly used in dining
rooms so that couches for the diners could be disposed conveniently
around the walls. The floors were of hard-packed clay. The middle room
was entered not directly from the colonnade but through a narrow ante-
chamber inserted between this room and its neighbor on the east. This
arrangement recalls the *andron* or men's diningroom found in commodious houses. Several other features suggest that meals were taken
in some at least of these rooms. The fifth from the east has a raised
border constructed in cement studded with pebbles, of a kind used to

[42] *Theages* 121a; *Eryxias* 392a; E. Vanderpool draws my attention to a similar
occurrence in a fragment of a Socratic dialogue in *Oxyrrhynchus Papyri* 39, 1972,
48.

[43] Diogenes Laertius 6.2.22.

[44] *Hesperia* 37, 1968, 43–56; *Agora* xiv 75–78; Travlos *PDA* 534ff.

support couches. The most probable users of such rooms in a prominent public building on the agora are the various boards of magistrates; and it is significant that in one room the excavators found an inscription concerned with the activities of the Metronomoi, the inspectors of weights and measures.[45] Communal eating was a regular feature of Athenian life; the same room might serve as office and diningroom.

We cannot safely identify this so-called South Stoa I with any building known from literature. It can best be explained as an attempt to provide more compact and convenient accommodation for the various magistrates and boards, who by the end of the fifth century had become very numerous.

This was the last stoa to be built in the agora before the Hellenistic period. It will be noted that all these buildings were of different architectural types. Each had a distinct character of its own, and as in the rest of the agora there was only a very limited coordination of plan.

We can assume that before this the magistrates concerned had been accommodated in sundry buildings scattered about the agora region, principally in the *archeia* to the southwest. The author of the *Constitution of Athens* (3.5) tells us that of the nine archons the Basileus originally used the so-called Boukoleion, near the Prytaneion; the archon (the one called *eponymos*) used the Prytaneion itself, the Polemarch the Epilykeion (named after the man who rebuilt it), and the Thesmothetai (the six lesser archons), the Thesmotheteion; but in Solon's time, he adds, they all came together in the Thesmotheteion.[46] Though attributions to Solon are always open to suspicion, we can well believe that curious traditional offices were superseded by a more compact and convenient arrangement; and we can think of the South Stoa as a further move in this direction, at a time when the administrative machinery had become more complex. Perhaps in this period it was a section of this building which was known as Thesmotheteion.

The Prytaneion remains elusive. As its name implies it was for some purposes the successor of the king's house. It contained the representative hearth of the city, with the cult of Hestia, and in it the city's guests were entertained.[47] Possibly it was on the Acropolis in early times; but the only Prytaneion for which we have definite evidence is the one seen

[45] E. Vanderpool, *Hesperia* 37, 1968, 73–76.

[46] *Agora* III 177f; *Agora* XIV 77f.

[47] L. B. Holland, "The Hall of the Athenian Kings," *AJA* 43, 1939, 289–98 (on Acropolis); *Agora* III 166; XIV 46f.

by Pausanias (1.18.3) as he proceeded from the agora to the Acropolis. The site has not yet been identified and excavated. The Prytaneion remained somewhat detached from the agora and the more active centers of public life.

Magistrates' offices are naturally difficult to identify among the scanty remains unless by good luck some relevant inscription is found. One building which can be recognized with probability lies just outside the agora proper, to the southwest, though it can still be considered as belonging to the *archeia*.[48] It was an irregular quadrilateral measuring about 26m north to south and 21m east to west. The northern part seems to have been an open court; the southern contained a series of rooms on either side of a passage. Originally erected in the middle of the fifth century, it continued to be used until Roman times. Clearly it served some important function; more tentatively the suggestion has been made that it was occupied by the *strategoi* or generals, who by the middle of the fifth century overshadowed the archons even in political matters.

A comparable building, of similar date, has been found about 70m farther south and labeled "Poros Building" because of the scanty foundation blocks which survive. Measuring 37.4m long north to south and 16.5m wide at the southern end, it consists of a series of rooms on either side of a north to south corridor, a courtyard on the south and a semidetached annex of four rooms, probably with an upper story, on the northeast. Eugene Vanderpool now makes a good case for installing the Desmoterion or Prison in this building, on grounds of location, form, and interior appointments, the annex being the quarters of the prison officers and the "Eleven," the magistrates in charge of the prison and of executions. The Desmoterion was used for the temporary housing of offenders and suspects, not for long terms of punishment. Andokides (1.48) and Plato in the *Phaedo* give vivid scenes within its walls, and Vanderpool shows

---

[48] For the "Strategion" see *Agora* xiv 73; cf. iii 174ff. In *Agora* iii 177, I suggested that the Hipparcheion too was here, but H. A. Thompson now suggests to me that it was to the northwest, possibly in a 5th century building of which slight remains are behind the Stoa of Zeus—the cavalry met in this area, *Agora* xiv 73, and n. 29 above.

For the "Poros Building" see *Hesperia* 20, 1951, 168–87; *Agora* xiv 74; Vanderpool's view has been put forward in a symposium in memory of Rodney Young at Philadelphia in May 1975, and in a paper to the American Archaeological Institute at Washington in December 1975; and *Illustrated London News* June 1976. On the prison see Agora iii 149f. The so-called "Prison of Sokrates" on the Mouseion Hill is a cutting in the rock presumably for a house.

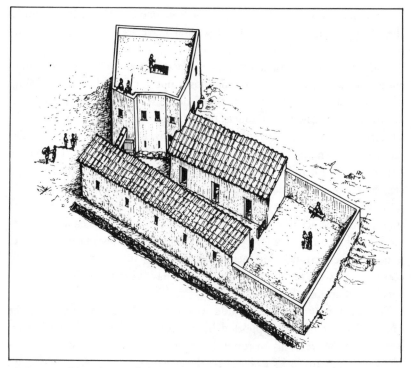

16. Poros Building (Prison?) (Restoration by J. E. Jones, after Travlos)

that this building accords very well with what they say. He notes that in the annex were found a set of thirteen small "medicine pots," suitable for holding the carefully measured doses of hemlock, and the upper part of a Hellenistic statuette of Sokrates, as though the Athenians at a later date, besides making amends to Sokrates by erecting a statue of him in the Pompeion, placed a small replica in the building where he died.

Another building which can be considered in this context, though it was more of an *ergasterion* or workshop than an office, is the mint.[49] It occupied the extreme southeastern corner of the square, beyond the fountain house, and it is identified beyond doubt by the discovery of bronze blanks and other debris. It was a large structure, over 27m north to south and nearly 39m east to west. It was built in the latter part of the fifth century, with solid poros foundations; though its plan is not altogether clear (it was partly built over by the later Nymphaeum), one can see that

---

[49] *Agora* III 160f; XIV 78f.

it contained a number of rooms and at least one courtyard. It was under the control of a board called the Epistatai (Overseers) of the Argyrokopion.

The Tholos or Skias, a rotunda of modest size in the southwestern corner of the agora, was one of the most important and famous buildings of Athens, and a vital focus of its political life.[50] It was built about 465 B.C. to accommodate the Prytaneis, the rotating standing committee of fifty Councilors which attended to the day-to-day business of the city. The old building on the site seems to have been repaired after the Persian destruction and kept in service for a few years; and even after it had been cleared away, its irregular shape, partly due to the adjacent streets, was preserved to some extent in the form of the enclosure in which the Tholos stood. The precinct was very probably what the Athenians called the Prytanikon; this can be deduced from the fact that the stones bearing decrees honoring the Prytaneis for their services, which in the third and second centuries B.C. were set up in the Prytanikon, have been found in large numbers in and around the area.[51]

The inner radius of the rotunda was 8.45m. The entrance was on the east, and the roof was supported by six columns. The wall, resting on bedrock on the west and on rough limestone blocks on the east, was made of hard gray poros in its lower part; the surviving stumps of columns are of the same material. Marble blocks from a stringcourse, belonging to a reconstruction after a serious fire towards the end of the fifth century, show by their treatment that the upper part of the walls was of unbaked brick, pierced by windows. The original floor, sloping down to a drain on the east, was of brown clay. Thus the building was plain and simple in both design and construction. The original roof was of diamond-shaped clay tiles, or half-diamonds at the eaves; many fragments survive, and they show that the face of the eaves, brightly painted in a pattern of a double braid and small palmettes, with the addition of large palmettes on the antefixes, gave the building a touch of ornament and color. This roof must have been destroyed in the fire, and the later form is conjectural; but the conical effect was presumably maintained since writers compare the roof of the Tholos to a parasol or sun hat.

[50] H. A. Thompson, *Hesperia* Suppl. 4, 1940, 44ff; Travlos *PDA* 553ff; *Agora* III 179–84; XIV 41–46. P. J. Rhodes, *The Athenian Boule*, Oxford 1972, 18, associates the building of the Tholos with the institution of the system of Prytaneis, which he attributes to Ephialtes rather than any earlier statesman.

[51] E. Vanderpool, *Hesperia* 4, 1935, 470–75; *Agora* III 184; XIV 41f; XV 3 (in this volume all the decrees are now published by B. D. Meritt and J. S. Traill).

The severe elegance of the building was somewhat marred by a small excrescence on its north side, several times remodeled, which cannot have been anything but the kitchen in which the Prytaneis' meals were prepared. The porch on the east, of which only the foundations survive, and which probably had four columns, was not added till the time of Augustus.

There was no obvious reason, traditional or practical, why the Prytaneis should have been housed in a round building. Perhaps it was simply an architect's fancy. We can only imagine how the Prytaneis and the officials associated with them sat at deliberation or reclined at dinner, and how the third of the Prytaneis which remained on call at night was accommodated.

The building had a sacred character of course; we learn something of the cults in which the Prytaneis were concerned from the decrees in their honor, of which we have a long series, set up in the third and second centuries B.C. though no doubt the principal cults are much earlier. They regularly sacrificed to Apollo Prostaterios and to Artemis Boulaia, whose altar may have stood on a bedding found in the southeastern part of the Tholos precinct. (Another altar base, which seems to be contemporary with the rebuilding of ca. 400 B.C., stands in the middle of the Tholos itself.) Artemis Phosphoros (the Light-bearer, an epithet also given to Hekate) is sometimes added to the list, and with her are associated certain obscure female divinities called the Phosphoroi.[52] A small marble plaque, found just southeast of the Tholos, bears an inscription dated as late as A.D. 200, giving a dedication of plants to the Phosphoroi by a certain Olympos.[53] Apparently in this epoch at least the precinct had a small garden.

The Skias contained a set of standard weights and measures, under the care of a public slave (*demosios*); we know from an inscribed decree that this was so, and that there were similar sets at Peiraeus and Eleusis.[54] The inscription can be dated late in the second century B.C., but one can assume that the Tholos was used for this purpose long before. Official weights and measures of earlier dates have been found in the agora, many of them in the region of the Tholos; they are usually inscribed *demosion* and carry some device. Three square bronze weights, of which one has an astragalos (knucklebone) in relief, one a shield, and the third a turtle, antedate the Tholos by some years, and may have come from its predecessor. Two bronze dry measures of about 400 B.C. were recovered from a well in the

---

[52] *Agora* III 57ff; XIV 45.
[53] *Hesperia* Suppl. 4, 1940, 137ff; *Agora* III, 58.
[54] *IG* II² 1013; *Hesperia* Suppl. 4, 141; *Agora* III 182f; XIV 44f.

southeast corner, a finding place which suggests that they may have been produced by the bronze-workers of the mint. Most of the weights are of lead, and most of the dry measures are terracotta vessels of simple mug-like form, usually stamped with an owl or a head of Athena. Many of them were probably not the original basic standards, which according to the decree were strictly confined to the repositories, but duplicates prepared and issued for use in the agora.

The Tholos continued in use throughout antiquity as a focal point of Athenian life and retained its original form, though damaged and extensively repaired many times. In the Roman period it was given a floor first of marble chips, then of slabs; in the second of these phases it lost its interior columns. It was even patched up after the Herulian sack A.D. 267, for what purpose we do not know. Thus this modest building of the fifth century B.C. outlived its more pretentious Hellenistic and Roman neighbors.

Towards the end of the fifth century a second large rectangular hall was built, just to the west of, i.e. behind, the Old Bouleuterion.[55] The remains are very scanty, but there are enough to reveal the plan and to show that this building too was designed as a Council chamber. It measured ca. 22.5m north to south by 17.5m east to west. The few surviving wall blocks are of hard gray poros, carefully worked; the wall, about 1.5m thick, rested on foundations which are mostly of a softer creamy poros. Again there were four interior supports for the roof; and a bedding running north and south indicates that the two on the east stood in the line of a wall, which probably served as a retaining wall for the auditorium. The long narrow section thus marked off on the east formed a kind of vestibule, with entrances probably at either end and possibly in the middle too. In the main chamber bedrock was treated so as to slope down gently from the north, west, and south. Sections of curved marble benches and their poros beddings have been found which do not belong to the first phase but to a later reconstruction, probably Hellenistic. The original seating presumably consisted of wooden planking, in what arrangement we cannot say precisely. The *bema* or speakers' platform too was no doubt of wood.

A small open courtyard was left to the south, and towards the end of the following century the building was given an extension in this direction, probably in the form of a long Ionic colonnade. At the same time a propylon was built, in the common form of a gateway with an inner and

[55] *Hesperia* 6, 1937, 140–72; W. A. McDonald, *The Political Meeting Places of the Greeks*, Baltimore 1943, 170–79; *Agora* xiv 31ff; Travlos *PDA* 191ff.

an outer columnar porch, at the eastern entrance to the passage which led to the New Bouleuterion between the old building and the Tholos.

It was probably in the New Bouleuterion that a dramatic scene described by Xenophon took place in 403 B.C. in the time of the Thirty.[56] Theramenes takes refuge at the hearth (*hestia*) while Kritias' armed henchmen stand menacingly at the barriers (*dryphaktoi*); then Theramenes is dragged from the *altar*, which here seems to be the same as the hearth. Where these barriers were is not clear, perhaps at the outer entrances, perhaps at the entrance from the vestibule to the main chamber. There is also some evidence of a lighter, outer fence controlling public access, though certain post beddings found south of the Old Bouleuterion seem to be related to the earlier rather than the later building.

The altar-hearth mentioned by Xenophon seems to have been sacred to Zeus Boulaios. The Councilors offered prayers to this deity and to Athena Boulaia as they entered. Pausanias (1.3.5) saw in the Bouleuterion a wooden statue of Zeus Boulaios, one of Apollo (probably the god known as Prostaterios) by Peisias, and a Demos by Lyson (both artists of unknown date).

The Bouleuterion, and with it the city's record office, maintained a close connection with the Mother of the Gods, her cult and shrine.[57] The old temple had not been replaced, but Pheidias, or else his pupil Agorakritos,[58] had made a splendid new statue for the goddess, showing her seated, with a tympanon in her hand and a lion or lions at her feet, as she is shown in many small dedicatory figures. After the New Bouleuterion was built, the two halls stood for a time side by side; this fact, which is not known from our authors but deduced from the remains, can best be explained if one assumes that the old building was now reserved for the cult of the Mother and for housing the archives which were under her tutelage. Thus more adequate provision was made for the various

---

[56] *Hellenika* 2.3.50–56. For the barriers note also Aristophanes, *Knights* 640ff. See *Agora* III 133ff; Rhodes, *The Athenian Boule*, 33ff; recently G. Roux, *BCH* 100, 1976, 475ff, has sought to deduce that the facade of the Bouleuterion, both the Old, on the south side, and the New, on the east, consisted of a row of columns with barriers between, as in the Bouleuterion at Assos.

[57] *Hesperia* 6, 1937, 115–40, 172–217; *Agora* III 150–60; XIV 35ff; Travlos *PDA* 352ff. Note I. K. Papachristodoulou, *ArchEph* 1973, 189–236, for the cult and another shrine, at Moschato south of the city; cf. *Ergon* 1974, 7–10; *Praktika* 1975, 5–10. For Athena Boulaia see now *Hesperia* 40, 1971, 96 (D. J. Geagan).

[58] G. I. Despinis, *Contribution to the Study of the Work of Agorakritos*, Athens 1971 (in Greek), discusses the problem and gives the statue to Agorakritos.

functions of the composite precinct, and this sufficed until the erection of the much more elaborate Hellenistic Metroon transformed the scene. How public archives had been kept in the fifth century, whether there was even then an organized central record office, is a matter of doubt and dispute.[59] Magistrates and their secretaries must have accumulated material. Laws, financial documents, and so forth were increasingly inscribed on stone and set up in large numbers within and in front of the Bouleuterion and various other public buildings appropriate to the nature of the business. But these were copies for public display and reading, not the primary documents, which were no doubt written on papyrus. The fourth-century orators and other writers show that in their time it had become the established practice to place copies of laws, and many other official documents, in the Metroon. They were in the care of a *demosios*; inscriptions mention an *antigrapheus* or copy clerk who provided copies when needed, for example by the stonecutter who carved the stelai. Besides political, financial, and legal documents, copies of the plays of the great tragedians were probably kept in the Metroon, though our authority merely says "in an official place."[60]

Even marble stelai did not last forever. They were damaged, or superseded, or became superfluous or even objectionable; clearances were effected from time to time; otherwise the agora, and the Acropolis and various other shrines, would have been cluttered up intolerably. But there were also many public notices which were purely ephemeral, and for these *leukomata* or whitened boards were used. Most important were drafts of proposals which were to come before the Council and the Assembly; impending lawsuits and lists of men required for military service were also published in this way.[61] As we learn from many references in the orators, beginning with Andokides (in the *De Mysteriis* 83; 399 B.C.) the usual "notice board" was "before the Eponymoi," the ten heroes after whom the ten Attic tribes were named by Kleisthenes. Aristophanes takes the practice back into the fifth century; in the *Peace* (1183; 421 B.C.) the chorus tells how a citizen, "standing in front of the statue of Pandion, saw his own name" on a military list. Early in the excavations, a long base, running north and south, enclosed in a stone

---

[59] *Agora* xiv 35; most recently, A. L. Boegehold, *AJA* 76, 1972, 23–30; E. Posner, *Archives in the Ancient World*, Cambridge, Mass. 1972, Ch. 3.

[60] Ps. Plutarch *Lives of Orators* 841f; *Agora* iii 160. A new inscription says that counterfeit coins were kept in the Metroon, *Hesperia* 43, 1974, 174.

[61] *Agora* iii 85ff.

fence, was found a little to the east of the Bouleuterion and the Metroon, just across the street. It is entirely suitable for the Eponymoi, and one need not hesitate to place the ten bronze figures on it. But the archaeological evidence now shows that it was not constructed till the middle of the fourth century, and that this cannot have been the original site of the Eponymoi. Where they first stood is not at all clear; possibly on a base supported by a large foundation found some distance farther south, near the west end of the site later occupied by the Middle Stoa, apparently built some time after the middle of the fifth century and destroyed in the fourth.[62]

Its form and its place in Pausanias' description (1.5) leave little doubt about the later monument. The enclosure measured originally 18.4m by 3.58m; it was made of poros, and consisted of a sill, a series of posts (15 x 4), and a continuous line of capping stones. Little of the inner structure survives; the foundations are of poros, and several crowning blocks of Pentelic marble have been found, bearing traces of a bronze statue and a tripod. We can imagine that the base was a tall one, that the notices were affixed to it, and that people leaned on the fence to read them.

In later periods Attalos I of Pergamon, one of the Ptolemies, and Hadrian were added to the ten original Eponymoi; and there are traces of extensions to the monument, giving it in the end a total length of 21m. In the time of Hadrian a new fence of marble was constructed.

In the agora and its immediate neighborhood one would expect to find some at least of the law courts, including the Heliaia, the great parent court of democratic Athens, and some of its offshoots. Archaeologically the buildings have proved extremely elusive.[63] Yet the law courts were thought of in ancient times as specially characteristic features of the city of Athens —the Athenians were notorious for their persistent litigiousness; besides private differences, the great political battles were fought out in the courts. "Here is Athens," says the student in the *Clouds* (207), pointing to the map; "I don't believe you," replies Strepsiades, "I see no jurymen sitting." The courts were numerous and required a good deal of space since juries were very large—a minimum of 201 persons served, commonly 501, often several times as many, especially in important political trials. Each jury was theoretically the Demos sitting in judgment. Odd

---

[62] *Hesperia* 2, 1933, 137–39; 21, 1952, 91–92; 37, 1968, 64–68; 39, 1970, 145–222; *Agora* xiv 38ff; Travlos *PDA* 210ff.

[63] *Agora* iii 144–50; xiv 52–72. For a general brief account of the courts see now A.R.W. Harrison, *The Law of Athens, Procedure*, Oxford 1971, 36ff.

buildings in odd places were occasionally used, for example the Odeion of Perikles on the south slope of the Acropolis, which was normally intended for musical contests;[64] and the curious ancient homicide courts, which remained outside the general system, met in various traditional places according to the nature of the case.[65] But we know that there were law courts adjacent to the agora, and there surely must have been some in the area excavated, in addition to the stoas which, as we have seen, could be used in this way. In locating them the trouble is that one does not know what one is looking for; once again there is no definite building type, with recognizable features. A law court, like a political assembly or a festal gathering, needed nothing but a suitable piece of ground; one would expect this to be enclosed by a wall, and a few rooms for the use of officials and the storage of equipment (urns, ballots, and so forth) would have been a useful appendage.

We have noted how the square enclosure built in the southwestern part of the agora early in the fifth century may well have been a law court, perhaps even the Heliaia. This is no more than a reasonable conjecture however, and there is no precise evidence. Like the Bouleuterion, the old building continued in use after the Persian Wars. In the fourth century a series of rooms was built in its western part, with a light colonnade in front facing the court; and a large water clock was constructed in stone against the outer face of the north wall towards its western end.[66]

The discovery of large numbers of objects concerned with legal procedure confirms the presence of law courts in the agora region.[67] These include jurors' bronze identity tickets, and ballots consisting of a bronze disk with a hub which is hollow for condemnation, solid for acquittal. Fragments of *klepsydrai* or water clocks have been found too, in the form of bucket-like vessels with small spouts at the base through which flowed the water allotted for each speech. Most interesting are the *kleroteria* or allotment machines, by means of which the jurymen were empaneled from the general body to serve in the courts which were sitting by an ingenious

[64] Aristophanes, *Wasps* 1109 (see D. MacDowell's edition, Oxford 1971, for the evidence of Aristophanes); *Agora* III 147.

[65] Pausanias 1.28; D. MacDowell, *Athenian Homicide Law*, Manchester 1963, see pp. 167, 168 below.

[66] A stone shaft with an aperture at the bottom; the falling water level must have operated some kind of visible indicator; *Hesperia* 33, 1954, 37-38; *Agora* XIV 65, 202.

[67] *The Athenian Citizen*, 1960 (Excavations of the Athenian Agora, Picture Book No. 4) figs. 21ff; *Agora* XIV 52ff.

process which precluded bribery. They take the form of marble stelai; indeed one side might be used for inscribing an honorary decree. On the other side were columns of slots in which the dikasts' tickets could be inserted, and an attachment for a funnel into which black and white balls

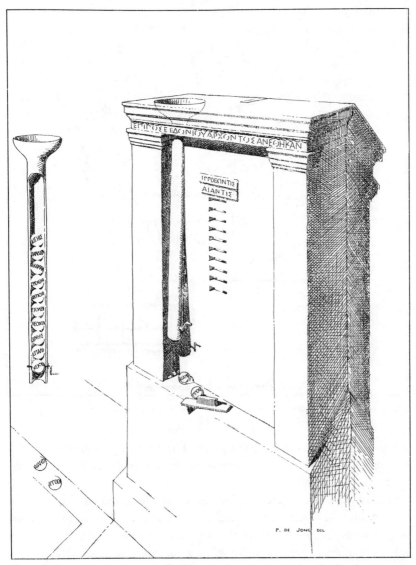

17. Kleroterion, 2nd c. B.C.; simple device for determining order of tribes for prytany duty (Restoration, *Hesperia* Suppl. 1, 1937, 201)

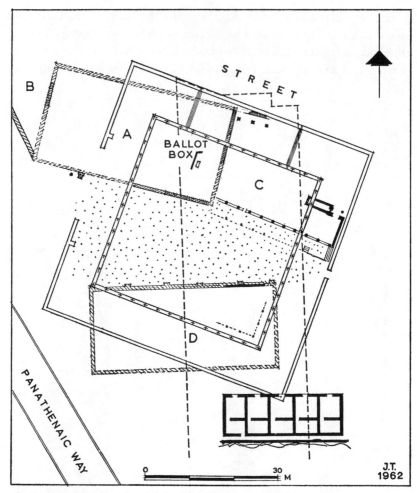

18. Court Buildings on site of Stoa of Attalos (*Agora* xiv 58 fig. 17)

could be fed, to be ejected one by one. The surviving examples are Hellenistic in date, but no doubt similar machines, probably of wood, were in use in earlier times.

Bronze ballots and jurors' tickets have been found in significant numbers in the southwestern part of the agora; and in the northeastern sector, towards the north end of the site later occupied by the Stoa of Attalos, a particular group was found in a context which strongly suggests that here indeed was situated a law court.[68] The ballots lay in or near a

[68] *Agora* xiv 56ff; Travlos *PDA* 520ff.

19. Ballots and Ballot Box Stand, with foundations of 5th c. building (front), 4th c. building (across middle) and Stoa of Attalos (top right) (Photo: Agora Excavations)

curious receptacle formed by two up-ended water channels of rectangular section set in the floor of a room. These are not contiguous, making a solid box, and they may have supported a kind of table on which were placed the urns intended to receive the ballots. Makeshift though they are, they are fixtures, and indicate that voting took place near this very spot.

(57)

Several other ballots and a number of dikasts' tickets were found in the same general area. Of the room in which the main bunch of ballots was found only the northwest corner survives; the walls had socles of rubble, no doubt originally supporting sun-dried brick. The room is associated with a walled enclosure, which can be dated late in the fifth century; very little of the walls survives, but the dimensions are clear—about 22m north to south by 41m east to west. One can imagine a court of at least 500 sitting here. Stretching eastward is an extension in the form of a kind of stoa, with a solid wall on the north side, and on the south a row of columns joined (presumably not to their full height) by a screen wall. About 3.5m farther south again is a row of holes presumably for wooden posts supporting some kind of light barrier. This feature too is appropriate for a law court, and the extension may have accommodated one of the smaller juries. South of the whole group is a graveled area, obviously much trodden; and beyond it are the remains of another east-to-west wall, and in front of this a water channel with basins; the line is not parallel with the northern buildings but converges towards the east. Though little else is preserved, there are slight indications that the wall was the north side of another rectangular enclosure of about the same size, erected probably half a century or more later.

All these buildings were of simple construction, with much re-used material. Unimpressive as they are, and hardly symbolical of the majesty of the law, we can accept them with probability as a group of law courts. Here in the time of Demosthenes took place the processes which were the very essence of Athenian democracy; but in visible form they provide a good example of what one might call non-architecture, of the basic simplicity of Athenian public buildings.

Someone, perhaps Lycurgus, who did so much to give various elements of the city a more impressive architectural form, was not satisfied, and later in the fourth century initiated an attempt to replace the old buildings, on the same site, with something more satisfactory in appearance and in use, namely a large square peristyle. This was never finished—on the west side, in the middle, not even the foundations were laid; and in another section the foundation trench was filled, after some blocks had been laid, with contemporary rubbish. In spite of this, what existed of the building was used for some time until finally the site was cleared for the erection of the Stoa of Attalos. The outer wall was about 39m square, and the colonnades on all sides were about 9m deep; the columns were of hard limestone, and Doric in style. The foundations are of conglomerate and the euthynteria of a hard gray poros. The floor of the inner area was made of brown clay and given a slight slope down towards the north side, where two drains laid beneath the colonnade carried off the water. The building differed in orientation from the later stoa, accommodating itself to the road which ran along the north side of the agora. The principal entrance was obviously on the west, from the agora, and one can imagine that a monumental propylon was originally planned; opposite this point on the east was a narrower entrance. There is no evidence of subsidiary rooms incorporated in the peristyle.

If the old buildings were indeed law courts, one's first thought is that the new building served the same purpose too; and there is no reason why this should not have been so, except perhaps that one would expect rooms to be provided for official use and storage of dicastic equipment. One significant feature is reproduced—in the southeastern part of the court has been found a series of holes, apparently intended again for posts which would carry a rope barrier set about 1m in front of the stylobate of the colonnade; this may well have been taken around all sides, to form a veritable *perischoinisma*.[69] The object would be to segregate persons not immediately engaged in the business which was being transacted in the colonnades. It has been calculated that there would be ample room in the spacious colonnade on one side for a court with a jury of at least 500. Thus several courts could have been sitting simultaneously; complete seclusion would not have been thought necessary, any more than in educational establishments; and partial seclusion could have been obtained by means of wooden screens. This was by no means the ideal court building, but it was a practicable arrangement, and architecturally a great improvement; the peristyle court, like the simple stoa, could be made to serve many various purposes.

Literary evidence is peculiarly difficult to correlate with archaeological. Authors, inscriptions, and lexica (especially Pollux)[70] give a number of different names, but just what these courts were and where they were located is usually quite uncertain. Of the Heliaia itself we are told only that it was near the Agora of the Kerkopes, a kind of thieves' market (a nice example of the curious jumble which made up the city of Athens), that it was open to the sky, and that juries two or three times bigger than the norm of 500 sat there. Aristophanes in the *Wasps* (1108–1109) gives a miscellaneous list: "Some sit where the Archon (sits), some with

[69] *Agora* iii 163–65.
[70] 8.21; *Agora* iii 147.

the Eleven, some in the Odeion, some by the walls." In the same play (120) he mentions the New Court (Kainon); and in the *Ekklesiazousai* (681) he implies that various stoas could be used as courts. Antiphon (late 5th century) mentions a court called Parabyston,[71] a name which means something like "pushed in alongside" (perhaps beside some larger building, possibly another court); and implies that it was in the agora, and that unlike the homicide courts it was under a roof; we are also told that the Parabyston was the court in which the officials called the Eleven presided. An inscription of 392/1 B.C. mentions "the First of the New Courts" and "the Middle Court (Meson) of the New Courts."[72] This suggests a block of three built as a unit; but before inferring that they were built early in the fourth century, one should reflect that towns, streets, and buildings can bear the title "New" for many, many years. Various other names are mentioned, some referring to physical characteristics, such as Trigonon or Triangular, some to persons (statesmen or architects). It may be that in some cases we have two names belonging to the same court.

Finally, we have the account given in the Aristotelian *Constitution* (63), which presumably refers to the procedure in the latter part of the fourth century. "There are ten entrances to the *dikasteria*, one for each tribe," says the author. One need not, in the present context, discuss the process of sortition as he describes it; it is sufficient to note that he appears to use the term *dikasteria* in a collective sense, implying that the courts were arranged in a compact group, adjacent to the area used for sortition, i.e. the allocation of jurors by lot to particular courts. Nothing quite like this has been found. The three "New Courts" of the inscription perhaps point the way to a greater concentration. Something like the system described could have been partially operated in the square peristyle, with the aid of *perischoinismata* and wooden barriers; sortition could have taken place in the courtyard and then the juries could have been dispatched to sections of the colonnades. But the building could not have accommodated all the courts. One wonders whether such a degree of concentration and regularization as our author seems to imply was ever attained. Certainly it was very different when some sat in the Poikile, some in the Odeion, some "by the walls" and in diverse other places.

The Ekklesia, as we have seen, had detached itself somewhat from the agora and found a more secluded place in a kind of primitive theater

[71] *Agora* III 146; XIV 59.
[72] *Hesperia* 5, 1936, 393f; *Agora* III 147.

on the slope of the Pnyx hill to the southwest. Plutarch tells us that the Thirty, in the oligarchical revolution of 404 B.C., turned the bema or speakers' platform round so that it faced the land rather than the sea, "since sea power was the origin of democracy, whereas oligarchy was less repugnant to agricultural people."[73] This does not sound very convincing; but archaeological evidence shows that at the end of the fifth century the assembly place was indeed reversed, so that the bema faced

20. Pnyx from North, with Mouseion Hill and Monument of Philopappos behind (Photo: Alison Frantz)

north and the audience was accommodated on a great embankment facing southward—a very unusual arrangement since theaters and theater-like structures were seldom made in defiance of the natural contours. One advantage was gained in that the assembled citizens were now sheltered from the northeast winds. In the fourth century the auditorium was en-

[73] Themistokles 19.4; K. Kourouniotes and H. A. Thompson *Hesperia* 1, 1932, 90–217; 5, 1936, 151–200; W. A. McDonald, *Meeting-Places of the Greeks*, Baltimore 1943, 44–61, 67–80; Travlos *PDA* 466ff; *Agora* xiv 48ff; M. H. Hansen, *GRBS* 17, 1976, 115–34.

larged so as to accommodate 10,000; the features which are conspicuous today, the massive retaining wall and the bema projecting from a rock-cut scarp, belong to this phase. There was still no permanent stone seating. On the south side of a terrace above the bema two long stoas were begun but never finished. In later times the theater of Dionysos was to take over the function of the Pnyx; better sheltered and more commodious, it might have done so earlier but for Athenian conservatism and the desire to remain within easy distance of the political heart of the city.

To turn to the religious aspects of the agora—most of the public buildings we have looked at were in some sense sacred, had associations with one or more deities, and housed various cults, by reason of tradition or function. But the agora as a whole, or at least the inner square, was considered sacred ground to a certain extent. This is implied by the erection of *horoi*. The stones mentioned above gradually disappeared as the ground level rose in the course of the fifth century; no replacements have as yet been found, but we do hear of *perirrhanteria* or lustral basins set up in the agora in the later periods, and several examples have been found in the excavations.[74] A common form is a marble pillar with a basin for the purificatory water cut in its spreading top. Persons suffering from some pollution were not allowed within the bounds thus defined. Aischines (3.176) tells us that the law kept all who were guilty of certain misdemeanors "outside the *perirrhanteria* of the agora."

One factor which increased the sanctity of the agora was the consciousness in the minds of the later Athenians that from very early until comparatively recent days the ground had been used for burials. Certain cults, for example at the triangular shrine found southwest of the agora, may in fact go back to graveside offerings of prehistoric times. From time to time ancient graves were disturbed in later leveling and building operations; and there are several curious pieces of evidence to show that when this happened they were treated with respect, and offerings were made—in one case on the immediate occasion, in another over a long period—to placate the dead whose rest had been broken.[75]

Two curious little cult spots found in the northern part of the agora deserve mention in this context. One is a small circular pit, constructed early in the fifth century of various re-used blocks, apparently to serve as a receptacle for offerings in a hero cult which extended far back into the archaic period. Besides the bones of victims, a bearded snake, a faience

[74] *Agora* III 218; XIV 117f.
[75] *Agora* XIV 119f; for the triangular shrine see p. 192 below.

21. Rock Altar and Enclosure (Photo: Agora Excavations)

hawk, arrowheads, fragments of terracotta chariot groups, of a bronze shield, and of a terracotta shield have been found in or near the pit.[76]

In the northwest corner of the agora, in front of the Stoa Basileios, has recently been found a small enclosure, barely 3m square inside, made of poros slabs, around an outcrop of rock which apparently served as a ready-made altar or table of offerings. Again many small dedicatory objects have come to light, and since these include miniature squat *lekythoi*, loom weights and spindle whorls, jewelry, and mirrors, one deduces that the occupant or occupants were female. The enclosure and the offerings are dated in the latter part of the fifth century; but that is not to say that the cult of this primitive little shrine was not in some form a good deal older. The excavators with great caution avoid giving the place a name; but it is worth while to ask whether it may be the Leokorion, shrine of the daughters of Leos, who according to legend were sacrificed for the good of the city. This was a familiar landmark in the center of the city; archaeologically it has hitherto proved very elusive; the evidence is puzzling, but at least the site near the northwest corner suits very well the

[76] *Hesperia* 27, 1958, 148–53; *Agora* xiv 119.

lively scene depicted by Demosthenes (54.7-8), in which the Leokorion figures prominently.[77]

With these modest and makeshift little shrines, typically Athenian in their way, one may contrast the most famous *heroon* of all, the true Theseion, where Kimon laid the hero's bones, bringing them from Skyros about 475 B.C. This was a spacious precinct—Peisistratos held an armed muster there—with a *sekos* or inner sanctum. We have no good evidence for a temple; but there were walls on which were displayed paintings by Mikon and possibly Polygnotos. From Pausanias' account one infers that the site of the shrine was east or southeast of the agora, still beyond the reach of the excavators.[78]

The Altar of the Twelve Gods, established as we have seen in 521 B.C., remained a focal point in the religious life of the agora.[79] Here, in the middle of the square and in full view of the populace, suppliants took refuge, making a display of their wrongs. In front of the altar, according to Xenophon, choruses danced at the Dionysia.[80]

The old altar and its enclosure, badly damaged by the Persians, was reconstructed in a slightly different form towards the end of the fifth century. A new sill of hard gray poros, 9.05m east to west by 9.86m north to south, was set on top of the old blocks of yellow poros. Though nothing of the superstructure survives, the marks on the upper surface of the sill show that there were eight posts on each side, with slabs between them which because of their thinness one can imagine as being of marble, and presumably with a capping rail above.[81] Open entrances were left in the middle of the east and west sides. The panels on either side of the entrances were made a little thicker than the rest, perhaps with the intention of carving them in relief. Nothing has been found of the new

[77] *Hesperia* 42, 1973, 126ff, 360ff; *Agora* xiv 123; for the Leokorion see Judeich 338; *Agora* iii 108-13; xiv 121-23; S. Brunnsaker *Opuscula Atheniensia* 8, 1968, 77ff; Travlos *PDA* 3, 5, 578; p. 98 below.

[78] *Pausanias* 1.17.2-6; Aristotle *Ath.Pol.* 15.4; Plutarch *Theseus* 36.2; Judeich 351; *Agora* iii 113-19; xiv 124-26; Travlos *PDA* 234, 578-79; W. R. Connor, "Theseus in Classical Athens," in *The Quest for Theseus*, ed. A. Ward, London 1970, Ch. 8. On the date see J. D. Smart, *JHS* 87, 1967, 136-37; A. J. Podlecki, *JHS* 91, 1971, 141-43; for the paintings see J. P. Barron, *JHS* 92, 1972, 20-45; S. Woodford, *JHS* 94, 1974, 158-65.

[79] M. Crosby, *Hesperia* Suppl. 8, 1949, 82-103; H. A. Thompson, *Hesperia* 21, 1952, 47-82; *Agora* iii 119-22; xiv 129-36.

[80] *Hipparch* 3.2.

[81] A bit has recently been found, *Hesperia* 40, 1971, 278.

altar; fragments of the old one came to light under the slabs of yellow poros with which the enclosure was paved in this period.

An attractive but unprovable suggestion concerning the sculptures which may have adorned the thicker panels is that they were the originals of a group of four three-figure reliefs, known from numerous copies, representing Hermes, Eurydike, and Orpheus; Medea and the daughters of Pelias; Peirithous in the underworld seated between Herakles and Theseus; and Herakles seated on a rock between two of the Hesperides.[82] Since they were frequently copied, and accurately too, to judge by the very slight variation between different versions, the originals must have been well known and readily accessible. The style and date are right; and in form and dimensions the slabs would fit the parapet very well. The themes are very varied and have no special relevance; but undoubtedly sculptors ranged very widely in mythology in search of subjects with which to adorn the shrines of the gods, and thought very largely in terms of decorative effect.

The Athenians had something which they called the Altar of Eleos or Pity, which is frequently mentioned by writers from the first century b.c. onwards. The nature of the literary evidence suggests that this Eleos was an idea and an abstraction rather than a genuine old deity with an independent cult of his own, and that "Altar of Eleos" was an alternative title given in these periods to an already existing altar.

Our authors bring to the Altar of Eleos various legendary personages such as Adrastos and the Herakleidai, besides historical figures such as Demosthenes; but of course this proves nothing about the antiquity of the cult of Eleos, and it is significant that the fifth-century dramatists in handling the legends make no mention of the altar. The question arises to which altar the title was given. Wilamowitz and several recent investigators have maintained that the most likely candidate is the Altar of the Twelve Gods.[83] The identification cannot be proved outright, and

---

[82] H. A. Thompson, *Hesperia* 21, 1952, 60ff; E. B. Harrison, *Hesperia* 33, 1964, 76ff.

[83] *Aus Kydathen* 201; see, in addition to authorities in n. 79 above, *Agora* III 67–74; R. E. Wycherley, *CQ* ns 4, 1954, 143ff.

E. Vanderpool, *Hesperia* 44, 1975, 308–10, suggests that when Pausanias (1.17.1) says that the Altar of Eleos was "in the agora" he means the Roman Market; but even though in other contexts he seems to call the old agora "Kerameikos" (see p. 254 below), surely when he says "in the agora" he means not a special new market building (and hardly a suitable place for the altar) but as on so many other sites, the true main city center.

there are possible alternatives such as the altar of Zeus Agoraios. But the Altar of the Twelve is appropriate in its situation and in its character as a prominent suppliants' altar. Pausanias does not mention the Altar of the Twelve by name, but inserts the Altar of Eleos at the very end of his account of the agora (1.17.1), after describing the north side, without giving any clear indication of its site. Statius describes the altar of "Clementia" as surrounded by trees, and it is curious that there is evidence of tree planting around the Altar of the Twelve, in the form of pits and a basin hollowed out in a sunken poros block, fed by a pipeline, presumably to irrigate the grove.[84]

Cults of deities concerned with the ancestry of the Athenians—of the people as a whole and of the *phratriai* or clans—naturally found a place in the agora. We have already noted the small archaic temple in the middle of the west side, probably dedicated to Apollo, who as the father of Ion was regarded as Patroos or ancestral god by the Ionians in general and the Athenians in particular. This was not replaced in immediately post-Persian times, though a statue of Apollo Alexikakos (Averter of Evil), by Kalamis, was dedicated in the shrine. Just after the middle of the fourth century a tiny temple, a *naiskos*, was built a little to the north of the site, near the south end of the Stoa of Zeus.[85] It consisted of a simple cella, 5.2m east to west by 3.65m north to south. The foundations are of conglomerate, with an eastward extension added two centuries later obviously for the purpose of giving the temple a columnar porch. The walls, of which several blocks survive on the south, were of hard gray poros. A conglomerate block at the western end no doubt belonged to the statue base. A poros block found *in situ* to the east of the temple supported the altar; and an altar of Hymettian marble found on the east side of the agora, bearing the inscription "[Altar] of Zeus Phratrios and Athena Phratria," in letters of appropriate date, fits the base perfectly and has been confidently restored to its place. Thus the identification is confirmed.

The new temple of Apollo Patroos, clearly identifiable by its place in Pausanias' description (1.3.4) between the Stoa of Zeus and the Metroon,

---

[84] Statius *Thebaid* 12.481ff; *Hesperia* 21, 1952, 50; 22, 1953, 46. On Statius' treatment of the Altar see J. F. Burgess, *CQ* NS 22, 1972, 339–49.

Note also, immediately south of the shrine of the Twelve Gods, an *eschara* or ground altar, an area 1.76m by 3.77m, enclosed by a poros curb, surrounded by a paved area bounded by a wall; see *Hesperia* 22, 1953, 43ff; *Agora* III 49; XIV 132; a very tentative suggestion is that it was the hero shrine of Aiakos of Aigina, mentioned by Herodotus 5.89.2.

[85] *Hesperia* 6, 1937, 84–90, 104–7; *Agora* III 52; XIV 139f.

was built a little later, to judge by the archaeological evidence.[86] To make the maximum use of the limited space, the architect gave the shrine a kind of inner sanctum or possibly treasury by building an annex on to the west end of the north side, immediately behind the little temple of Zeus and Athena. The main cella measured 8.64m by just over 9m internally; the annex was about 4.5m square. The foundations were again of red conglomerate; Acropolis limestone and the hard yellowish limestone of Kara are both found in the extant sections of the walls. In the porch the euthynteria is of hard gray Peiraeus limestone, and certain blocks of Hymettian marble probably belong to the steps. The form of the porch is not entirely clear—it probably consisted of four Ionic columns between *antae*. The east wall of the cella was given exceptional thickness, at least in its lower part; the reason may be that only the western or inner section of this socle carried a high wall, while the eastern or outer section provided a ledge on which stood, on either side of the door, the two statues of Apollo seen by Pausanias, the Alexikakos of Kalamis and another made by the fourth-century sculptor Leochares. Pausanias locates them "in front of the temple," and this may mean "in the *pronaos* or front porch."

Two poros slabs in the western part of the cella must belong to the base of the cult statue, and the figure which stood upon the base was probably a colossal Apollo Kitharoidos (Lyre-player) in Pentelic marble which was found long ago about 20m to the south. The head is missing, and without it the figure stands 2.54m high. The god wears a peplos which hangs down to his feet in heavy folds, and a cloak on his back. A number of small copies are known, and show in a general way how the missing parts can be restored. The kithara, of which only slight traces survive in the original, was held against the left side. The figure shows very fine workmanship, and may be dated in the third quarter of the fourth century B.C. Pausanias attributes the cult statue to the painter-sculptor Euphranor; and though it is a little surprising that he should have represented Apollo Patroos as a lyre-player, style, quality, and scale make the identification probable.

A slab of Pentelic marble found in northern Athens, with a late fourth-century inscription reading "(Altar) of Apollo Patroos," no doubt belongs to the altar of this shrine;[87] and two omphaloi of Delphian type, half-egg-

[86] *Hesperia* 6, 1937, 90ff; *Agora* III 50ff; XIV 137ff; Travlos *PDA* 96ff; on the statue see H. A. Thompson, *ArchEph* 1959, 30–34; S. Adam, *BSA* Suppl. 3, 1966, 94–97; O. Pelagia, *AAA* 6, 1973, 323–29.

[87] *IG* II² 4984; *Agora* III 52.

22. Agora, West Side from Southeast (Photo: Agora Excavations)

shaped blocks of Hymettian marble, found some distance to the south near the Metroon, may well have stood in front of the temple of Apollo.

In this period the temple of Apollo Patroos, modest though it was, was the biggest temple in the agora. No great peristyle temple stood in the square or on its edges till Roman times. But the Hephaisteion, though it stood aloof, on the low rocky hill to the west, the Kolonos Agoraios, belonged in a sense to the agora.[88] It was the most prominent feature of the scene, and it was dedicated to Athena herself, as goddess of the city and as patron of the arts, along with Hephaistos, divine smith and god of arts and crafts.

"Theseion" is the popular name given to the building in comparatively modern times, no doubt because of the representation of Theseus in the sculptures. Though there are still a few doubters, the identification as temple of Hephaistos is now generally accepted;[89] one piece of evidence

[88] W. B. Dinsmoor, *Hesperia* Suppl. 5, 1941; Travlos *PDA* 261ff; *Agora* iii 98–102; xiv 140–49; W. B. Dinsmoor, Jr., *AJA* 80, 1976 223–46 (on roof).

[89] R. E. Wycherley, *JHS* 79, 1959, 153–56; H. Koch, *Studien zum Theseustempel in Athen*, Berlin 1955 (important for the general study of the temple) assigns the temple to Theseus and Herakles jointly; cf. also M. Delcourt, *Hephaistos*, Paris 1957.

is the discovery on the slopes of the hill of traces of the shops of metal workers, who plied their trade under the eye of their patron.

Pottery and traces of burning on top of the hill probably indicate that there was a simple shrine here, destroyed by the Persians. The temple was part of the great Periklean building program; Dinsmoor's date of 449–444 B.C. is generally accepted,[90] but before the building was completed there was some kind of delay, probably through concentration of the work force on the Acropolis. The final details, including the sculpture, were not added, and the cult statues were not installed, until some twenty years later.

The building measures 13.7m by 31.8m on the stylobate, and has a peristyle of 6 by 13 Doric columns; the cella has a pronaos and a back porch, each with two columns between the *antae*. Investigations by the excavators of the agora have shown that there was an interior colonnade, probably with five columns along the sides and three along the back, possibly with seven and four.[91] The relation of the foundations of this inner colonnade to those of the walls shows that it was inserted as an afterthought, perhaps in imitation of the plan of the Parthenon. Indeed the whole temple was built from the outside inwards, the foundations of the peristyle being laid first, as the archaeological evidence shows—this was common practice. The principal material was Pentelic marble, but most of the sculpture and some architectural details were of Parian. The foundations and the lowest step were of three different grades of poros.

The scheme of the sculpture seems to be a reduction, in the interests of economy, of the more complete and elaborate scheme of the Parthenon.[92] Sockets cut in the floors show that there were pedimental groups, and various fragments have been conjecturally assigned to them. In the east even the subject is doubtful, in the west it was probably a Centauromachy. The sculptured metopes are confined to the east end. Ten on the front of the temple show the labors of Herakles; and four each on the north and south sides, in the eastern part, the labors of Theseus. Like the Parthenon, the Hephaisteion has some typically Ionic details to

[90] Dinsmoor ascribes the temple to the same architect as the temple of Ares, the temple of Poseidon at Sounion, and the temple of Nemesis at Rhamnous; *Architecture of Greece*, 181ff; cf. A. T. Hodge and R. A. Tomlinson, *AJA* 73, 1969, 185; *Agora* XIV 142f; H. Knell, *AA* 1973, 94–113, who distinguishes two architects. On the date see now B. D. Meritt, *Proceedings of the American Philosophical Society*, 119, 1975, 272f.

[91] For different opinions on this see *Agora* XIV 142 n. 122; 145.

[92] H. A. Thompson, *Hesperia* 18, 1949, 230–68; *AJA* 66, 1962, 339–47; C. H. Morgan, *Hesperia* 31, 1962, 211–35; 32, 1963, 91ff; *Agora* XIV 147–49.

enliven its Doric severity, notably a frieze within the peristyle but limited in this case to the ends. The eastern frieze, running over the pronaos and extending to the outer colonnade, shows a combat taking place in the presence of the gods, interpreted as Theseus subduing the rebel sons of Pallas; the western, confined to the width of the porch, develops the theme of the pediment and shows more Lapiths and Centaurs. The themes of the external sculptures have no particular reference to the cult; sculptors were allowed much latitude in their choice.

There has been endless argument about the treatment of the walls of the cella[93]—the date of the plaster on them, the purpose of the stippling of the blocks, and whether there was ever any intention of having mural paintings. It now seems certain that no such paintings were ever carried out, especially since the inner columns were placed so close to the walls; and of course the paintings by Mikon and possibly Polygnotos in the Theseion must be sought elsewhere.

The inevitable total loss of the great bronze cult statues is not so hopeless as one might think. Two blocks of dark Eleusinian stone from the base survive, and one has holes for the attachment of figures in relief, no doubt of white marble. A hint in St. Augustine, of all people,[94] suggests that the subject was the miraculous birth of the Attic hero Erichthonios.

Another bronze-casting pit, very probably used for making the statues, has been found just southwest of the temple; and an inscription about the making and erection of two bronze statues, giving accounts dating from 421 to 415 B.C., almost certainly refers to Hephaistos and Athena. Besides various materials and technical processes, we are told of wooden crates and scaffolds used in installing the figures.[95]

Cicero attributes a fine Vulcan at Athens to Alkamenes,[96] and even if the identification is not certain these statues must have been in the best Pheidian tradition. In Homer's Olympos Hephaistos was a figure of fun; his sexual relationship with Athena was ambiguous and undignified; here he stood beside her as an equal partner, watching over the craftsmen, the agora, and the city.

The temple stood in an enclosure of the irregular fortuitous shape

---

[93] Summarized in *Agora* xiv 147.

[94] 18.12; cf. S. Karouzou, *AthMitt* 69–70, 1954–1955, 68–94.

[95] *Hesperia* Suppl. 5, 1941, 109–10; *IG* i² 370–71; *Agora* xiv 145f.

[96] *On the Nature of the Gods* 1.30 (83). F. Brommer, *Der Gott Vulcan auf provinzialrömischen Reliefs*, Köln-Wien 1973, suggests that the type is derived from Alkamenes.

which is characteristic of Athenian shrines. Along the north, west, and south sides rows of shrubs were planted; many holes in the rock have been found and fragments of plant pots. These traces are of Hellenistic date, but the "garden of Hephaistos" may have existed in some form much earlier.[97]

Every visitor to Athens is impressed by the miraculous state of preservation of the temple, especially when one contrasts it with the bits and pieces in the agora below. This is only partly accounted for by its long-continued use as a church. Such things depend on chance. In mediaeval and Turkish times the colonnades and even the cella were used for burials—this accounts for the bad preservation of the marble pavement. Looking for the bones of Theseus in the middle of the temple, the French archaeologist Fauvel found instead the remains of the English traveler John Tweddell. Nearby lay George Watson, whose Latin epitaph, still on view, was written by his friend Lord Byron.[98]

Another notable shrine which can best be treated as an appendage of the agora is the Eleusinion in the City, counterpart of the great shrine of Demeter and Kore at Eleusis. It stood to the southeast, high up on the slope leading to the Propylaia, with the Panathenaic Way on its west side.[99] Starting here, the Eleusinian procession passed through the agora on its way to Eleusis. The western part of a spacious enclosure has been found; the eastern side is still unexcavated. Within are the foundations of a temple of simple form and modest size, 17.7m north to south and 11m east to west, consisting of a main room on the south and an *adyton* or inner sanctum on the north, dated early in the fifth century; there are slight remains which may belong to an earlier shrine. To the east are the remains of an altar and of a long base which may have carried the remarkable series of marble stelai on which was inscribed the record of the sale of the property of Alkibiades and others found guilty of sacrilege in 415 B.C.[100] Many dedications have been found in the area, confirming

[97] D. B. Thompson, *Hesperia* 6, 1937, 396ff; *Garden Lore of Ancient Athens*, 1963 (Excavations of the Athenian Agora, Picture Book No. 8), figs. 11–14; *Agora* XIV 149.

[98] *Hesperia* Suppl. 5, 16ff.

[99] *Agora* III 74–85; XIV 150–55; Travlos *PDA* 198ff. A small enclosure at a lower level adjacent to the north side may have been some kind of appendage or subsidiary shrine.

[100] *IG* I² 325–34, with many additions from the excavations; W. K. Pritchett, "The Attic Stelai," *Hesperia* 22, 1953, 225–99; 25, 1956, 178–328; *Agora* XIV 153. See *Hesperia* 44, 1975, 319–21 for a new piece.

the identification of the shrine; among them, most surprisingly, is a Herm of an Epicurean philosopher Phaidros.[101] A simple propylon at the south end was added in the fourth century, and a stoa on the south side in Roman times. Thus the shrine of the Two Goddesses, in spite of its sanctity, spaciousness, and fine situation, was architecturally simple, and, unless the eastern section has some surprises in store, by no means equivalent to the sanctuary at Eleusis.

23. Fragment of Stele recording sale of property of Alkibiades (Photo: Agora Excavations)

In this context we may also note the Pompeion,[102] though it stood some distance away to the northwest of the agora, on the south side of the Panathenaic Way, inserted between the Dipylon and the Sacred Gate. It was used for the preparation of the great processions (*pompai*), especially the Panathenaic, but no doubt also the Eleusinian, and for the storage of the necessary equipment. Built at the beginning of the fourth century, though there may well have been simpler installations for the same purpose on the site much earlier, it took the form of a rectangular peristyle, enclosing a court about 45m by 17m, with a columnar porch at the southeast end, and an odd assemblage of rooms, laid out as dining rooms, attached to the northwest section and fitted in somewhat awkwardly

[101] *Hesperia* 18, 1949, 101–3; *Agora* III 83, XIV 154.

[102] Judeich 361; *Agora* III 85; D. Ohly, *AA* 1965, 286–301; Travlos *PDA* 477ff; W. Hoepfner, *Das Pompeion* (Kerameikos Heft 1) Athens 1971.

between the peristyle and the adjacent city walls. The building suffered badly in the time of Sulla and was replaced in the second century A.D. by a three-aisled structure resembling a basilica. Like so many Athenian buildings, the original Pompeion was versatile in function; in Demosthenes (34.39) we hear of a distribution of corn being conducted there; Diogenes' remark that it provided him with yet another home implies that when not in official use it was open to the general public. It contained a statue of Sokrates by Lysippos and portraits of Isokrates and the comedy writers.

Still to the northwest of the agora, at a distance of about 50m on the south side of the Sacred Way, are slight remains of what seems to be a small temple, obliterated on the north by the railway. This may be the shrine of Aphrodite Ourania noticed by Pausanias immediately after the Hephaisteion.[103] The remains are of early Roman date, but if the identification is correct there must have been a much earlier shrine, containing the statue of the goddess seen by Pausanias, which was made by Pheidias of Parian marble. A little to the east, during the construction of the railway, a handsome altar was found *in situ*, dedicated in 197–196 B.C. "to Aphrodite Leader of the Demos and to the Charites (Graces)." Other inscriptions show that in Hellenistic times honorary statues of certain foreigners were set up in the shrine of Demos and the Charites, and we learn from Josephus that a Jewish high priest, Hyrkanos, was among them.

We have seen several cult statues and others closely associated with the shrines and public buildings. It remains to look at some of the more remarkable of the statues which stood detached in the open square. Most prominent and most famous were the Tyrannicides.[104]

Harmodios and Aristogeiton assassinated Hipparchos, younger son of Peisistratos, in 514 B.C. Their attempt to end the tyranny was abortive and they were killed; but after the restoration of democracy in 510 B.C. they were given heroic honors, including bronze statues by Antenor in the middle of the agora. Carried off as a trophy by the Persians in 480 B.C., they were eventually sent back to Athens by Alexander the Great or one

[103] 1.14.7; *Agora* III 50, 59–61; XIV 142, 159f; Travlos *PDA* 79ff; altar *IG* II² 2798; Josephus *Antiquities of Jews* 14.8.5.

[104] S. Brunnsaker, *The Tyrant-Slayers of Kritios and Nesiotes*, Lund 1955; B. Shefton, *AJA* 64, 1960, 173–79; *Agora* III 93–98; XIV 155–58; C. W. Fornara, *Philologus* 114, 1970, 155–80; Richter, *Sculpture and Sculptors*, 154f; copies fig. 602f. On Theseus and the Tyrannicides see E. Hudeczek, *Jahreshefte des oesterreichischen archäologischen Instituts* 50, 1972–1973, 134ff. Note also Hölscher (see n. 32) 85ff.

of his immediate successors to stand henceforth alongside their replacements. We do not know much about these earlier figures, but we can assume that they were a more archaic version of their successors. The latter, erected soon after the Persians had gone, were by two sculptors in association, Kritios and Nesiotes. We know them from full-size copies and representations in minor arts, on vases and coins; and it is generally agreed that two figures of Theseus, one in the middle of the east frieze of the Hephaisteion, one in a similar position on the west, reflect the statues of the Tyrannicides down below. In spite of this evidence there has been much dispute about the composition of the group; but at least we know that they were heroic figures, somewhat more than life-size but not colossal, advancing menacingly upon their victim, the younger Harmodios with his sword arm raised, the older bearded Aristogeiton with his cloaked left arm outstretched to guard his friend. We are told that they stood in the old orchestra, which probably means right in the middle of the square.[105] In Roman times both groups may have stood on a foundation in front of the Odeion; but we do not know how they were placed in relation to one another. Not far away two fragments of a marble base have been found, bearing a few letters which with the help of a quotation in a writer on meters, Hephaistion (4.6), can be restored as part of the dedicatory inscription, reading, "A great light for the Athenians rose when Harmodios and Aristogeiton killed Hipparchos . . . made their fatherland" presumably "free" or "with equal laws" as the famous song composed in their honor has it.[106] The couplets are attributed to Simonides by Hephaistion, but this has been disputed by some modern writers. The fragments leave room for differences of opinion about the precise size of the base, and so about the restoration of the group; nor is it certain whether they belong to Antenor's group or to Kritios', probably to the latter's. What is clear is that the figures had a uniquely prominent place in the Athenian scene, as Harmodios and Aristogeiton had in the hearts of the Athenians.

To be "set up in bronze in the agora" was a very great honor, and indeed conferred upon a man the status of a hero. Themistokles and the other great generals of the fifth century did not receive it in their lifetime. Demosthenes (20.70) tells us that Konon was the first man after the Tyrannicides to be publicly honored thus, though, as we have seen in

---

[105] Timaios *Lexicon Platonicum s.v. orchestra*; Arrian *Anabasis* 3.16.8; cf. *Agora* III 94, 97; XIV 157.

[106] *Hesperia* 5, 1936, 355; 6, 1937, 352; *Agora* III 97f.

the case of Leagros, near the Twelve Gods, statues of men could be dedicated privately. The distinction began to be given more freely in the course of the fourth century. Plutarch tells how Diogenes wandered among the statues begging and explained to wondering onlookers that he was "practicing failing to get what he wanted."[107] The general Chabrias was shown as a heroic figure, his shield supported on his knee and his spear thrust forward. The famous statue of Demosthenes by Polyeuktos was not set up till long after his death, in the northwestern sector of the agora. Amends were made to great men of the more distant past; Pausanias saw the figure of Solon in front of the Stoa Poikile (1.16.1) and Pindar near the temple of Ares (1.8.4). In Hellenistic and Roman times the honor was cheapened and became a form of flattery; the honorands stood in serried ranks, cluttering the agora. But for a long time the Tyrannicides kept their special place, and decrees about the setting up of statues were apt to specify, "not beside Harmodios and Aristogeiton."

Of the statues of gods which we have not yet had occasion to notice probably the finest was the group of Eirene (Peace) holding the infant Ploutos (Wealth) made early in the fourth century by Kephisodotos, who was probably Praxiteles' father. The statue was seen by Pausanias immediately after the Eponymoi, on the west side of the agora, presumably a little to the south of the place where, curiously, the temple of Ares was later built.[108] It is known from late copies and representations on coins; and we can see that Kephisodotos combined a new fourth-century subtlety with the old fifth-century Pheidian dignity. We are told that the Athenians established an altar of Eirene in 374 B.C., the year of the peace arranged by the King of Persia.[109] But the cult may be earlier. In the late fifth century, as the Peloponnesian War dragged on, many Athenians were obsessed by the thought of peace. Aristophanes says that the altar of Eirene is not stained with blood;[110] Euripides calls her bringer of prosperity, nurturer of youth, giver of deep wealth, fairest of the blessed gods.

[107] *On Shamefacedness (Dysopia)* 7. For all these see *Agora* III 207–17; cf. p. 73 above. For Chabrias see now J. Buckler, *Hesperia* 41, 1972, 467, who denies the kneeling posture usually inferred from Cornelius Nepos, *Chabrias* 1.2–3.

[108] 1.8.2; *Agora* III 65–67; XIV 168; A. H. Borbein, *Jahrbuch* 88, 1973, 115ff; Richter, *Sculpture and Sculptors*, 197ff; E. la Rocca, *Jahrbuch* 89, 1974, 112–36.

[109] Philochoros frag. 151, Jacoby *FGH* IIIb 1, 523ff; Plutarch *Kimon* 13.6 associates the altar with the peace of 449 B.C.

[110] *Peace* 1020; Euripides *Kresphontes* frag. 453 (Nauck).

24. Decree against Tyranny, 336 B.C., with relief of Demos and
Demokratia (Photo: Agora Excavations)

Finally, alongside the statues, and in far greater numbers, stood the inscribed stelai, the best of which were true works of sculptural art, made of fine marble, well-proportioned and carefully designed, with the text meticulously set out in elegant lettering. Some had a simple pediment at the top, some had suitable ornament in relief; a few had a sculptured panel showing a relevant subject. Fortunately for our studies, the Athenians became more and more addicted to having all their activities inscribed on stone for public scrutiny, and the stelai accumulated in hundreds and eventually in thousands, standing within or in front of the various public buildings and shrines. Some were in time discarded and incorporated in later constructions. Very few have been found *in situ*. After the final destruction of the agora there was a clean sweep, and the stones, mostly shattered or deliberately cut up, were widely dispersed for use as building material. Many found their way into the post-Herulian wall. Re-used again and again, some have been found built into modern house walls. In classical Athens they formed a basic component of the scene in the agora.

HELLENISTIC AND ROMAN AGORA

The later history of the agora can be briefly summarized. The place was no longer one of the centers of the earth, but it had a peculiarly interesting architectural history. For more than a century after the time of Lycurgus there was no important change, and little was built. Then in the second century B.C. the scene was transformed by the erection of vast new stoas, of great length in the contemporary fashion. Attalos II King of Pergamon (159–138 B.C.) had studied at Athens in his youth, at the Academy; along with another monarch, Ariarathes of Cappodocia, he honored his old teacher Karneades with a statue. The base has been found in front of the Stoa of Attalos, and on it the two kings modestly described themselves as demesmen of Sypalettos, with reference to their honorary citizenship.[111] To show his gratitude to the Athenian Demos as a whole, Attalos donated the great two-storied stoa which bears his name; bits of the epistyle bearing the dedication have been found and leave the

[111] *IG* ii² 3781; *Hesperia* 19, 1950, 318; *Agora* iii 46; xiv 107. H. B. Mattingly, *Historia* 20, 1971, 29ff, maintains that the dedicators were indeed ordinary Athenian citizens, named after the kings; he rejects, curtly and with no good reason, Diogenes' statement (4.65) about correspondence between Karneades and King Ariarathes. Between the Attalids and the Academy Diogenes shows that there was a long and close association (4.60; 5.67).

25. Rebuilding of Stoa of Attalos; on right, part of original wall; in foreground, part of dedicatory inscription (Photo: Agora Excavations)

identification beyond doubt.[112] The stoa, rebuilt in the 1950s to provide a museum for the agora, reproduces the ancient building with great accuracy, except for a few details such as larger windows.[113] The facade was of marble, the walls of Peiraeus stone, the roof was of terracotta tiles of impressive size. On the ground floor the outer columns were Doric, the inner Ionic; in the upper story the Ionic order was used in the facade, and the inner columns were surmounted by a variety of Egyptian palm capital ("Pergamene"). It is assumed that the rooms behind the colonnades were superior shops, no doubt owned and rented out by the city. The colonnades themselves provided spacious promenades, supplemented at ground level by a broad terrace. Now at last Athens had a splendid market building, contrasting strongly with the old ramshackle shops and *skenai* or booths.

[112] *Hesperia* 26, 1957, 83–88, 104f; *Agora* III 46; *The Stoa of Attalos II in Athens*, 1959 (Excavations of the Athenian Agora, Picture Book No. 2), fig. 33.
[113] Picture Book No. 2; *Agora* XIV 104ff; Travlos *PDA* 505ff.

(78)

26. Stoa of Attalos, South End, with Apollo of Euphranor (Photo: Agora Excavations)

27. Stoa of Attalos, North End, with Nike from Stoa of Zeus (Photo: Agora Excavations)

The Stoa of Attalos was in itself a complete architectural unit. Even in the Hellenistic period the Athenians did not construct an agora of "Ionian" type with a closely knit complex of colonnades. The "Middle Stoa," built at about the same time, was placed at right angles to the Stoa of Attalos, but it was a very different type of building, single-storied, with Doric columns on both sides and both ends, and a central row.[114] The interior columns, and probably some of the exterior, were joined except at the top by curtain walls. The building was vast in extent, being greater in ground area than any other in Athens, but comparatively simple in construction, the principal material being brown Aiginetan stone. Since it was two-faced, this stoa formed both the south side of the main square of the agora and the north side of a smaller square which was now cut off on the south. The old South Stoa was demolished, and a simple, single-aisled Doric building, "South Stoa II," 93m long, was erected parallel to the Middle Stoa. Its west end adjoined the old court building, which was now given a lantern roof supported by an interior peristyle. Its east end was linked to the Middle Stoa by the "East Building." A north-south wall divided this building lengthwise, with a single narrow hall to the east,[115] and five rooms to the west. The middle room, containing a stairway descending westward, probably provided the principal entrance to the area.

The purpose of this "south square" and its component buildings cannot be determined beyond dispute. For some time after its discovery it was labeled "Commercial Agora," and so it may have been. In some cities in Hellenistic times there was a tendency to segregate market from political agora. But there is no particular confirmatory evidence, and a good case has been made by H. A. Thompson for installing the law courts in these buildings. The fact that the old court building was adjacent does not in itself prove anything; as we shall see in the next chapter, at Athens markets and law courts were apt to be mixed up. But it is perhaps significant that the new buildings were erected just at the time when the old court enclosures in the northeastern area were abandoned to make room for the Stoa of Attalos; and in particular a great deal of material from the northeastern peristyle was re-used in South Stoa II. If these buildings were indeed law courts, there was ample space, but we do not know how

[114] For a conspectus of the southern buildings see now *Agora* XIV 65-71; 103f.

[115] Note in this a row of marble bedding blocks with sockets in the corners, perhaps for the feet of chests in which equipment and documents were kept; *Agora* XIV 70.

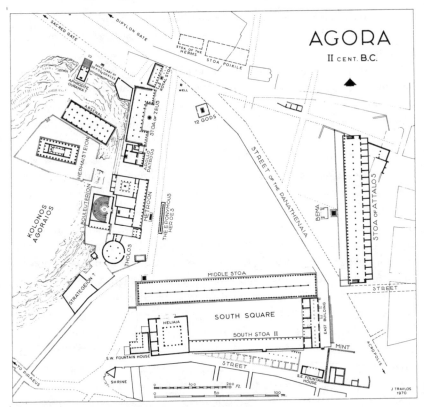

28. Agora in Hellenistic Period (*Agora* xiv pl. 7)

it was used; perhaps the arrangements were, as we have suggested for the peristyle, by no means ideal but practicable. The fact is that even in this architecturally sophisticated age the Athenians and the Greeks in general still made great use, for a wide range of purposes, of open spaces with large stoas and where necessary simple rooms attached. This is apt to make the precise identification of buildings difficult or impossible, in default of the discovery of inscriptions or other specific evidence.

In the middle of the South Square are two rectangular foundations suitable for small temples; we do not know what cults they may have housed.[116] They may be dated about 100 B.C.; both buildings were destroyed in the sack by Sulla, in 86 B.C., when the whole of this area suffered very badly. For a time it was even invaded by workshops. Eventually the South Square was restored to order and dignity; but only the

[116] *Hesperia* 37, 1968, 41–43; *Agora* xiv 70f.

western temple, the smaller, was rebuilt, and the South Stoa was abandoned, except that its back wall was restored to form the southern boundary.

The main agora to the north even in the Hellenistic period remained an open square, free from large buildings. Minor monuments accumulated; statues were set up in ever greater numbers, and many Hellenistic princes, friends and patrons of Athens, were honored in this way.[117]

The north and west sides, in contrast with the east and south, were still an assemblage of miscellaneous public buildings and shrines; but the old Metroon, with the shrine of the Mother of the Gods and the city's archives, was given a splendid new form in the second century B.C.[118] The facade consisted of a marble Ionic colonnade nearly 39m long; behind this were four rooms, a large square one on the north and three smaller oblong ones to the south. Some of the walls were built on foundations provided by the Old Bouleuterion and the archaic temple. If any final proof of identification is needed, it is provided by the discovery on the site of tiles inscribed: "Dionysios and Ammonios (dedicated this) to the Mother of the Gods."[119] These men presumably made the tiles. We cannot be sure how the new building, which has some resemblance to the great library at Pergamon, was adapted to the dual purpose of the Metroon. The second room from the south has a temple-like facade and may have housed the cult statue, leaving the rooms on either side for the archives, stored in chests or on shelves. The large northern room contained a peristyle round a small court; in front was a columnar porch with a small room on either side, and behind were three small narrow rooms. To the east of the building, just opposite the room which we have identified as the inner shrine, are foundations which probably carried the main altar.

On the opposite side of the western street, near the Eponymous Heroes, are the remains of what must have been one of the handsomest altars in Athens. In the Hellenistic period altars tended to assume a more imposing and elaborate form, to be works of architecture rather than simple and modestly decorated slabs. In this case, on conglomerate foundations, four marble steps were built, measuring about 8.6 by 5.3m. Of the altar proper a large marble orthostate is preserved, and fragments of a second;

---

[117] *Agora* III 207ff.

[118] *Hesperia* 6, 1937, 172–203; Travlos *PDA* 352ff; *Agora* XIV 37f.

[119] *Hesperia* 6, 1937, 191–93; Suppl. 4, 1940, 150f; *Agora* III 159.

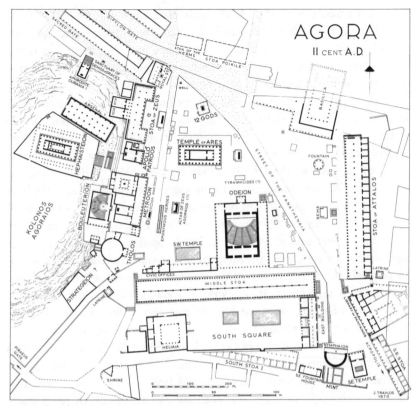

29. Agora in Roman Period (*Agora* xiv pl. 8)

at top and bottom are elaborate moldings. The altar may be dated late in the fourth century B.C., but it had obviously been moved from some other site and was not erected here before the first century B.C. A very important deity must have been worshiped here; and the most likely suggestion is that it was Zeus Agoraios, who, we are told, was "established in the agora and in the ekklesia"; and in fact a bedding of suitable size, from which the altar may have been transferred, has been found on the Pnyx.[120]

The most characteristic development of the Roman period was the erection of large buildings right in the middle of the square. Most prominent was the covered theater called Odeion or Agrippeion, built in the time of Augustus.[121] It was placed in the middle of the southern

[120] Schol. Aristophanes *Knights* 410; *Hesperia* 21, 1952, 91–93; *Agora* iii 122–24; xiv 160–62.
[121] See p. 216 below.

(83)

part of the agora, with the Middle Stoa immediately behind it. A large temple might well have been built here in the manner of Roman imperial fora; but in fact a temple was placed in a less central and less dominating position, farther north and in the western part of the square. It can be identified, chiefly on Pausanias' evidence, as belonging to Ares.[122] The site is marked by solid foundations of re-used poros at the east end, cuttings in the rock elsewhere (the whole has now been built up to make a neat level platform). Numerous fragments make it possible to reconstruct the temple as a Doric structure of marble, very similar in size and general plan to the temple of Hephaistos above, with six columns by thirteen. Dinsmoor ascribes it to the same architect and dates it a little later. But the foundations are unmistakably of Roman date, probably of the time of Augustus. Obviously the temple was transferred to the agora from some other site, and this is confirmed by the fact that many of the blocks have letters carved on them to ensure that each one was replaced in precisely the same position. One wonders where the temple originally stood. The name of Ares suggests the Areopagus, but we have no record or trace of a temple there, and it is difficult to see why in that case there should have been a removal. Other sites in the city have been suggested, but the most acceptable theory is that it stood in a known shrine of Ares at Acharnai, several miles north of Athens.[123] As we shall see, in the Roman period monuments were removed from several sites in the Attic demes and brought into the city. A number of fragments of relief sculpture in marble have been found to the east of the temple, a bearded head and several female heads and draped torsos.[124] They are of very fine quality, contemporary with the building, but are too badly preserved even to determine the subject. At first they were naturally assigned to a parapet round the altar, but then it was shown that this altar, which stood on a foundation to the east, was made a century later than the temple. A place must be sought for them within the building, perhaps on a frieze above the pronaos, as in the Hephaisteion, though they are inconveniently large for the purpose. Easier to place is a beautiful draped figure, headless, found when the railway cutting was made in 1891; two more bits were found in the later excavations, just east of the temple, and one need not

---

[122] 1.8.4. W. B. Dinsmoor, *Hesperia* 9, 1940, 1–52; H. A. Thompson, 21, 1952, 93ff; M. McAllister, *Hesperia*, 28, 1959, 1–64; *Agora* III 54f; XIV 162–65; Travlos *PDA* 104ff.

[123] *Agora* XIV 165; cf. B. Holtzmann, *BCH* 96, 1972, 73ff.

[124] Besides n. 122 above note a new fragment, *Hesperia* 40, 1971, 273.

doubt that we have here an akroterion.[125] There is no clear evidence for pedimental figures; and nothing is left of Alkamenes' cult statue of the god; but a marble torso found nearby may belong to an Athena, made by Lokros (otherwise unknown), which Pausanias saw in the temple.[126] The Athenians seem to have taken the opportunity afforded by the rededication of the temple to pay a further tribute to the family of their benefactor Augustus; his adopted son C. Caesar is honored in an inscription as the "new Ares."[127]

In the Periklean high noon the Athenians had had the resources and the will to build temples not only in the city but in various country demes. In the Hellenistic and Roman republican period some of these had become neglected and dilapidated. When under the peace and patronage of Augustus happier times returned, instead of patching up the buildings on the spot the Athenians brought material from some of them for reerection in the city. Two temples in southern Attica made their contribution, the temple of Athena at Sounion and the temple of Demeter and Kore at Thorikos. Of the former a number of Ionic architectural members, found in the southern part of the agora, are usually assigned to the "Southwest Temple," which was built in the early imperial age just in front of the western part of the Middle Stoa; we do not know who was worshiped here—perhaps some imperial figure.[128] From the temple of Demeter Doric columns were brought to adorn the facade of the "Southeast Temple," which was built, probably in the first century A.D., at the far corner of the agora area, facing north across what was now a separate little *plateia* east of the South Square.[129] We need not doubt that this too was dedicated to the Two Goddesses and was a kind of appendage of the Eleusinion above. Fragments of a large draped standing figure, probably one of the original cult statues, were found on the site. The material of both these temples is a peculiar type of marble quarried in southern Attica and not used in the city in earlier times. Another set of marble

[125] P. N. Boulter, *Hesperia* 22, 1953, 141–47; *Agora* XIV 164.

[126] *AJA* 40, 1936, 199; *Hesperia*, 9, 1940, 1; *The Athenian Agora: A Guide*, 2d edn 1962, 131.

[127] *IG* II² 3250; *Hesperia* 9, 1940, 49; *Agora* III 55. The two cella-like rooms now built behind the Stoa of Zeus may also have housed cults of Augustus and his family; *Hesperia* 6, 1937, 59–64; *Agora* XIV 102–3.

[128] *Hesperia* 21, 1952, 90–91; *Agora* XIV 166; for the temple at Sounion see A. Orlandos, *ArchEph* 1917, 183–87.

[129] *Hesperia* 29, 1960, 339–43; *Agora* XIV 167; for Thorikos see most recently H. Mussche et al., *Thorikos* II, Brussels 1964, 73–75.

30. Agora Model (Photo: Agora Excavations)

Ionic columns, three in number, has been found in the post-Herulian wall.[130] They were made in the fifth century, but mason's letter marks, possibly of Augustan date, show that these too were moved. Where they originally stood, and how and where they were re-used, we do not know.

Besides these old structures, new buildings characteristic of the Roman period were added to the astonishing miscellany of the agora. We have already noted the Odeion. What seemed to be a simple colonnade was found long ago at the eastern end of the north side of the agora. The extension of the excavations beyond the railway showed that in fact it was the southern facade of a great rectangular building with an interior peristyle, probably a basilica, of Hadrianic date.[131]

Hadrian's greatest benefactions to the city which he loved so well were elsewhere.[132] But his Library was not far away, standing alongside the

[130] *Hesperia* 29, 1960, 351ff; *Agora* xiv 166. The capitals rely largely on paint for decoration.

[131] *Hesperia* 40, 1971, 261–64; 42, 1973, 134–44. Note also an elaborate bathing establishment, replacing a simpler one of the 2d century b.c., southwest of the agora on the slope of the Areopagus *Hesperia* 38, 1969, 394–415.

[132] In general see A. Kokkou, "Works of Hadrian at Athens" (in Greek) *Deltion* 25A 1971, 150–73; P. Graindor, *Athènes sous Hadrien*, Cairo 1934.

31. Hadrian, Marble Statue found near Metroon. Breastplate shows Athena, with Victories, owl, and serpent; and she-wolf with Romulus and Remus (Photo: Agora Excavations)

Roman Market, to the east of the agora.[133] It was a great peristyle court, nearly 60m by 82m inside, built of poros richly adorned with marble, with a columnar facade and a propylon on the west, three exedras on the north and three on the south, and a large room for the books in the middle of the east, flanked by rooms for lectures and reading. During the Hellenistic period large libraries had been accumulating, notably in the gymnasia and the philosophical schools, but we do not hear of purpose-built libraries at Athens, as at Pergamon and Alexandria, till Roman times. Early in the second century A.D. a library was built at the south-eastern corner of the agora, facing west on the little *plateia* mentioned above.[134] It was much smaller than the Library of Hadrian, but similar in general plan, with a peristyle court and what appears to be the main book room on the east. On the west was a colonnade facing the Panathenaic Street, and behind it, on either side of the entrance, were rooms which, since they face outwards, were probably not used for pur-poses of the Library. Fortunately a lintel block of Pentelic marble has been found, bearing an inscription which tells us that T. Flavius Pantainos, "priest of the philosophic Muses" (whatever that means—probably not a specific office), dedicated to Athena Polias, to the Emperor Trajan, and to the city of the Athenians, the outer stoas, the peristyle, the library with the books, and all the embellishment. Another inscription adds a nice touch, saying, "No book shall be taken out, since we have sworn; it shall be opened from the first hour to the sixth."[135] Two female figures in armor, representing the Iliad and the Odyssey, were found a little to the north; we may assume that they stood in the library, probably flanking a statue of Homer.

Another stoa extended southeastwards along the Panathenaic Way, with rooms behind, which may have been shops. Also on the north side

---

Besides buildings mentioned in our text note also the Pantheon, shrine of all the gods; this is now plausibly identified as a building of which sections of the north side have been found on Hadrian Street east of the Roman Market and the Library; it is tentatively restored as a large three-aisled cella with a massive porch on the east; *AAA* 1, 1968, 221–24; 2, 1969, 1–3; *Deltion* 24, 1970, B1, 19–23; Travlos *PDA* 439ff.

[133] Judeich 377; Travlos *PDA* 244ff; *Deltion* 25, 1972, B1, 28ff. The ruins of a building with apses in the center of the court belong to a church built early in the 5th century A.D.; originally there was a long basin or pool here.

[134] Travlos *PDA* 432ff; *Agora* XIV 114–16; *Hesperia* 42, 1973, 145f, 385f; cf. C. Callmer, "Antike Bibliotheken," *Opuscula Archaeologica* 3, 1944, 174f.

[135] *Agora* III 150.

of the Library was a colonnade facing outwards, towards the south end
of the Stoa of Attalos, with rooms of irregular shape fitted in somewhat
awkwardly behind it.[136] The colonnade continued eastward along the
street which led to the columnar gateway of the Roman Market. In
the Roman period important streets in many Greek cities were lined with
colonnades. Pausanias (1.2.4) tells us that there were stoas along the street
leading from the main gate (the Dipylon); these have now been investigated in the section adjacent to the agora, and it has been revealed that
the colonnade on the south side of the street was backed by another
which faced the parallel street leading to the Sacred Gate.[137] Thus the
approaches to the agora were given a more monumental character.

So too were the hydraulic installations. Hadrian devoted much thought
and money to the water supply of Athens. A great reservoir was built on
the slope of Lykabettos, where remains can still be seen.[138] Water was
brought in by channels from the direction of Mt. Parnes and passed on
to the city below. As a terminal for the system in the agora, a handsome
Nymphaeum was built just north of the old southeast fountain house.
The massive concrete foundations show that the building was semi-
circular, but we have to imagine the elaborate architectural and sculptural
decoration, characteristic of the period and contrasting with the simple
old fountain houses. The overflow was still carried northward and supplied a small fountain house of quite different form, a round building
with a ring of columns of mottled green marble.[139]

In the same period, the second century A.D., a curious little building
was placed in front of the west end of the Middle Stoa. On the east was
a room with a columnar porch; to the west were three more rooms, each
set back a little from its neighbor, no doubt to avoid narrowing the southwestern exit from the agora. In the angle between the Middle Stoa and
the Odeion another building with a porch was placed, joined to the group
of four by a colonnade. These rooms are reasonably labeled "Civic Offices," and we may imagine that they supplemented the resources of the
old *archeia*.[140]

[136] *Hesperia* 42, 1973, 370, 385; 44, 1975, 332ff.
[137] *Hesperia* 40, 1971, 260ff.
[138] Judeich 203–4; Travlos *PEA* 116–20; *PDA* 242f.
[139] *Hesperia* 21, 1952, 102–3; 24, 1955, 57–59; 43, 1974, 410–27; *Agora* xiv 202–3.
[140] *Hesperia* 17, 1948, 151–53; 21, 1952, 90–91; *Agora* xiv 79–80. In front of
the building stood marble slabs, of which fragments have been found, which served
as standards for the making of tiles.

Pausanias, visiting Athens in the middle of the second century A.D., saw the agora in this Indian summer of its life; and he found a most extraordinary assemblage of buildings, accumulated over a period of eight centuries, widely varying in type and style, never united into a single architectural whole.

A century later, with the incursion of the Herulians in 267 A.D., came the final destruction. Some of the buildings were patched up once more, but probably not for their original purpose. They were no longer in the center of the city but on its periphery. The area, no longer an agora, was worked over and built over again and again. The ancient monuments disintegrated, their members were dispersed and widely and repeatedly re-used. The process continued through Byzantine, Turkish, and more recent times, leaving the modern archaeologists a task unique in its complexity.[141]

BIBLIOGRAPHY

Judeich 328ff

W. Dörpfeld, *Alt-Athen und seine Agora*, Berlin 1937–39

H. A. Thompson, "Buildings on the West Side of the Agora," *Hesperia* 6, 1937, 1–226

R. Martin, *Recherches sur l'agora grecque*, Paris 1951

The Athenian Citizen, 1960 (Excavations of the Athenian Agora, Picture Book No. 4). Other booklets in the series deal with special aspects of the agora

R. E. Wycherley, *The Athenian Agora* III, *Literary and Epigraphical Testimonia*, Princeton 1957

H. A. Thompson and others, *The Athenian Agora, a Guide to the Excavation and Museum*, 3d edn, Athens 1976; *The Athenian Agora: A Short Guide*, 1976 (Excavations of the Athenian Agora, Picture Book No. 16)

A. N. Oikonomides, *The Two Agoras in Ancient Athens*, Chicago 1964

R. E. Wycherley, "The Agora of Pericles," *Journal of Historical Studies*, 1, 1968, 246–56

Travlos *PDA* 1ff

H. A. Thompson and R. E. Wycherley, *The Athenian Agora* XIV, *The Agora of Athens, the History, Shape and Uses of an Ancient City Center*, Princeton 1972

[141] For the later history of the site see *Agora* XIV 208–19.

CHAPTER III

The Market

Athenaeus[1] quotes from the *Olbia* of Euboulos, the Middle Comedy poet, some lines which say, "Everything will be for sale together in the same place at Athens, figs, summoners, bunches of grapes, turnips, pears, apples, witnesses, roses, medlars, haggis, honeycombs, chickpeas, lawsuits, bee-stings-pudding, myrtle berries, allotment machines, irises, lambs, water clocks, laws, indictments."

These lines, comic though they are, have a certain literal truth in them. The "Agora of the Kerkopes," the "thieves" market, was near the Heliaia;[2] Plutarch in an amusing passage brings box makers, Herm carvers, law courts, and pigs into juxtaposition.[3] Curious finds made recently in the excavation provide illustrations and will be described more fully below. Shops and a law court are side by side on the south side of the agora and at the northeast corner; the shop of Simon the shoemaker is not far south of the Eponymous Heroes;[4] beneath the Stoa of Attalos, which was a market hall, are unmistakable traces of a law court.

Athenian life was a fascinating mixture, from which it is almost impossible to separate the elements, and the intricate nature of this mixture was particularly striking in the agora. When Euboulos says "in the same place" he means of course in the agora, using the term in its widest sense. The meaning of the word is elastic. For certain political and religious purposes, as we have seen, there were formal and comparatively narrow limits, marked by boundary stones. The great bazaar quarter of Athens, which in a very real sense belonged to and indeed *was* the agora, must have extended far in probably every direction. So many things were sold, some of them in special quarters; in its fullest extension the agora must have been immense and ill-defined. One could hardly say with

---

[1] 14.640 b-c; Edmonds *FAC* II 114 Fr. 74.

[2] Hesychios *s.v. Agora of Kerkopes*; p. 94 below.

[3] See p. 97 below.

[4] See p. 237 below. In front of the Eponymoi notices of lawsuits were posted; this place was probably what Aristophanes *Knights* 979 calls the *deigma* of lawsuits, the place where lawsuits were displayed, as wares were displayed for sale, the term having the same kind of implication as Euboulos' gibe.

precision whether a given shop was in the agora or near. Again, should one include the Kolonos Agoraios, the Market Hill to the west, with the temple of Hephaistos on top and the shops of bronze-workers around? Normally one thinks of it as beyond and above, and rightly so; but Pollux (7.132–33) speaks of it as being in the agora. One need not be very precise, especially for our present purpose.

If law courts were embedded in market districts, political activity too was not confined to council house and magistrates' office but was carried on vigorously in neighboring shops just as in the cafés of modern Athens. Strangely enough, we hear nothing of the wine shops in this connection. The barbershops are naturally mentioned, and the shops of cobblers or leather-workers; and above all the perfume shops, the favorite resort of the more fashionable, of the young men-about-town.[5] "Each of you is in the habit of frequenting some place," says Lysias (24.20); "a perfumer's shop, a barber's, a cobbler's and so forth; and the greatest number visit those who have their establishments nearest the agora, the smallest number those who are farthest from it." According to Demosthenes, Aristogeiton, because of his antisocial habits, "did not frequent any of the usual barbershops in the city, or the perfume shops, or the other shops"[6] (*ergasteria*). "In what stoa," says Theophrastos, "in what shop, in what part of the agora do they (the Newsmakers, 8.14) not spend the day?" "We sit in the shops," says Isokrates (7.15), "denouncing the present order," though deeper and more dangerous political plotting would no doubt be carried on in private houses at club meetings. The talk would not of course be entirely political; it would range from the lowest of gossip to the highest of philosophy. But at Athens it was impossible to get away from politics. The most scandalous gossip about the depravity of a Kallias or a Timokrates found its way into political comedy or into rhetorical invective. At the other end of the scale we find Sokrates discoursing with his friend the cobbler-philosopher.[7] Xenophon's account of the behavior of Euthydemos is interesting:[8] "because of his youth he did not yet go to the agora, but if he wanted to get anything done went and sat in one of the reinmakers' shops near the agora," and there Sokrates sought him

[5] *Agora* III 200, 202f. The metal-workers' shops were also frequented by loungers; see Andokides 1.40; cf. Hesiod *Works* 493.

[6] 25. 52. The word *ergasterion* may be translated simply 'shop'; it includes places of business and industry of all kinds.

[7] Diogenes 2.13. 122; see p. 97 below.

[8] *Memorabilia* 4.2.1 and 8.

out. Much of this activity would ultimately find its expression in the law court or the assembly.

Our information about the Athenian market of the fifth to third centuries comes from the orators and, much more plentifully, from comedy; this information, though colorful, is of a general character and does not give a very precise idea of the form, arrangement, and topography of the market; nor do archaeological discoveries in the agora help very much—the market of these centuries has left few recognizable traces, and in any case it must have been largely beyond the field of excavations. Only here and there can contacts be made with known monuments. The great market buildings of Athens belong mainly to the Hellenistic and Roman ages.

What struck the ancient commentators most was the way in which the names of the various commodities were used for the places in which they were sold. Enumerating the parts of a city, Pollux says:

> The Attic writers named places after the things sold there; for instance they might say, "I went off to the wine, the olive oil, the pots"; or again in the words of Eupolis, "I went around to the garlic and the onions and the incense, and straight on to the perfume."[9]

If this idiom, found *passim* in comedy and occasionally elsewhere, is taken quite literally, it suggests an astonishing degree of specialization. Some of the items are more comprehensive and comprise a number of subdivisions. The fish market was a great institution among Athenians of all classes.[10] The extravagant spent money lavishly "at the fish" on favorite delicacies. The more frugal or penurious passed by this part of the market and resorted to the *membrades* (a cheap sea fish). Strangely enough, we do not hear of "the meat," in general; but in particular, besides "the asses' flesh" mentioned by Pollux, there was also the *kenebreion* where carrion was sold.[11] "The birds" in Demosthenes (19.245) is taken by some editors to mean the cockpits, but it may mean the bird market, "aux oiseaux," as in Aristophanes' *Birds* (13), where poultry was set out on clay tablets (*pinakes*). "The vegetables" or "greens" had a number of subdivisions for particular vegetables; there was also "the sesame," "the nuts," "the hard-shelled fruit" (*akrodrya*). In the clothes market we hear of "the sleeveless tunics" in particular.

[9] 9.47-48; Edmonds *FAC* I 418.
[10] *Agora* III 195f.
[11] 9.48; *Agora* III 197.

The list can be extended to include almost all varieties of a great range of goods.[12] Theophrastos' Boastful Man (23.7) would "go to the good horses and pretend that he wanted to buy"; to make a real purchase he would presumably have gone to another part of the market where the horses were not so good.

Ehrenberg refuses to accept this manner of speaking at its face value and thinks that the comic poets give an exaggerated impression of specialization and concentration in the market district.[13] No doubt they do; and one would not expect to find rows of stalls or shops full of garlic with not an onion to be seen. But the usage must correspond fairly closely to something in real life; it is introduced naturally by the poets as a current colloquialism, without any particularly comic effect. People said to one another, "Meet me at the so-and-so," and they knew just where to go.

We also hear of several special "agoras" included in the market district —the *ichthyopolis* for fish, and the *himatiopolis* or *speiropolis* for clothes.[14] The "women's agora" (*gynaikeia*)[15] was probably the place where one bought articles of feminine interest, and perhaps largely of feminine manufacture—it was no doubt to the *gynaikeia* that the singer of the Euripidean parody in the *Frogs* would take her work (1346-51, "I was intent upon my work . . . making yarn, so that I might take it to the Agora before daylight and sell it"). The "Agora of the Kerkopes," where stolen goods were sold, and where the appearance of Arkesilaos the Academic philosopher called forth sarcastic comment,[16] was proverbial for a den of thieves.

Yet Xenophon too must be exaggerating in the *Oikonomikos* (8.19-22) when he makes Ischomachos lecture his young wife on the virtue of having "a place for everything and everything in its place," in the home as in the agora. Shoes, clothes, bedding, bronze vessels, tableware, pots, should all be kept separate and in good order, each like a well-drilled cyclic chorus, with a clear space in the middle. "The whole city contains altogether an infinite number of things; and yet when you order any servant to buy something from the agora and bring it, not one of them will have any difficulty; every one will plainly know where he must go

[12] See Judeich 359-60; *Agora* III 193ff.
[13] *The People of Aristophanes*, Oxford 1951, 133.
[14] Ps. Plutarch *Lives of the Orators* 849e; Pollux 7.78.
[15] *Agora* III 201.
[16] See p. 231 below; Diogenes 9.12.114; *Agora* III 201.

to get each class of goods. The reason for this is simply that they are kept in their appointed places." Ischomachos is working the comparison for more than it is worth. One cannot believe that the Athenian agora really provided the scrupulously tidy housewife with a good model, or that it exhibited the impeccable neatness and marvelous organization of the Great Phoenician Ship which Ischomachos describes.

The tendency for certain branches of trade to concentrate in certain streets and parts of the agora was natural and may be observed in striking form in modern Athens too. But it must have been far from systematic and complete. Wine was sold both in the agora and "at the gate," and so were sausages and fish.[17] No doubt trade was distributed about the city to some extent.[18] But one can safely assume that most of the quarters mentioned by our authorities were in the agora and its immediate environs, even though we shall find very little evidence for the location of particular spots.

Another section of Pollux (10. 18-19) introduces the subject of *kykloi* (rings) in the agora.

The part of the agora where utensils were sold was called "rings," as Alexis seems to indicate in his *Kalasiris*[19]—"Where are you taking me through the rings?" Diphilos shows the usage more clearly in his *Mainomenos*[20]—"And, in addition, hearth, couch, jar, bedding, spear, knapsack, pouch, so that one might think that it was not a soldier but a ring from the agora standing up and walking about; such is the rubbish which you carry around with you."

Elsewhere (7.11) Pollux says, "The name *kykloi* is given in New Comedy to the places in which slaves are sold; probably," he adds with some apparent doubt, "other merchandise too." Some modern writers maintain that all the different parts of the market, named after the wares sold

[17] Isaios 6.20; Aristophanes *Knights* 1247. For wine see *Amphoras and the Ancient Wine Trade*, 1961 (Excavations of the Athenian Agora, Picture Book No. 6); cf. *Agora* III 199; *Agora* XIV 172.

[18] Lysias 24.20 implies that there were shops in other parts of the city. A. Boethius, *AJP* 69, 1948, 396ff, contrasts the typically Greek concentration of shops in a bazaar quarter, in and around the agora, with the Roman system of shops in the ground floor of residential *insulae*, distributed about the city. The contrast is real but should not be pushed too far. There were shops let off from houses at Athens (p. 238 below) and at Olynthos; see *AJA* 55, 1951, 232.

[19] Fr. 99, Edmonds *FAC* II 418.

[20] Fr. 55, Edmonds *FAC* III 124; cf. *Agora* III 187.

there, were what were known as *kykloi*. But it seems safer to assume that the name was used primarily of certain marts where household furniture and slaves were sold, with perhaps a limited extension to other quarters. That is the impression which one gets from Pollux and the comedy writers, especially from Diphilos' description of a figure who seems to be the ancient equivalent of the White Knight.

In spite of the mass of literary material it still remains impossible to describe with any precision the situation and arrangement of the pre-Hellenistic market. The scraps of evidence which we have would seem to indicate that the commercial area impinged upon the public buildings and shrines of the central agora at many points, and probably on every side. Perhaps one may tentatively infer that the main bulk of the bazaar quarter was on the east. Official buildings were concentrated on the west. On the northwest was the Stoa Poikile. On the south was a series of public buildings—though there may have been shops too—and the ground rose steeply towards the Areopagus. The eastern side was the most open, and the ground here was fairly level; and it was in this direction that the Stoa of Attalos and the great Roman Market were ultimately built.

Points of topographical interest can quickly be given; it will be seen that they usually involve difficulty and obscurity and do not help very much. Wine was sold, according to Isaios,[21] in the Kerameikos "beside the postern gate" (*pylis*), which may be a small gate found to the southwest of the Dipylon. This takes us well away from the agora proper; but we may perhaps assume that the market extended towards the Dipylon along the street that in later antiquity was lined with stoas in which goods were sold.[22] Judeich conjectures that even much earlier than this the Alphitopolis Stoa,[23] mentioned by Aristophanes in the *Ekklesiazousai* (686), stood on this street, since he identified it with the Makra (long) Stoa, which can with some reason be placed here; but the identification is very uncertain. In the Alphitopolis flour was sold, and according to Eustathios a picture of Helen by Zeuxis was set up there.

On the north side of the Agora, we hear in Lucian of a moneylender behind the Poikile.[24] There is no evidence that the two most famous ancient stoas of Athens, the Poikile and the Basileios, were ever used for

---

[21] 6.20; see Judeich 137 Abb. 10.

[22] Himerios *Oration* 3. 12; Pausanias 1.2.4–5, cf. *Agora* III 20; XIV 108.

[23] 364; *Agora* III 21f and 194; Eustathios on *Iliad* 11.630.

[24] *Dialogues of Hetairai* 8.2; cf. *Ship* 13. We also find a moneylender at the Diomeian Gate, Alkiphron *Epistle* 3.3.

trade; they seem to have been reserved for political and judicial uses, and for recreation. But the barbershop frequented by the Deceleans must have stood near by, since Lysias (23.3) tells us that it was by "the Herms," which stood in the northwestern part of the agora.

One of the informers in the case of the Mutilation of the Herms, seeing a conspirator "sitting in the bronze-foundry, took him up to the Hephaisteion" for a confidential chat.[25] We are told that bronze was sold "where the Hephaisteion is"; and there is now little doubt that the temple of Hephaistos was the so-called "Theseion" on the hill to the west. On this same hill, according to the commentators, was the place where men for hire stood and offered their services.[26] The spot was near the shrine of Eurysakes, son of Ajax, the site of which can perhaps be approximately established by the discovery of a group of inscriptions southwest of the Hephaisteion. On the other hand slaves for hire stood at the Anakeion, the shrine of the Dioskouroi, which was certainly to the southeast of the agora, close to the slopes of the Acropolis.[27]

Immediately southwest of the agora are the remains of a shop which has been identified by means of a large number of boot nails as belonging to a cobbler, perhaps Sokrates' friend Simon.[28] Some distance farther in this direction, in the hollow extending southwestward from the agora between the Areopagus and the Hill of the Nymphs, is the "Industrial District of Ancient Athens" excavated and described by Rodney Young. There were bronze-workers' establishments here too—the major trades were widely distributed; but in particular there was a street apparently devoted mainly to marble-working. Young tentatively places here the scene of a curious incident in which Sokrates was involved, described by Plutarch.[29] Sokrates, walking with a group of friends, suddenly checked himself and took a different road—through "the box-makers"; some of his friends laughed and went straight on through the *hermoglyphoi* (the name is used of sculptors in general, not merely of "Herm-carvers") past the law courts; there they became involved in a herd of pigs, no doubt going to market or coming from it, and emerged dirty and disheveled and with a new respect for Sokrates' "divine sign," which had

[25] Andokides 1.40; Bekker, *Anecdota Graeca* 1.316.23.

[26] Pollux 7.132–33; *Agora* III 90; for Eurysakes see *Hesperia* 7, 1938, 1ff; *Agora* III 90, 92.

[27] Demosthenes 45.80; see p. 177 below.

[28] See p. 237 below.

[29] *De genio Socratis* 10. 580 d–f; *Hesperia* xx 1951, 139, 151; see p. 238 below.

warned him to change course. Without placing much faith in the truth of the story, one may still take the topography quite seriously; but of course the identification of the scene is uncertain. The law courts in question remain highly elusive, and with them the "Agora of the Kerkopes."

So far we have mostly been touching various peripheral points of the agora area. In the heart of the square itself the great Odeion was built in the time of Augustus; and on or near this spot is a likely site for the ancient Orchestra, which was in any case in the agora; and from the Orchestra, Plato tells us in the *Apology*,[30] one could buy for a drachma at most the books of Anaxagoras.

Such scraps of evidence do not add up to much. There is nearly always some doubt, and hardly any points can be located even approximately. But at least one receives an impression of the extensiveness and ubiquity of shops and marts in this part of Athens, and of their close attachment to various shrines and public buildings. It appears that at Athens, at least in the earlier phases, the state of affairs was quite contrary to what is recommended by Aristotle in the *Politics* (7.11.2), where he says that there should be an entirely separate agora for buying and selling.

One more passage deserves detailed attention. Somewhere in the agora, according to Demosthenes (54.7,8) was the well-known but mysterious shrine called the Leokorion. We hear of a *hetaira* staying near by—they no doubt had their recognized places in the agora district.[31] The plaintiff in the speech of Demosthenes narrates a lively incident. He was taking his usual evening stroll in the agora with a friend, when Konon's son passed him, drunk, "by the Leokorion, near Pythodoros' place," and went up towards Melite; later he returned to the agora with a party, met the speaker "turning back from the Pherrephattion and walking just by the Leokorion again," and attacked him. Melite was on the high ground to the southwest of the agora; the Pherrephattion, a shrine of Persephone, may have been associated with the Eleusinion to the southeast of the agora; and, as we have seen, a possible site for the Leokorion has now been found towards the northwest.[32] Since Pythodoros was called *Skenites*,[33] his establishment in the agora was presumably a shop or booth, or a group of booths, apparently in a conspicuous place where it could serve as a landmark or point of reference.

[30] 26d; see p. 204 below; cf. J. Ferguson, *CP* 65, 1970, 172.
[31] Alkiphron *Epistles* 3.5 (3.2); *Agora* III 109, 222.
[32] See p. 63 above.
[33] Isokrates 17. 33; cf. *Agora* III 191.

Skenai or booths constructed of flimsy materials were a great feature of the early market, and no doubt continued in use to some extent even after monumental stone buildings had been constructed. They figure in a famous incident of 338 B.C. described by Demosthenes in the *De Corona* (169). When news came that Philip had taken Elatea, the Prytaneis, determined apparently to put a stop to all commercial business and to have everything ready for deliberation on the crisis, excluded the people from the *skenai* about the agora. One gets the impression that normally the *skenai* were allowed within the central square of the agora (perhaps mainly on the open east side). Just what they were like or how they were set out we can only imagine. A very simple form is suggested by Pherekrates' picture of a man "selling perfume, sitting aloft beneath a sunshade (*skiadeion*) providing a meeting place for young men to talk in all through the day."[34] Wine sellers brought their product into the agora on waggons and sold it from these;[35] presumably this was the local wine brought in from the country, not expensive imported varieties. Many traders no doubt merely set out their wares on tables, or even on the ground. "The tables" in the agora, by which Sokrates could be heard talking, are frequently mentioned, and it is not always clear whether the reference is to the *trapezitai*, the money-changers, or to market stalls generally.[36] Certainly it is not always the former; the Shameless Man of Theophrastos (9.4) "snatches up some guts from the table and goes off laughing." At the lowest end of the scale was Aristophanes' sausage seller in the *Knights* (152, 169), who carried around a sort of tray or portable table, which he could set down when he wished.

Of course many trades were carried on, many goods both manufactured and sold, in the modest houses, shops, or workshops in the neighborhood of the agora, such as those discovered in the "Industrial District" to the southwest. One would not describe this district as being "in the agora," even using the word in its extended sense; on the other hand, it hangs on closely to the agora and is in what one might call the sub-agora area, of which it is typical. The products could either be sold on the spot or taken to the agora itself for display and sale.

[34] Fr. 64, Edmonds *FAC* I 230; for *skenai* see *Agora* III 190ff.

[35] Pollux 7.192–93; *Agora*, III 199.

[36] Plato *Apology* 17 c; *Hippias Minor* 368 b; Theophrastos *Characters* 5.7. On the other hand Demosthenes 19. 114 certainly refers to money-changers; see *Agora* III 192; an inscription recently found in the north-western part of the agora is concerned with coinage and was set up near "the tables," *Hesperia* 43, 1974, 167.

The Market

More intimately connected with the agora is a double row of rooms found at the east end of the north side.[37] These were no doubt shops; built originally in the late archaic period, they were restored after the Persian War, and with several remodelings continued in use till Roman times when they were partly obliterated by the basilica. Another row of shops, built in the latter part of the fifth century B.C., has recently been found on the south side of the street which led east from the southeast corner of the agora, on the site where in Roman times, when the area was given more monumental treatment, the outer stoa of the Library of Pantainos was built. The material discovered, notably the filling of a large well, includes cooking vessels and tableware, bones of animals, oyster and mussel shells, drinking cups and amphoras of various types which show that Samian, Chian, and other imported wines were available; from this one may infer that part at least of the building was occupied by a thriving tavern. The basic plan consisted of two rows of rooms, somewhat irregular in shape, running east and west; but as happened so often in shops and houses there was repeated adjustment of the interior divisions. On sites like this, as Shear says, "Craftsmen, eating establishments, and shopkeepers crowded together in the cramped rooms of rambling buildings which were freely altered and remodeled to accommodate the needs of a new tenant."

In course of time men's ideas turned towards making more handsome and efficient provision for buying and selling. Xenophon not only liked to think of the agora as a vast well-organized department store; he thought it would be a good thing "if buildings and marts for the market people were constructed both in Peiraeus and in the city"; these would not only be an adornment to the city but would bring in large revenues.[38] Such buildings were known in Greece as early as the fifth century; the "North Building" at Corinth provides an example; it had a row of shops behind a columnar hall and seems to have been a fish market.[39] When large market halls or well-designed blocks of shops first appeared at Athens is not certain. The Alphitopolis is the first commercial stoa of which we know, and we first find it mentioned in Aristophanes' *Ekklesiazousai* (686), 391 B.C.

---

[37] *Hesperia* 42, 1973, 138ff; see also 40, 1971, 265 for slighter remains of a similar structure a little farther west; and 44, 1975, 346ff for shops to the southeast.

[38] *Poroi* 3.13 (possibly not by Xenophon).

[39] *Corinth: Results of Excavations* 1.1, Cambridge, Mass. 1932, 212ff.

The Market

Of the excavated remains none earlier than the second century B.C. can be definitely assigned to a substantial market building. Several buildings at first thought to be market halls have been shown by further evidence to have served another purpose. "South Stoa I" when first discovered was called "South Shops," but now everything seems to indicate that it was designed for and used by the various boards of magistrates. Even so, at some stage of its existence some of the rooms may have been shops. The large square peristyle built in the fourth century in the northeast part of the agora seemed appropriate for a market, but later finds have shown that its simple predecessor of the fifth century was used by law courts.

On the grounds given above we may still reasonably think of this general area on the east as devoted to the market; and the juxtaposition of a law court will offer a striking example of the truth of part at least of Euboulos' gibe. But we still cannot feel that we have a safe example of a substantial pre-Hellenistic market building in the agora. One would naturally assume that the fourth-century peristyle was designed to continue the function of its predecessor; and it is worth noting that the Hellenistic buildings thought to have served the needs of trade were planned on different principles—it was not until the Roman age that Athens was furnished with a market laid out as a great peristyle enclosure.

Early in the second century B.C. a row of five rooms, opening northwards, with small rooms behind, was built just south of the square peristyle.[40] These may well have been shops with storerooms. But a few years later far bigger architectural schemes eclipsed all such tentative creations and transformed the market of Athens into something quite different from what Aristophanes and Euboulos had known. The east side of the agora was cleared of earlier structures to make way for the stoa which the Athenians owed to the generosity of King Attalos II of Pergamon. As we have seen, the rooms behind its vast columnar halls on both floors were commodious shops. Along the front of the stoa, as on the north side of the Middle Stoa, was a terrace which on days of festival would make an excellent grandstand for crowds watching the processions pass along the Panathenaic Street. Before 88 B.C. a large bema, from which harangues could be delivered, was built in front of the middle of the stoa.[41] Two inscriptions record that honorary paintings of worthy officials were set up inside the building, and many honorary monuments were

[40] *Hesperia*, 19, 1950, 320; 21, 1952, 101.
[41] *Hesperia*, 7, 1938, 324; Athenaeus 5.212 e, f.

set up in front.[42] Thus the stoa and its appendages served a variety of purposes and belonged in some degree to both market and civic center.

Though it may well have housed the law courts, one still cannot dismiss outright the possibility that the stoa complex which made a separate square of the southern part of the agora served at some time as a market. One would expect something in the nature of a distinct commercial agora at Athens in this period, in accordance with contemporary practice, but its location and its very existence remain questionable. Once again we are faced with the problem of the indeterminate character of so many Athenian buildings.

Alongside the splendor of the Hellenistic agora one can safely assume that to some extent the old market district survived and retained its characteristic features. Throughout its history the city of Athens has been given its peculiar character by the retention of the old in startling contrast with the new. The "tables," the *skenai*, the *kykloi* would still be there; and crowding around the fringes would still be narrow tortuous streets, with small shops and workshops. The history of the "Industrial District" has indeed been traced down to Roman times, and the district retained its character throughout.

One further stage remains to be noted briefly. Towards the end of the first century B.C., under Roman patronage, a brand new market place, complete and self-contained, was built at a little distance to the east of the agora.[43] It was a great peristyle court, about 112m by 98m, with shops behind the colonnade on at least the east side, and with a columnar gateway in the middle of the west side and a smaller one towards the south end of the east. An inscription on the main gate records that the people dedicated the building from the gifts of Julius Caesar and Augustus to Athena Archegetis. Another inscription, of Hadrianic date, concerns the sale of oil, which, one may infer, was sold in the great market, along with many other commodities. But though the same activity tended to continue

---

[42] *Agora* III 46; XIV 107.

[43] *IG* II² 1100 and 3175; Judeich 371ff; H. S. Robinson, *AJA* 47, 1943, 291–305; Travlos *PDA* 28ff.

A rectangular building just east of the Roman Market, with three arched doorways, has usually been identified as the Agoranomion of the Roman period, the office of the market officials called Agoranomoi, Judeich 374, on the basis of an inscription on a similar arch, *IG* II² 3391; Travlos however, *PDA* 37, questions the identification, noting that the block on which the inscription is carved, found *west* of the Roman Market, is different in some details from the others.

in the same place for many centuries at Athens, it would be rash to assume that one of the people of Menander is referring to this same spot when he says, "Wait for me by the olive oil."

The building of Pentelic marble which we call the Tower of the Winds, a little to the east, may now be seen as an appendage of the Roman Market, though in fact, as we know from Varro, it was built a few years earlier and was the gift of Andronikos of Kyrrhos in Syria.[44] It is an octagonal structure, each side measuring 3.2m, with two columnar porches facing northwest and northeast, and a circular annex on the south. A frieze of figures representing the eight winds ran round the top of the wall; the roof was surmounted by a weather vane in the form of a bronze Triton according to Vitruvius; and within was an elaborate mechanism by which a *horologion* or clock was worked by water power. This area was obviously an important center in Roman times. The Tower is miraculously preserved; in the Turkish period it was used as a meeting place of dervishes.

BIBLIOGRAPHY

V. Ehrenberg, *The People of Aristophanes*, Oxford 1951, Ch. v "Traders and Craftsmen."

R. E. Wycherley, "The Market of Athens," *Greece and Rome* 2d Series 3, 1956, 2–23 (the present chapter is a shortened version of this)

An Ancient Shopping Center, 1971 (Excavations of the Athenian Agora, Picture Book No. 12)

Agora III 185–206

Agora XIV 170–73

[44] Varro 3.5.17; Vitruvius 1.6.4; *IG* II² 1035 line 54: cf. Judeich 374–75; Robinson, see n. 43; J. Noble and D. J. de Solla Price, *AJA* 72, 1968, 345–55; Travlos *PDA* 281ff; A. Stamelman, *ArchEph* 1975, 221–23.

32. Acropolis from Southwest (Photo: Alison Frantz)

CHAPTER IV

The Parthenon and Its Setting

The Parthenon is the culmination of Greek architecture and the climax of every book on the subject. In the present context it can be treated briefly, with the emphasis on its place in the architectural scheme of the city and in the life of the people. The temple dominated the Acropolis and was the crowning glory of the city as a whole. It was elaborately designed, and no care or expense was spared in building and decoration to make it a worthy offering to Athena and a splendid symbol of the power and achievements of Athens.

Already in the early decades of the fifth century the Athenians had attempted to build a great temple of Athena on the south side of the Acropolis, as a complement to the old temple on the north, but the attempt was cut short by the Persian invasion. Whether there was an earlier and smaller temple on the site has been much disputed; the evidence is uncertain, depending not on remains found *in situ* but on the interpretation of the names used in inscriptions and the attribution of archaic sculpture.[1]

The remains of the immediately pre-Persian building are solid enough, consisting of foundations and architectural members from the superstructure. A substructure of limestone was built, nearly 77m long and 32m wide—dimensions somewhat ampler than the temple itself required—rising at one point, on the south, to as much as 10m above the rock of the Acropolis. A terrace was raised on the slope to the south, but even so several courses of the great foundation on this side were carefully dressed, and clearly designed to be visible above ground level. On this spacious platform the steps of the temple were laid, with a broad border left free on all sides. The lowest step was of Kara limestone, the other two were of Pentelic marble, and so were the columns; this material was now used on a greater scale than ever before. The temple was apparently designed to have six columns on the ends, sixteen on the sides, with a long main cella, a back chamber opening to the west, and inner porches which probably had four columns each in prostyle arrangement. The plan was

[1] See p. 145 below.

a simpler version of what was used in the later building. Many column drums were roughly shaped, and some perhaps partly built up; some at least of the "refinements" introduced so subtly in the later building were already present in the earlier. Thus in scale, material, and design this was a worthy prototype.

It is not clear whether the temple was begun before or after the Battle of Marathon, 490 B.C. The Persians in 480 B.C. must have wrecked everything above the foundations. There was no question of simply resuming the work where it had been left off, even if Perikles' architects had not had new and more grandiose ideas on temple design. Some of the blocks were re-used in the later building, some were incorporated in the foundations or in the terrace; many drums can still be seen in the north wall of the Acropolis, along with architectural members from other buildings; and these were not simply thrown in as building material but carefully arranged, no doubt with the intention that they should stand as a memorial of the great war.

Lycurgus quotes the oath which was said to have been sworn by the Greek allies at Plataia in 479 B.C.—"Of the shrines burnt and overthrown by the barbarians I will rebuild none, but I will allow them to remain as a memorial to those who come after of the impiety of the barbarians."[2] This may be a rhetorical fiction, based on the fact that for some years Athens and other cities had not sufficiently recovered and acquired the surplus of economic resources which was necessary if they were to undertake the vast labor and expense of major temple building. However that may be, just after the middle of the century the Athenians felt themselves free to resume work on the Acropolis under the inspiration of Perikles; peace had been made and honor satisfied.

The new Parthenon was begun in 447 B.C.; the necessary decrees may have been passed and plans worked out a little earlier. The temple was designed in the Doric order, with unusual complexity of plan and great refinement of detail and with certain Ionic touches. For the principal architectural facts and figures a brief recapitulation will be sufficient.

The building was both longer and wider than the old, but it did not completely cover the old platform. The site was shifted a little to the

---

[2] *Against Leokrates* 80–81; P. Siewert, *Der Eid von Plataiai*, München 1972, discusses the oath, with full bibliography of earlier work. On the much disputed Peace of Kallias, the authenticity of which I accept, see now R. Meiggs, *The Athenian Empire*, Oxford 1972, 129ff and 487ff (on the oath, 504ff); A. R. Hands, *Mnemosyne*, Series 4, 28, 1975, 193–95.

33. Foundation of Older Parthenon, South Side (Photo: German Archaeological Institute)

northwest, so that a strip of the foundations was left unused on the east and south, but additions had to be built out on north and west. The increase in the size of the temple was greater in width than in length, the object being to provide for a very wide cella to contain the cult statue. The dimensions on the stylobate were now 69.51m by 30.86m, a proportion of 9 to 4 (a basic figure in the dimensions of the Parthenon). The terrace on the south had earlier been greatly extended and raised, in successive stages; and precious fragments of archaic sculpture, smashed by the Persians, were laid to rest in the fill, to be unearthed by modern excavators.[3]

All three steps of the new Parthenon were of Pentelic marble, and this was the material used for the whole structure. The outer columns numbered eight by seventeen; their normal diameter at the foot was 1.9m; the proportion of height to lower diameter was 5.48, which meant that the columns were slightly heavier than many of their contemporaries but much lighter than most archaic examples. Above the massive architraves all 92 metopes were carved in high relief, and above the triglyph-metope frieze was a beaded astragal, one of several unusual details in the moldings. The wall of the pediment was set well back to leave plenty of space for the sculpture. The marble akroteria crowning the pediments were not in the form of figures but of great floral ornaments, terminating in palmettes.

The principal room, the cella, was entered from the east through a prostyle porch of six columns, of lighter proportions than the main colonnade, set above two steps; and a similar porch formed the opisthodomos. Above the architraves in place of triglyphs and metopes was the continuous frieze which ran round the whole of the inner building, seen only by much craning of the neck from within the colonnade or in fitful glimpses from outside. The interior colonnades, in two stories, did not merely divide the cella into a central nave and two aisles, but continued round the back, behind the statue. The floor of the central area, as compared with the side and back passages, is sunk by nearly 4cm. In the area occupied by the base of Pheidias' great statue, poros blocks replaced the marble of the pavement. In the cella and the small back room the ceiling was of wood, in the outer colonnade and in the front and back porches the beams and coffered slabs were of Pentelic marble; and marble tiles covered the

[3] Judeich 249f; Hill 147ff; A. Tschira, *Jahrbuch* 87, 1972, 158–231; cf. *AA* 1965, 422.

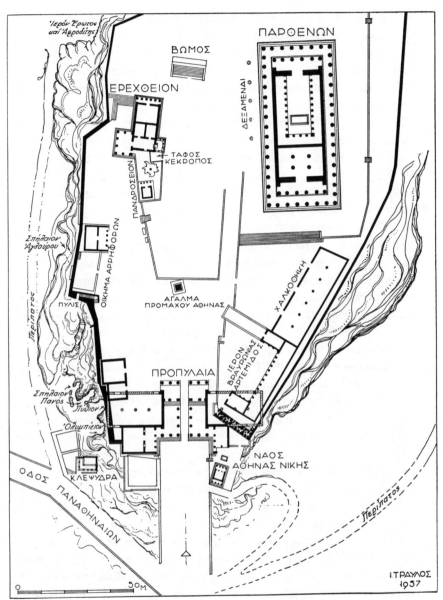

Ἱερόν Ἔρωτος
καί Ἀφροδίτης

ΒΩΜΟΣ

ΠΑΡΘΕΝΩΝ

ΕΡΕΧΘΕΙΟΝ

ΔΕΞΑΜΕΝΑΙ

ΤΑΦΟΣ
ΚΕΚΡΟΠΟΣ

ΠΑΝΔΡΟΣΕΙΟΝ

Σπήλαιον
Ἀγλαύρου

ΟΙΚΗΜΑ ΑΡΡΗΦΟΡΩΝ

ΑΓΑΛΜΑ
ΠΡΟΜΑΧΟΥ ΑΘΗΝΑΣ

ΧΑΛΚΟΘΗΚΗ

Περίπατος

ΠΥΛΙΣ

Σπήλαιον
Πανός

ΠΡΟΠΥΛΑΙΑ

ΙΕΡΟΝ
ΒΡΑΥΡΩΝΙΑΣ
ΑΡΤΕΜΙΔΟΣ

Πύθιον

Ὀλυμπίειον

ΝΑΟΣ
ΑΘΗΝΑΣ ΝΙΚΗΣ

ΟΔΟΣ
ΠΑΝΑΘΗΝΑΙΩΝ

ΚΛΕΨΥΔΡΑ

Περίπατος

ΙΤΡΑΥΛΟΣ
1957

0   50M

34. Acropolis (After Travlos *PEA* 55 fig. 21)

massive timbers of the roof. For the back chamber, where there was hardly space for superimposed Doric colonnades, four tall slender Ionic columns were used as supports. This room, entered separately from the west, was what was originally designated as Parthenon or Maiden's Chamber, but at least as early as the fourth century the name was extended to the whole temple.[4]

The Parthenon provides the supreme example of the so-called refinements of Doric architecture, those tiny deviations from the straight, the vertical and the horizontal, and from normal dimensions, which gave the temple greater beauty, anticipated optical illusions, and at the same time, at least in some cases, served a practical purpose. From the very foundations the main horizontal lines were given a slight upward curvature, in the stylobate a mere 11cm on the sides and 6cm on the ends.[5] This upward lift, continued in the entablature, was not only aesthetically pleasing but enhanced the building's appearance of great strength; in the stylobate, the curvature also served the simple and obvious purpose of getting rid of the rainwater. The vertical lines of the building too are not in fact absolutely vertical. Not only the individual columns, but the whole of the main structure of the temple, including the walls as well as the colonnades, tapers slightly upwards. The inward inclination of the columns is barely 6.5cm; it has been calculated that if the lines of the columns on the north and south flanks were prolonged, they would meet at a height of a mile and a half. The shafts were given a very subtle entasis or convex vertical curvature, involving barely 2cm in their height of 10.4m. Another refinement was the thickening of the columns at the angles of the peristyle, by a fortieth of the normal diameter; the reason for this was that otherwise, seen against the bright sky instead of the cella walls, they would have seemed to be lighter than their neighbors, and in the corner columns this would have given an unfortunate appearance of weakness.

Some of the deviations which we now call refinements have in the past been attributed to chance, to subsidence, or to negligence. Even the builders of the Parthenon were human and, because of miscalculation or careless workmanship, the building has its faults. But in general, accurate measurement and detailed study have left no doubt that the features we have been examining were deliberate and that they were produced by careful

[4] Judeich 247. M. Robertson and A. Frantz, *Parthenon Frieze*, London 1975, 6.
[5] A. D. Mavrikios, *AJA* 69, 1965, 264ff, with bibliography; S. Sinos, *AA* 89, 1974, 157–68.

mathematical calculations on the part of the designers and exquisite craftsmanship on the part of the stone-carvers.

A peculiar feature more recently dealt with by G. P. Stevens is worth adding to the list.[6] Penrose had already noted long ago that the west facade of the Parthenon was built at a very slightly higher level than the east; the difference was already present in the foundations of the older Parthenon and it was not eliminated in the new. Naturally it has sometimes been explained as due to simple error. But as Stevens reminds us the builders could lay their stones with an astonishing degree of accuracy. The centers of the bases of the northeast and southeast columns, he observes, are at precisely the same level; the corresponding points on the northwest and the southwest are respectively .035m and .052m higher. The object was to enhance the impressiveness of the building from two crucial viewpoints. The finest view of all was as one approached from the northwest, from the Propylaia. Similarly at the southwest corner the additional height increased the visual effect on the spectator as he stood on the southwest slope and looking up saw the Parthenon towering above the wall of the Acropolis. Of course the difference of levels is very small indeed; but in all these deviations the architects were dealing in quite tiny dimensions. One cannot be sure as in the case of the other features; but perhaps we have in this matter of the horizontal levels a refinement of a refinement.

All this added greatly to the time, trouble, and expense of building the Parthenon. Consider for example the shaping of the bottom drum of a column; it was by no means a simple cylinder. Its underside conformed to the curvature of the stylobate; its upper surface was not horizontal but cut at right angles to the inward-sloping axis of the column; its outer surface followed the taper and entasis of the shaft. In addition, the twenty-one flutes were cut to a delicate and subtle curve, carefully modified and diminished as the column rose. Thus each drum was a work of complex art and science requiring great care and skill in design and execution.

In other ways too the Parthenon represents the highest point of refinement of the Doric order. The decorative moldings, with their painted details, of which faint traces remain, are seen in their most exquisite form.[7] In particular the echinus of the capital, which terminates the shaft, has

---

[6] *AJA* 66, 1962, 337f; cf. F. C. Penrose, *Principles of Greek Architecture*, London 1888, 32–34.

[7] L. T. Shoe, *Profiles of Greek Mouldings*, Cambridge, Mass. 1936.

a delicately curved profile which contrasts with the more extravagant bulge of archaic capitals and the uninspired straight profile of many later examples.

Fortunately we know a good deal, from literary and epigraphical sources, and from the stones of the building, about the processes technical and political by which the Parthenon came into being.[8] Just about the middle of the fifth century, having already rehoused themselves, made their defenses secure, and erected various public buildings, the Athenians turned their minds to the task of creating worthy shrines of the great gods of the city, especially Athena, and in particular to the beautification of the Acropolis. Pheidias is often said to have been Perikles' Minister of Works; but it is not clear that he held any regular or semipermanent position over and above his special commissions. "Pheidias managed everything for him," says Plutarch, using a word which implies the allocation of tasks, in reference to Perikles' great program of public works and the army of craftsmen of various kinds needed to carry it out. "He was the overseer (*episkopos*) of everything, even though the various works required great architects and artists." Just what this means is a matter of conjecture. The Parthenon has been described as a sculptor's temple. There is some exaggeration in this—the Parthenon would have been a work of marvelous art even if sculpture had been confined to the minimum. But certainly provision was made right from the beginning for a well-thought-out scheme of decoration, and the main room was designed to contain Pheidias' great chryselephantine Athena. Pheidias was not as yet the dominant figure which he now appears to be in the history of sculpture—recent finds at Olympia have shown that the climax of his work, the Olympian Zeus, came after the Parthenos. But he had a great reputation, and no doubt he was on good terms with Perikles.

Iktinos, who designed the temple of Apollo at Bassae and had a hand in the great Hall of Initiation at Eleusis, is named as architect of the Parthenon. Kallikrates, known to have worked on walls and on the temple of Nike on the Acropolis, was associated with him. A third architect, Karpion, is mentioned—Vitruvius says that with Iktinos he wrote an account of the Parthenon—but nothing more is known of him.[9]

---

[8] *Parthenos and Parthenon*, Greece and Rome Supplement to 10, 1963, 36–45, R. Meiggs, "Political Implications of the Parthenon"; (cf. *The Athenian Empire*, 154, 289); 23–35, A. Burford, "The Builders of the Parthenon"; (cf. *Proceedings of Cambridge Philological Society* 191 [NS 11] 1965, 21ff).

[9] 7 Pref. 3. For Kallikrates see I. M. Shear, *Hesperia* 32, 1963, 375ff; for Iktinos, H. Knell, *Jahrbuch* 83, 1968, 100ff.

The Parthenon and Its Setting

We cannot tell how these architects worked together, or in what precise relation they stood to one another, or to Pheidias, or to Perikles, or to other officials political, financial, or priestly. There must have been consultations at a high level; in some sense the Parthenon must have been the work of a committee. In a very real sense it was the work of the whole Athenian people, not merely because hundreds of them had a hand in building it but because the assembly was ultimately responsible, confirmed appointments and sanctioned and scrutinized the expenditure of every drachma.

The Demos, besides having the first and the last word, exercised control at every point, as in other enterprises, through the medium of a board of *epistatai* or commissioners, five in number, who saw to it that the plans were well laid and the money well spent, and that professional license was not carried too far. There were those who thought that the whole project was too extravagant and that the money could have been better spent on other things. In particular some people—including Thucydides son of Melesias, leader of the opposition to Perikles until his ostracism in 443 B.C.—felt guilty, or for political purposes pretended they felt guilty, because raids were made on the funds contributed by the allied cities for the purpose of winning and maintaining their freedom from the domination of Persia. "Greece seems to be the victim of monstrous and manifest tyranny," they said, "when she sees us using what she is forced to contribute for the war to gild and deck out our city like a wanton woman, decorating her with costly stones and statues, and thousand-talent temples." Plutarch's account of the debate may contain an element of later rhetorical fiction but there is no doubt some truth in it.[10] The more authentic speeches in Thucydides the historian hint at the nature of Perikles' reply (2.40–41). He claimed that the Athenians pursued beauty without extravagance and that Athens was a city which others might be proud to acknowledge as mistress. One need not imagine that the protesters were numerous or received much popular support. Most citizens no doubt showed both interest and pride in the progress of the work. Besides, it provided steady employment and satisfactory pay for large numbers, craftsmen and laborers, quarrymen, haulers, workers in stone, metal, ivory, and wood, and indirectly for many others.

We have a number of fragments of the annual building accounts of the Parthenon, but the information which they give is limited.[11] They are

[10] *Perikles* 12 and 14.
[11] *IG* I² 339–53; cf. *BSA* 68, 1973, 350–51.

not specifications or working instructions, such as we have for certain other buildings, for example the naval arsenal built at Peiraeus by Philon in the fourth century. No doubt such documents were constantly in use on the Acropolis too, and they probably formed the basis of the published work of Iktinos and Karpion. But the inscriptions which we have were carved and published to show what money had been received and how it had been spent on the building and the statue. In one year, for example, when the temple was nearly complete, large sums came in from the treasurers of Athena and from the Hellenotamiai, the treasurers of the Delian League, something from the treasurers of Hephaistos at Laurion, and a little from the sale of surplus gold; ivory was bought, stone was cut on Pentelikon, carted, hoisted, and carved, and wages were also paid for work in wood, gold, and silver.

Industry in the Greek cities was on a comparatively small scale, and in the execution of a big public job numerous small contracts were apt to be involved. But in the case of the Parthenon Miss Burford infers from the accounts that the *epistatai* themselves acted as contractors, and employed labor direct. We do not have full details of the allocation of tasks and the payment of individuals, as in the case of the Erechtheion. Penalties were fixed for those who did not do their work properly or failed to fulfill their contracts.

From the accounts, from the evidence of the fabric itself, and from comparable evidence on other sites, we can get a good general idea of the stages by which the work was carried out. Extensive workshops must have been erected on the Acropolis, perhaps on the terrace to the south. When the foundations were ready, the temple was built from the outside inwards, with the main colonnade rising first, though gaps might be left for a time through which material for the inner structure could be safely carried. The metopes were carved on the ground and then set between the triglyphs in the outer frieze. The inner frieze was carved in position high up on the wall.[12] Thus the sculpture was by no means an excrescence or an afterthought but was knit into the very fabric. The great doors were hung, the marble paving was laid, and the temple must have been complete in all essentials, with inner colonnades and roof, when in 438/7 B.C. the statue was finally completed and dedicated. But for four or five more years the quarrymen continued to cut for the Parthenon, and the waggons still brought in their loads, though some were sold off along with other superfluous equipment and material, until in 433/2 B.C. the most difficult

[12] R. Stillwell, *Hesperia* 38, 1969, 231–41, discusses position and visibility.

job of all, the carving and setting in position of the pedimental sculptures, was finished. For this last addition only the finest artists were used; one need not be surprised that the work required half as long as the whole of the rest of the temple. And even then something went wrong, someone miscalculated the dimensions of certain figures, and some awkward hacking and pushing around was needed before they were all in place on the pediment floor. Meanwhile the main labor force under a different architect, Mnesikles, had been transferred to the Propylaia.

We do not know who was responsible for the choice of subjects in the sculpture. A good deal of freedom was commonly allowed to the artists in this matter. Some relevance to the cult might be called for, or some reference to a local legend; but there was also a repertoire of favorite subjects to which the sculptors recurred again and again in very diverse contexts—the exploits of the major heroes, the legendary battles of Gods and Giants, Lapiths and Centaurs, Greeks and Trojans. Over the course of the last century and a half these had been ingeniously adapted to the requirements of the various types of architectural sculpture; to a certain extent they provided ready-made designs, which the sculptor could develop as he wished. The Parthenon, incorporating traditional material of this kind alongside more unusual and peculiarly Athenian subjects, surpassed all other temples in the richness and variety of its sculpture, and in the way in which each element formed part of a single coherent scheme, produced, one likes to think, by the mastermind of Pheidias and carefully worked out by his pupils and subordinates.

The metopes were the most conventional part of the sculptured decoration. Their subjects, as far as we can tell, were taken from the common repertoire. On the south side was the battle of Lapiths and Centaurs, resolved of course into a series of duels. Even here there is doubt about the middle section, destroyed by the great explosion of 1687.[13] The drawings of Jacques Carrey, made a few years earlier, show that these central metopes represented not more Centaurs but a different subject, perhaps Erechtheus and the setting up of the ancient image of Athena. This gives a very unusual composition for the southern series. On the north side most of the metopes are lost; on the east, west, and north, nearly all of those which survive are in a deplorable state. This is due much more to defacement by human hands than to weathering, and subjects can be recognized only with difficulty. The eastern metopes certainly showed

[13] F. Brommer, *Metopen*, 233ff; cf. W. Schierig, *Jahrbuch* 85, 1970, 82–93; E. Simon, *Jahrbuch* 90, 1975, 100–20; M. Moltesen, *AA* 1976, 53–58.

35. Parthenon, Metope and Cornice at West End of North Side (Photo: German
Archaeological Institute)

Gods and Giants; the western probably Greeks and Amazons, possibly Persians—even the sex of the combatants is difficult to determine, but the types of composition used find parallels in Amazonomachies painted on vases. On the north appear to be scenes from the sack of Troy. The westernmost metope on this side, showing two female figures, one standing and one seated, with drapery in the best Parthenon style, is astonishingly well preserved by comparison with its battered neighbors, except that the heads are lost; one suspects that it was given a Christian interpretation, perhaps as the Annunciation, and so was spared defacement.[14] The metopes measure about 1.2m square. They are carved in high relief; both figures and background were colored, and details were added in bronze.

In technical and artistic quality, which of course has to be judged mainly from the southern examples, the metopes vary much more widely than the frieze and the pediments. The sculptors owed much to the wrestling school and the pankration; some were capable of superb designs finely executed, some sacrificed grace and harmony to vigor. One gets the impression that in the metopes the sculptors were allowed a little more freedom in working out their versions of the basic designs and preliminary sketches. Perhaps at this stage the master plans had not yet been so fully and clearly formulated; and probably Pheidias had not yet gathered together a team of uniformly excellent artists, capable of working harmoniously together for the achievement of a single grand design.

For the next element, the frieze, such a team was indispensable. On all four sides a single subject was represented, the Panathenaic procession. The long frieze was skillfully punctuated and subtly varied; no doubt definite lengths were allocated to each sculptor, as in the Erechtheion. But there were no clear-cut breaks; the whole was carefully integrated, and though various hands can be detected there is remarkable uniformity of treatment and style. The total length was 160m; and since about four-fifths of this survives, the general effect can be appreciated better than in the metopes or the pediments. The height of the frieze is about one meter; it is carved in low relief, with great technical virtuosity, with horses superimposed for example, and the figures nowhere project much more than 5 cm from the background. Color was again freely used.

There is no doubt about the subject, but the manner in which it is represented raises questions. It is hardly true to say that here, in contrast with the mythical themes of the other sculptures, we have a scene taken directly from contemporary life. The procession may have been conceived

[14] F. Brommer, *Metopen*, 59ff.

as taking place in the legendary past, perhaps at the time when the rite was first instituted by Erechtheus. Even if this is not so, what we have is not a realistic representation of an actual procession, but rather what Robertson calls "the ideal image of a recurrent event."[15] By a curious method which had earlier been employed in the great painting of the battle of Marathon in the Poikile, in which successive phases of the struggle were combined into a seemingly contemporaneous whole, the procession was shown at different stages in different parts. On the west end many of the horsemen are making preparations and are not yet mounted; most of the procession is in motion, sometimes brisk, sometimes stately; at the east end the rites on the Acropolis are already taking place, watched by the gods. Certain features were omitted altogether, notably the ship which was trundled from the Pompeion, the building for the preparation of processions near the Dipylon Gate, across the agora to the foot of the Acropolis, with the new robe for Athena carried on its mast. Perhaps for reasons of scale it would have been awkward to work into the design.

The procession moves northwards along the west side (though some figures face the other way), and eastwards along the north and south sides; then it rounds the northeast and southeast corners to converge upon the central part of the east side—an ingenious and indeed unique arrangement. In the present context one need not give a detailed description; it will be enough to note the endless variety of the scenes, which comprise more than two hundred human figures, besides the gods. The cavalry is predominant, the elite of Athenian youth, with their spirited mounts. There are also chariot groups, and victims are led to the sacrifice, some docile, some recalcitrant. Musicians are in attendance; other men carry offerings in jars and on trays. Dignified marshals punctuate the procession, and towards its head, at the east end, young ladies walk sedately, looking very like the Caryatids of the Erechtheion. In the middle of the east side are the priest and priestess with attendants. The folded robe which the priest is holding is generally thought to be the old robe of Athena which is being put away. The ceremony, though represented on the front of the Parthenon, in fact took place in the older temple to the north. On either side of the central scene are the Olympian gods, most of them easily recognizable. They are of superhuman stature; though they are seated, their heads are on the same level as the standing humans.

[15] *Greece and Rome* Supplement to 10, 56; cf. *Parthenon Frieze*, 11. On the gods in the east frieze see now E. G. Pemberton, *AJA* 80, 1976, 113–24. Cf. J. D. Mikalson, *Erechtheus and the Panathenaia, AJP* 97, 1976, 141–53.

Beyond them again to right and left are standing male figures; it has been suggested that while two of them are yet another pair of marshals superintending the arrival of the procession, the others are the eponymous heroes of the Athenian tribes. In all there is a representative gathering of mortals and immortals for the great occasion. Others might have been added, but at the cost of overloading an already crowded scene.

Many hands were at work in the frieze, and there were still some differences of quality. When the time came to add the pedimental sculpture, Pheidias had available a well-balanced group of true masters of the art, practiced in carrying out together a highly complex design, capable of working in harmony without loss of individual style and genius. Attribution to known artists is highly conjectural, and we cannot say even with probability that any particular piece was by the hand of Pheidias himself. We can believe that models were made, probably on a reduced scale rather than full size—the pediments were over 27m long and over 3m high in the middle. The old problems of creating a design to fill a flat triangular field, and the peculiar character of the two subjects, made

36. Parthenon, West End, Showing frieze in position (Photo: Alison Frantz)

37. Parthenon, Floor of East Pediment; the figure is a replica of one in the British Museum (Photo: F. Brommer)

constant and careful coordination essential, with perhaps just a little freedom in detail.

Much less is left of the pediments than of the frieze or even the metopes; the remains belong chiefly to subordinate figures which stood in the outer angles; the central group has perished entirely in the eastern pediment, and only fragments have survived from the west. Pausanias (1.24.5) tells us very briefly that on the east the birth of Athena was shown, on the west the contest of Athena and Poseidon to decide who was to possess the land of Attica. But for his testimony there would surely have been innumerable different theories about the themes of the pediments.

There is still plenty of scope for discussion about treatment, composition, and detailed arrangement; but the artist's general conception is in both cases fairly clear. Marks on the floor of the pediment give a little assistance, but their interpretation is often open to dispute. Drawings made shortly before the calamitous explosion of 1687, and commonly attributed to a French artist, Jacques Carrey, add something.

Athena, according to the story, was born from the head of her father Zeus, released by a blow of Hephaistos' axe. Happily the treatment of the theme in the lost central group of the east pediment is preserved in a relief now in Madrid, carved on an altar of Roman date which was later converted for use as a wellhead. Most writers believe that the sculptor took his design from the Parthenon. Zeus is enthroned in majesty, holding his scepter; Athena starts away to the right, and between them a winged Nike flies forward to place a wreath on her head. Hephaistos strides away to the right of Zeus. Athena is not shown, as in earlier vase paintings, as a doll-like figure in the act of emerging from her father's head—this would have been out of place in a splendid and prominent sculptural group; she is already full-grown, and fully clothed and armed. The figures which are still preserved or represented in Carrey's drawing belong to the northern and southern ends of the pediment, thus complementing the picture given by the Madrid puteal. In the present context one need only consider the general character of the composition, without going into details of the many problems of identification and arrangement. Various gods and heroes were shown as present at the birth; one gets the impression that excitement radiates outwards from the center as they become conscious of the great event. In the extreme southern angle the sun god Helios and the heads of his horses rise as if from the sea; in the northern angle the moon goddess Selene and her tired horses are sinking. These figures give the setting of the event in time as the river gods in the angles of the east pediment of the temple of Zeus at Olympia give the setting in place. Comparison with the Olympia pediments is inevitable.[16] In the Parthenon the composition is more elaborate and subtle; the two halves of each pediment do not correspond so closely; for example in the east pediment of the Parthenon the nude male figure reclining towards the southern end is balanced by a draped female figure. In older restorations of the principal group Zeus was placed a little to the left of center, Athena a little to the right; the whole group formed the centerpiece, rather than any single figure. More recently, after further examination of the pediment floor, Zeus on his throne has been placed in the exact center.[17]

In the west pediment Carrey's drawing shows that the centerpiece did indeed consist of two figures, Athena and Poseidon, striding away from one another, her left leg overlapping his right. Between them may be restored the olive tree, the gift of Athena to Athens. Poseidon's gift, which could hardly be represented in the pediment, was a miraculous salt spring. The figures in the narrowing angles, separated from the central group by the chariots and horses of the contestants, and their attendants, can best be interpreted as local Attic heroes and heroines, who are said to have constituted a panel of judges. The two solitary figures which still remain in position on the pediment may be Kekrops and his daughter. The splendid reclining male figure formerly in the extreme northern angle is generally said to be the river god Ilissos. His counterpart at the other end is not a similar figure, as in the east pediment at Olympia, but a draped female, seen in Carrey's drawing, who may be the fountain nymph Kallirrhoe.

The surviving pedimental figures show the art of the Parthenon sculptors at its finest, both in the powerful rendering of the masculine frame and in the subtle treatment of the women's drapery. One may prefer the grand simplicity of the Olympia sculpture, and think it more in keeping with the character of Doric architecture; one may see in the elaboration and refinement of the Parthenon the beginnings of the style which in the next generation of Attic sculptors was criticized as being "kata-

[16] And can best be made by using Ashmole, *Architect and Sculptor*.

[17] R. Carpenter, *AJA* 66, 1962, 265ff; cf. E. Lapalus, *Le Fronton Sculpté en Grèce*, Paris 1947, 181ff; E. Harrison, *AJA* 71, 1967, 27–58. On west pediment see now M. Brouskaris, *Deltion* 24A, 1971, 8–14.

texitechnic" (i.e. wasting art on details).[18] One may even doubt whether the peculiar beauty of the sculpture could be properly appreciated when it could only be seen from far below; but on the other hand it should be borne in mind that in bright sunshine, creating a lively play of light and shade, the effect which the sculptors aimed at would not be lost even from a distance. Pheidias and his associates aimed at nothing less than perfection in the execution of their designs. The Olympia sculptors left some of the figures rough at the back, using a technique which was something between relief and sculpture in the round, and one cannot blame their common sense and desire for economy. The Parthenon sculptors carved with great care even those parts of the figures which would never be seen as long as they remained in position in the pediments; and one can be grateful to them for the laborious efforts which were wasted on their contemporaries, and to the Athenian people who, though for many years the temple and its decoration had made great demands on their resources, gave their approval to this final extravagance.

We can now see how the whole great scheme added up to something more than the sum of its parts. Prominent on the east, the main front of the temple, was the birth of Athena, the eponymous deity of Athens and the embodiment of the spirit of the city. On the west front, which would in fact be seen first by people approaching from the Propylaia, the gods were shown in rivalry bringing gifts to the city, with Athena victorious. In their place on the Parthenon ancient legends took on a new significance. The metopes depicted the victories of the Greeks and their gods over lower and less civilized powers. In the frieze the people of Athens pay due homage to their goddess with lavish pomp and simple ceremony. Some of the themes, we shall find, were taken up and repeated in the elaborate subsidiary decoration of the great statue within.

The cult statue itself, the Athena Parthenos,[19] was taken to Constantinople in late antiquity and is irretrievably lost, more completely even than Pheidias' second masterpiece in chryselephantine technique, the Zeus of Olympia. In the area of the workshop of Pheidias at Olympia fragments of ivory and of clay molds for the golden parts, and tools used by the sculptors have been found, though the statue itself has vanished.

---

[18] See p. 146 below.

[19] F. Brommer, *Athena Parthenos*, Bremen 1957; Neda Leipen, *Athena Parthenos: a Reconstruction*, Royal Ontario Museum 1971; cf. J. W. Graham, *Greece and Rome* Supplement to 10, 77–83. F. Schiff, "Athena Parthenos, die Vision des Pheidias," *Antike Kunst* 16, 1973, 3–43.

The general appearance of the Athena is known from Pausanias' description, from representations on coins and from small copies.[20] The goddess was a majestic figure about 12m high. On her head was a triple-crested helmet of elaborate design; her peplos hung in heavy folds. A snake was coiled at her left side, and beyond it stood a shield, supported by her left hand which also held a spear. Her right hand rested palm upwards on the top of a column, and carried a winged figure of Nike 2m high. On the outer face of the shield a battle of Greeks and Amazons was shown in relief,[21] on the inside was a battle of gods and giants, probably painted rather than carved. The sandals of the goddess were adorned with figures of Lapiths and Centaurs; and on the front of the base of the statue was shown the myth of the creation of Pandora in the presence of the gods.

Thus the Parthenos was a work of highly elaborate design and great technical skill. The processes by which it was created were very different from the art of the sculptor in stone. Pheidias was a master of design in both media; and for the cult statue he must have had the assistance of yet another group of master craftsmen. To produce a large chryselephantine figure the first step was to shape a wooden structure which would serve as a base or core; to this carved sheets of ivory and molded plates of gold were attached to represent bare flesh and drapery respectively.[22] We know that the gold plates of the Parthenos could be detached on occasion. The cost of the statue was of course enormous, and the details figure prominently in the accounts.

The final effect of such a figure on the observer baffles the imagination. Though the Parthenos was the product of a wonderful and harmonious combination of several arts used with great virtuosity, one cannot help feeling that Pausanias[23] and Lucian may have been right in preferring another Athena which stood on the Acropolis, the so-called Lemnian, a bronze figure, simpler in technique, and perhaps less forbidding in aspect. Yet we know that the Athena Parthenos, like the Olympian Zeus,

[20] A.J.N. Prag, "Athena Mancuniensis," *JHS* 92, 1972, 96–114, produces another and compares it with known examples.

[21] Represented in copies, notably the reliefs found in the harbor of Peiraeus; for recent work on this see H. A. Thompson, *Hesperia* 28, 1959, 106–8; E. B. Harrison, *Hesperia* 35, 1966, 107–33; V. M. Strocka, *Piräusreliefs und Parthenosschild*, Bochum 1967; F. Preishofen, *Jahrbuch* 89, 1974, 50–69.

[22] G. P. Stevens, *Hesperia* 24, 1955, 240–76; 26, 1957, 350–61.

[23] 1.28.2; Lucian *Imagines* 4.

had a powerful impact on worshipers entering the temple; Pheidias is said to have added something to the accepted religion of the Olympians.[24] On the other hand a Christian writer remarked, with some malice, that these great figures, though splendid in outward appearance, harbored dirt and vermin within.

"The Parthenon," says Lawrence, "is the one building in the world which may be assessed as absolutely right."[25] It approached as near perfection as human handiwork is likely to go; it was complete in itself. Yet if one is to appreciate it properly one must look at it in its setting and its context. Sir Mortimer Wheeler once compared the temple to "a very superior ornament on a mantelpiece."[26] This simile is misleading. The Parthenon, decreed by the Athenian people and placed where it stands by the long-sustained efforts of many artists and workmen of many kinds, was part of the very fabric of the city and of the life of its citizens. It dominated Athens and the Acropolis in particular. Other major monuments of the Periklean and the succeeding period were carefully related to it but not wholly subordinated; and at the same time it was embedded in large numbers of cult spots and minor monuments.

It was conspicuous, as it still is, from most points in the city, but as one came up under the Acropolis slopes it was wholly or partly lost to view. Even after entering the Propylaia it was largely masked in ancient times by intervening monuments, as Stevens has demonstrated,[27] and not fully visible as now. Only after passing through a further small propylon, and entering the area immediately west of the temple, was one confronted with the final overwhelming view.

To glance down the later centuries[28]—in early Christian times the

24 Quintilian 12.10.9.

25 *Greek Architecture*, 3d edn, Penguin 1973, 295.

26 *Antiquity* 36, 1962, 6ff.

27 *Hesperia* 5, 1936, 443ff.

28 W. B. Dinsmoor, Jr., *AAA* 4, 1971, 264–68; *AJA* 77, 1973, 211; *Hesperia* 43, 1974, 132–55, on fragments recently found in the agora, including the first recognized fragments of the interior colonnade, deduces extensive damage in the 4th century A.D., involving the ceiling and the inner colonnade; cf. J. Travlos, *ArchEph* 1973, 218–36.

On the removal of the sculpture see W. St. Clair, *Lord Elgin and the Marbles*, Oxford 1972.

On excavation note J. A. Bundgaard, *The Excavation of the Athenian Acropolis* (with the original drawings), 2 volumes, Copenhagen 1974.

temple was converted into a church, of the Virgin, and in Turkish times into a mosque. Its main outer structure stood largely intact until 1687, when a Turkish powder magazine was exploded by the besieging Venetians, causing severe damage especially on the north and south sides; subsequently a complete small mosque was built in the interior. Early in the nineteenth century Lord Elgin bought much of the sculpture from the Turks and transferred it to London. After the liberation the Parthenon like the rest of the Acropolis was cleared of Turkish accretions. The questionable process of *anastylosis*, re-erection of columns and other elements, with cautious insertion of modern material, still continues.

The Propylaia was designed as a splendid prelude to the Parthenon. It was another great Doric building, with Ionic elements, constructed mainly of Pentelic marble, with details in dark Eleusinian stone; but it had a different architect, Mnesikles,[29] and we do not know in what relation he stood to the architects of the Parthenon, or to Pheidias. The Propylaia had no sculptured pediments, metopes, or frieze, whether by reason of economy or because the intention was to reserve such adornment for the temple. Its orientation was the same as that of the Parthenon, but it was not placed on the same east to west axis. It was no mere gateway to the precinct beyond but an imposing building in its own right. Yet its plan, though complex, was based on the simple type of propylon in which a porch was built on either side of a gate in a wall. Traces of a structure of this type, built early in the fifth century, with a different orientation, have been found on the site; and there were no doubt still earlier predecessors, going back to Mycenean times. In the Propylaia of Mnesikles the processional way ascended through a great central gateway, and on either side were two subsidiary doorways approached by flights of steps. The outer porch was made very deep, and the ceiling was supported by Ionic columns of elegantly simple form, three on either side of the roadway. The inner, eastern porch, standing at a higher level, was comparatively narrow; both had a facade of six Doric columns, nearly 9m high on the west, a little lower on the east. This central structure measured a little over 18m north to south and 25m east to west. To the northwestern corner was attached a temple-like wing with a porch of three Doric columns facing southwards across the road; the inner room was a

[29] J. A. Bundgaard, *Mnesikles* (Copenhagen 1957), is the most important work on the Propylaia; for further bibliography see Travlos *PDA* 483. On the older propylon see now H. Eiteljorg, *AAA* 8, 1975, 94–95, who dates it *after* the Persian invasion.

Pinakotheke or picture gallery, and the pictures were probably painted on detachable boards as in the Stoa Poikile. A similar columnar facade was built in the corresponding position on the south, but the structure behind it was reduced to a single small room, open on the west side too, with a single pier, facing the bastion on which the little temple of Victory was soon to be erected. The width of the whole building, north to south, amounted to about 48m.

The Propylaia was built between 437 and 432 B.C. That such a short period was required, even allowing for smaller size, in comparison with the Parthenon, shows how much less time and effort was demanded when elaborate sculptural adornment was omitted. The Propylaia was never completed as originally planned. The architect was confronted by various difficulties. Funds must have been much depleted as the Parthenon entered its final phase. An inevitable war was looming ahead. The site presented problems, owed partly to the natural configuration, partly to the existence of many old shrines at the western end of the Acropolis. The architects had to show respect for these even if it meant some sacrifice in aesthetic effect. The determination to develop the little shrine of Athena Nike in its own right was no doubt one of the reasons for the somewhat awkward amputation of the southwest wing. The plan was even more drastically curtailed on the east. There are clear architectural indications that large extensions were planned adjoining the central structure on the north and south, in the form of rectangular halls, probably storerooms. The southeastern room would have encroached on the sanctuary of Artemis Brauronia. The northeastern room would have roofed over the cisterns which occupied this area. Besides this evidence of omission of important elements in the design, details such as unfinished surfaces and the retention of lifting-bosses show that work on the Propylaia had to cease before completion.

The southwestern bastion, built upon a rocky spur, had been an excrescence on the face of the Acropolis since prehistoric times. Remains of a Mycenean wall have been found, and these were left visible at certain points, behind the later masonry. As at Mycenae, the projecting spur threatened the exposed right side of an enemy attacking the gate. It was appropriate that the protectress of the city should be worshiped on the bastion as well as on the summit of the hill, and by the middle of the sixth century a cult of Athena as goddess of Victory was established there. A poros altar of that date was found under the later pavement, bearing the inscription "Altar of Athena Nike. Patrokles made it."[30] To the west of the site of the altar were the remains of a small shrine, about 3.50m square, built of poros, probably early in the fifth century. Pausanias (5.26.6) mentions an old wooden image of "Wingless Victory," i.e. Athena Nike; this no doubt stood on the bastion.

In the middle of the fifth century, when grand schemes for the embellishment of the Acropolis were being worked out, the existence of this old shrine was scrupulously taken into account. Indeed before its requirements were satisfied it had diverted a good deal of effort to itself and may have been something of an embarrassment to the architects.

In 449 B.C. a decree was passed authorizing the erection of a temple for Athena Nike;[31] the architect was Kallikrates, who was soon to be engaged on the Parthenon, and plans were prepared for a small Ionic temple in Pentelic marble, with a prostyle porch of four columns at either end. But for some reason construction on the bastion had to be deferred for some years, and the plans were apparently adapted for use in building the Ionic temple on the bank of the River Ilissos southeast of the city. Meanwhile, probably soon after the middle of the century, the bastion was rebuilt, in ashlar masonry of poros; courses of headers and stretchers alternated, and the number varied according to the lay of the land, with a maximum of twenty-one at the southeast. The north wall conformed with the orientation of the Propylaia; the northern and western walls met in an obtuse angle, the western and southern in a right angle. Thus the general orientation of the bastion, and with it the shrine, remained independent of the Propylaia. At the end of the north side, a flight of steps, originally seven in number, gave immediate access to the bastion. In the west wall two large niches were left; what they contained is not known. The surface of the bastion was paved with marble slabs set on a poros bedding.

When the temple of Athena Nike was finally built is not altogether clear; it was probably in the middle 420s, a few years after work on the Propylaia had ended, to judge by architectural and sculptural style and the relation of the building to its big neighbor. A statue of the goddess was dedicated in 425/4 B.C.[32] Even in the war years fine architectural

---

[30] A. E. Raubitschek, *Dedications from the Athenian Acropolis*, Cambridge, Mass. 1949, 359; cf. B. Bergquist, *The Archaic Greek Temenos*, Lund 1967, 25f.

[31] *IG* I² 24; Dinsmoor, *Architecture* 185f; I. M. Shear, *Hesperia* 32, 1963, 377ff; R. Meiggs, *The Athenian Empire* 496ff, Appendix 9, "The Temple of Athena Nike."

[32] *IG* II² 403.

38. Southwest Bastion and Temple of Athena Nike (Photo: Alison Frantz)

work, on a comparatively small scale, could still be undertaken. The temple was similar in general character to the one originally planned, but different in details and somewhat smaller. In particular the length was curtailed and the inner porch omitted. The material was still Pentelic marble. The building was set as far north and west as possible, and was orientated with the west and south walls of the bastion, at an angle of 18 degrees from the line of the Propylaia. The little cella was squarish; its eastern front was open, consisting of two piers, with bronze screens between these and the antae. The porches back and front had four monolithic Ionic columns just over 4m high. Overall dimensions, on the stylobate, were 8.27m east to west by 5.64m north to south. The altar, of which little remains, stood on poros foundations a short distance to the east.

A continuous sculptured frieze ran round the temple,[33] and there are indications that the small pediments too contained figures, and were surmounted by akroteria. The frieze represented an assembly of the gods, and battles of Greeks and Persians. The combat scenes are vigorously

[33] E. B. Harrison, *AJA* 74, 1970, 317ff.

executed but variable in quality. The work of a much more distinguished group of sculptors can be seen in another frieze which was carved some years later, probably towards the end of the century, on the outer face of a marble balustrade about a meter high, supporting a metal grille, which ran around the edge of the bastion. It showed a number of figures of Victory, forming a kind of procession which ran westward along the north and south walls to converge on the west end—an idea no doubt adapted from the arrangement of the Parthenon frieze. There seem to have been sixteen slabs on the south side, nine on the west, eight on the north, and two which made a southward return along the east beside the stairway, giving a total length of nearly 42m. The figures of Nike are ingeniously and attractively varied. Some lead victims to sacrifice; others construct a trophy; one bends to fasten her sandal. On each of the three main sides was a seated figure of Athena. The composition and style of the frieze have been carefully studied;[34] half a dozen different hands have been detected, and the finest sections have been conjecturally assigned to some of the leading artists of the post-Pheidian era, such as Paionios. Whether there was a master mind directing these sculptors, as in the Parthenon, we do not know; but in any case, between them they produced a striking and harmonious composition, and the finer slabs represent the best in late fifth-century sculpture, especially in the treatment of drapery, combining strength of design with delicacy of detail. Yet there was a bungler among the sculptors who committed the unforgivable sin of appearing to cut into the flesh when carving deep folds.

The Nike shrine, and the treatment of the bastion in general, are very characteristic of the Athenian way of doing things, of planning and building. It is difficult to believe that any single architect or planner, given a free hand to develop the western end of the Acropolis and its approaches, would have produced what was in fact built. One can imagine that he would have given the Propylaia greater symmetry, and kept whatever he placed on the bastion in stricter subordination and conformity. As things were, natural features, ancient traditions and cults, and the efforts of several architects, combined to produce the effect which we see, lacking full coordination, yet not lacking harmony. In particular, the little Nike temple asserted a lively and prominent independence of the main scheme; yet it is not out of place, and one would not wish to have it otherwise.

[34] Most notably by R. Carpenter, *The Sculpture of the Nike Temple Parapet*, Cambridge, Mass. 1929.

Of course it was not possible to give a handsome temple to all the deities whose cults clustered round the entrance to the Acropolis on the west; but in one way or another each was taken into account, and given a niche, in some cases quite literally, in the new scheme. We do not know what happened to the shrines of Aphrodite Pandemos, and of Ge Kourotrophos and Demeter Chloe, which seem to have stood lower down the slope.[35] Immediately beside the Propylaia and the Nike temple, as we see in Pausanias' account (1.22.8), stood Hermes Propylaios, and the Charites (Graces); here too was the goddess variously called Artemis Hekate, Hekate Propylaia, Hekate or Artemis Epipyrgidia ("on the Tower"), and Artemis Phosphoros.[36] No doubt a Hermes had stood before the gateway to the Acropolis from very early times. As Thucydides tells us (6.27.1), stone Herms stood at entrances both private and sacred everywhere in Athens. This was the most important of gateways, leading to the most important shrine, and it could hardly fail to have its own Herm. A famous Hermes Propylaios, much admired and copied, was made by Alkamenes in the latter part of the fifth century, no doubt as an adornment for the new Propylaia.[37] A likely place for its dedication is in the niche between the northwest wing and the west end of the north wall of the main building; and here in fact are traces of a square bedding appropriate for such a monument. Hermes was associated with the Graces and appears with the three in some of the reliefs which were a common form of dedication to these deities. However we can probably assume that the Propylaios was an independent figure, a true Herm in fact. In the niche between the main hall of the Propylaia and the south wing, corresponding to the one mentioned above, marks have been observed indicating that a stele stood here, which may well have carried a relief showing the Graces and possibly Hermes too. A popular tradition, mentioned by Pausanias (1.22.8) and others, said that the sculptor of the figures of the Graces near the Propylaia was Sokrates the philosopher, but Pliny (36.32) denies this and certainly the ascription is open to doubt. The cult of the Charites was much older than the Propylaia; the shrine may have been in the forecourt of the earlier propylon; under the new dispensation it probably occupied the bit of spare ground east of the Nike shrine and south of the southwest wing of the Propylaia.

[35] See p. 178f below.

[36] For these shrines and the topography of the area see Judeich 223ff; Hill 185f; plan Travlos *PDA* 150.

[37] D. Willers, *Jahrbuch* 82, 1967, 37ff; *AthMitt* Beiheft 4, 1975, 33, 48.

Artemis-Hekate too was associated with the Charites; one of the official seats in the theater is inscribed as belonging to the priest of the Charites and Artemis Epipyrgidia.[38] Slight traces at about the middle point of the south wall of the wing have been taken to show that this is where she had her niche. Once again it was Alkamenes who produced a new statue for the ancient goddess, in triple form, the prototype of numerous small dedications which have been found in various parts of Athens.[39]

Probably within the Propylaia, alongside the heroic statue of the wounded general Diitrephes, Pausanias saw a figure of Aphrodite dedicated by Kallias and made by Kalamis. What is probably the base of this statue has been found far down the slope at the southeastern corner of the agora.[40] The name of the sculptor makes it clear that the statue antedates the Propylaia by some years. Where it stood originally we cannot say—possibly in the shrine of Pandemos. Obviously when the Propylaia was built and the western approach reorganized there must have been a good deal of dislocation and reshuffling.

Entering the Propylaia, turning right and halting before the southernmost column of the eastern porch, we find ourselves on much safer ground, in the precinct of Athena Hygieia, goddess of Health. The location, character, and history of this shrine are comparatively well attested by the monuments.[41] There is evidence in dedications that the cult existed in the early fifth century and perhaps even the sixth. The altar found a little to the east seems to have been set up at the time of the building of the Propylaia or shortly after, but it no doubt replaced an earlier one. The marble base is 2.6m square; of the altar proper only the southeastern corner survives, consisting of marble slabs which must have supported a table-like top. It occupied the eastern part of the base, leaving room for the officiating priest to stand on the western part.

Plutarch tells how, when the Propylaia was being built, an excellent workman fell from a height and seemed likely to die from his injuries.[42] Perikles was much distressed, and Athena herself appeared to him in a dream and revealed a cure which proved effective; in gratitude he set up "the bronze image of Athena Hygieia on the Acropolis beside the altar which, they say, had existed previously." This statue no doubt occupied the marble base immediately adjacent to the southernmost

[38] *IG* II² 5050.

[39] Pausanias 2.30.2. For shrines and figures of Hekate see p. 186 below.

[40] *Hesperia* 10, 1941, 60; *Agora* III 50.

[41] Judeich 242f; Travlos *PDA* 124, 126.   [42] *Perikles* 13.8.

39. Propylaia, Southeast corner, with Shrine of Athena Hygieia (Photo: M. Vernardos)

column of the porch, in shape something more than a semicircle, and possibly nearly one meter in diameter. The inscription, however, says, "The Athenians to Athena Hygieia; Pyrrhos of Athens made it,"[43] implying that the Athenian people in general, not Perikles in particular, made the dedication. The statue was a special offering, and the place for the cult figure would naturally be to the east of the altar, since the priest faced in that direction. But some time later Pyrrhos' Athena was given her own altar, or table of offerings, on a base which stands immediately to the east.

Plutarch's story may be garbled. Others tell a somewhat different tale. Pliny (22.44) says that the workman, a slave of Perikles, was engaged in work on a temple (probably the Parthenon), and does not mention the dedication of a statue to Athena Hygieia. Some modern writers have suggested that Pyrrhos' statue was a thank offering for release from the great plague of the early years of the Peloponnesian War. But one can still believe that Plutarch's story is true to the spirit in which the Periklean program was carried forward.

[43] *IG* 1² 395.

(133)

At a higher level to the east was the much more spacious precinct of Artemis Brauronia.[44] This was one of the many cults imported from the demes (in this case Brauron) and given a duplicate shrine in the city. The goddess had no temple; the main building was a stoa on the south side, 38.5m long, with its back to the Acropolis wall, and with projecting wings at either end in the form of rectangular chambers, in one of which no doubt stood Praxiteles' statue. Inscriptions mention an old image too. The stoa seems to have been built in the middle of the fifth century, and later, at about the time when the Propylaia was built, a shorter colonnade was added on the east side. Pausanias saw hereabouts a curious bronze statue of the Wooden Horse, with Greek warriors peeping out of it, and that this did in fact stand in the precinct is confirmed by the discovery of inscribed blocks from its base, which names as the sculptor Strongylion (late 5th century).[45] The west side of the shrine is formed by a well-preserved section of the Pelasgic Wall, which may indeed have been retained partly for the purpose of supporting the terrace. An oblique wall enclosed the north side, and towards its east end a stairway gave access.

Extending from the shrine as far as the rock-cut steps which lead up to the Parthenon are the very slight remains of a long hall, with interior columns, built probably in the middle of the fifth century B.C. and given a columnar facade early in the fourth. It can be identified as the Chalkotheke, a repository for armor, cauldrons, braziers, and many other bronze objects, mentioned in inscriptions of the middle of the fourth century.[46]

The area immediately east of the Propylaia and north of the shrine of Artemis was made into what G. P. Stevens calls the "Periclean Entrance Court to the Acropolis."[47] Because of the geography of the hill, with the approach inevitably from the west, in the case of the Parthenon there was not the usual emphasis on the area to the east of the temple, where the main altar commonly stood. The approach was from the rear, and even then oblique as we have seen; the eastern part of the hill was the "backyard," and comparatively unimportant in the scheme. The "Entrance Court" was bounded on the east by a massive wall, according

[44] Judeich 244; Stevens, *Hesperia* 5, 1936, 459–70; C. N. Edmonson, *AJA* 72, 1968, 164–65; Travlos *PDA* 124f; J. Kondis, *Deltion* 22A, 1967, 156–206.

[45] Pausanias 23.8; *IG* I² 535.

[46] *IG* II² 120, 1425, 1469 (cf. E. Schweigert, *Hesperia* 7, 1938, 281ff); Judeich 245: Stevens, *Hesperia* Suppl. 3, 1940, 7–19; Travlos *PDA* 196f.

[47] See Bibliography for this chapter.

to Stevens of Mycenean origin but still in being in the fifth century. Against this, at a point marked by a large square cutting and a few blocks, was placed the colossal bronze Athena Promachos of Pheidias, made about 460 B.C., towering above the countless smaller monuments.[48] Near the Promachos Pausanias (1.28.2) saw a chariot group, "a tithe from a victory over the Boeotians and the Chalkidians" won in 506 B.C. A large

40. Acropolis as seen from Northwest; Model in Stoa of Attalos, by G. P. Stevens (Photo: Agora Excavations)

square cutting immediately south of the Promachos probably marks the site. Herodotus (5.77.4) saw this same monument "on the left as one enters the Propylaia." It must have been moved, probably in the reshuffle of older monuments at the time of the construction of the Periklean Propylaia. What Pausanias and even Herodotus saw must have been a replacement. Such a group could hardly have survived the Persian destruction; and in fact fragments of two dedicatory inscriptions have been found, one in letters of the late sixth century, the other in letters of the mid fifth.[49]

[48] G. P. Stevens, *Hesperia* 5, 1936, 491–99; 15, 1946, 107–14; Travlos *PDA* 55.
[49] *IG* I² 394; Judeich 236ff; Stevens, *Hesperia* 5, 1930, 504–6; A. Raubitschek,

Even when we have considered the Propylaia and taken into account the relation of the Erechtheion to the greater temple, our picture of the setting of the Parthenon on the Acropolis will not be complete without adding the innumerable minor monuments, mainly sculpture, which were an essential part of the scene, a kind of continuous base from which the great buildings arose. We know them from Pausanias' account[50] (and he makes it clear though his list is long he is being highly selective) from bases and fragments of bases, some inscribed, and from cuttings in the rock. For present purposes one must be even more selective than Pausanias and briefly convey the general impression, with passing mention of a few particular monuments. The greatest concentration lined the road from the Propylaia to the east front of the Parthenon, crossing the "forecourt" and continuing along the north side of the temple. Works by the finest artists were exhibited here; Myron was particularly well represented by his Perseus and his Athena and Marsyas. The sculpture varied greatly in character and subject; there was no particular system or order—single figures and groups simply accumulated over a long period, and stood in a loose informal relation to each other and to their splendid architectural setting. There were statues of gods and of men, including generals—Phormion, Konon, and Timotheos—and several athletes. Mythological groups were numerous and covered a wide range. Theseus was naturally well represented, and so was Herakles. Prokne and Itys, dedicated by Alkamenes according to Pausanias, may be a group of mother and child which has been found;[51] doubt has been expressed whether the dedicator also made it, whether it is worthy of Pheidias' best pupil, and its state of preservation is hardly good enough to decide. Curiously, the subjects of both the Parthenon pediments, the birth of Athena and her contest with Poseidon, are found among the free-standing groups.

One point is fixed absolutely by letters cut in the Acropolis rock, a few yards north of the sixth column from the west in the north colonnade of the Parthenon. The inscription,[52] of Roman date, says "of Ge Karpophoros in accordance with an oracle," and Pausanias' "image of Ge beseeching Zeus to rain" must have stood nearby. Indeed the inscription

---

Dedications on the Athenian Acropolis, Cambridge, Mass. 1949, 191–94, 201–5; Hill 181.

[50] 1.23.9–24.4; cf. Raubitschek, *Dedications* 459f.

[51] Richter, *Sculpture and Sculptors* 183; Hill 188, 247; Stevens, *Hesperia* 15, 1946, 10–11.

[52] *IG* II² 4758; Stevens, *Hesperia* 15, 1946, 4.

may be the dedication of the statue—if as in vase paintings the goddess was shown rising from the ground, there would be no base on which to carve it. Just before this Pausanias mentions a cult of Athena under yet another title, Ergane (Worker);[53] he speaks of a temple, but an unfortunate obscurity in the text leaves it unclear whether he means that this cult had its own little temple, and it is difficult to see where such a building could have stood.

At the end of this series Pausanias notes two statues of Zeus, one by Leochares (4th century B.C.), the other called Polieus, god of the city. The altar of Zeus Polieus, the scene of the strange primitive ritual of the ox-slaying, was probably northeast of the Parthenon, where cuttings in the rock and slight remains may mark the site.[54]

"Opposite the temple," i.e. presumably the east front of the Parthenon, was another work ascribed to Pheidias, a statue of Apollo Parnopios, the locust god; Apollo both caused and warded off plagues of various kinds.

The eastern end of the hill, beyond the Parthenon, was more sparsely populated. The two most notable monuments in this area were of Hellenistic and Roman times. The figures from mythical and historical combats, dedicated by Attalos of Pergamon towards 200 B.C., replicas of groups which he set up at home to commemorate his victory over the invading Gauls, must have stood towards the southeast just above the theater, into which one of the statues is said to have fallen.[55] A short distance to the east of the Parthenon are the remains of a round temple, with nine Ionic columns and no interior structure, 8.6m in diameter, dedicated, as the inscription on its epistyle tells, to Rome and Augustus.[56]

Pausanias was only human, and he must have found the Acropolis overwhelming; he turns westward again, along the north side, with the remark, "I have all Greece to describe" (1.26.4). Before tackling the Erechtheion he notes a seated statue of Athena by Endoios of Athens. Since Endoios worked in the archaic period, this must have had a lucky

[53] Judeich 241; Stevens, *Hesperia* Suppl. 3, 1940, 54–57.

[54] Judeich 242, 257; G. W. Elderkin, *Hesperia* 10, 1941, 123.

[55] Pausanias 1.25.2; Plutarch, *Antonius* 60.2; Judeich 258; A. W. Lawrence, *Greek and Roman Sculpture*, London 1972, 221ff.

[56] *IG* II² 3173; Judeich 256f; W. Binder, *Der Roma–Augustus Monopteros auf der Akropolis in Athen*, Stuttgart 1969; cf. *Deltion* 22, 1967, 21–24; Travlos *PDA* 494ff. Binder finds evidence that the temple did not stand on the square foundation of poros blocks just east of the Parthenon, where the fragments now lie, but probably farther north, east of the Erechtheion.

escape from the Persian destruction; indeed it may be a figure which was found at the northeastern foot of the Acropolis.[57]

There are traces of an ancient rock-cut road leading from the Erechtheion to the northwest corner of the Propylaia. Here probably stood some of Pausanias' last series of statues, which he noticed on his way back, including, appropriately, Perikles, under whose inspiration the Acropolis attained its greatest glory, and yet a third Athena by Pheidias, the Lemnian.

The Athena Lemnia deserves more than a brief mention. It was a bronze (no doubt of modest size compared with the Promachos) dedicated by the Athenian colonists sent to the island of Lemnos about 450 B.C. Pausanias (1.28.2) says that it was "most worth seeing of all the works of Pheidias." Lucian as an art critic is more articulate when in the *Images* (4) he puts together his composite ideal beauty. "Which of the works of Pheidias do you praise most highly?" "Which but the Lemnian, on which Pheidias thought fit to inscribe his name? . . . The Lemnian and Pheidias will provide the outline of her whole face, and the softness of her cheeks and her finely proportioned nose." The Greek word used of the cheeks, and the fact that other features are taken from Aphrodites by Alkamenes and Praxiteles, suggest that this Athena had a certain seductive quality. After this, when Pliny (34.54) heads his list of the works of Pheidias with an Athena of such exceptional beauty that she received *formae cognomen*, i.e. she was popularly called, quite simply, Athena the Beautiful, we need not doubt that he means the Lemnia, and we can reasonably assume that when the rhetorician Himerios says that Pheidias did not always represent Athena armed, but also showed her without a helmet, he too had the Lemnia in mind.[58] A great bronze helmet does not enhance the facial beauty of a woman or a goddess (indeed it distorts the outline), but rather makes her more awesome. Most historians of sculpture believe that they can see the quality of the statue reflected, a little more clearly than in the case of most lost masterpieces, in copies in Dresden and Bologna.

If Pheidias' great cult statues "added something to the accepted religion,"[59] the Parthenos was certainly more than an exhibition of varied technical virtuosity, and a proud display of the city's power and wealth.

---

[57] Richter, *Sculpture and Sculptors* 36, 152. H. Payne, *Archaic Marble Sculpture from the Acropolis*, 2d edn London 1950, 46f.

[58] *Oration* 21.4.

[59] Quintilian 12.10.9.

Even the Promachos need not be put in a class with the Colossus of
Rhodes and the Statue of Liberty. Yet although it must have been
thrilling to get a glimpse of her spear point and helmet crest as one's ship
approached Peiraeus, to the visitor passing through the Propylaia she
must have seemed somewhat disproportionate, forbidding perhaps rather
than welcoming; and he may have turned with pleasure to the more
modest figure and delicate beauty of the Lemnia. Pausanias, confronted
like Paris with a choice between three, made the right award. With the
Parthenos and the Promachos Pheidias was executing state commissions,
and produced conventional representations of the goddess, even though
more splendid than any before, as the mighty protectress of the city.
Working for the Lemnian group, he perhaps felt freer to work out a
more personal conception. The Lemnia was Athena, less martial, more
womanly, revealing herself to a great favorite, as to Odysseus or to
Herakles in the Olympia metopes. This may be somewhat fanciful;[60]
but we can accept without question the Judgment of Pausanias, and of
Lucian. We can put her in her place in the setting of the Parthenon;
but as one stands before her she becomes a centerpiece, the peak of
achievement of Athens' greatest artist, in all Athens the thing "most
worth seeing." Nothing makes us more acutely aware of all we have
lost; apart from the architectural sculpture, which for Pausanias was
strictly subordinate, rating only a passing glance, the works of art seen
by him on the Acropolis have almost entirely vanished. But the acci-
dents of survival are astonishing. Because of the Persian destruction, and
the care with which the Athenians put away the fragments in the great
cache south of the Parthenon, we have a wealth of sculpture which was
invisible to Pausanias, and we can appreciate the beauty of the archaic
Acropolis as he could not. The Moschophoros, the Rampin Rider, the
korai, the Blond Boy, all have their own peculiar beauty and are as well
worth seeing as what Pausanias saw.[61]

[60] But I am encouraged by Ashmole, who in his fine appreciation of the Lemnia,
Architect and Sculptor, 74ff, 198, compares her with an Athena in an Olympia
metope; cf. Richter, *Sculpture and Sculptors*, 173–74; A. H. Buben, *Jahrbuch* 88,
1973, 113.
[61] See Payne, *Archaic Marble Sculpture*.

BIBLIOGRAPHY

A. Michaelis, *Der Parthenon*, Leipzig, 1870–1871

O. Jahn and A. Michaelis, *Arx Athenarum a Pausania Descripta*, Bonn
1891 (with texts, now re-edited by A. L. Oikonomides, Ares Press,
Chicago; I have been unable to obtain this re-edition, or the one mentioned on p. 279)

F. C. Penrose, *Principles of Athenian Architecture*, London 1888

G. P. Stevens, "The Periclean Entrance Court of the Acropolis of Athens,"
Hesperia 5, 1936, 443–520
"The Setting of the Periclean Parthenon," *Hesperia* Supplement III
1940

C. J. Herington, *Athena Parthenos and Athena Polias*, Manchester 1955

J. A. Bundgaard, *Mnesikles, a Greek Architect at Work*, Copenhagen
1957 (Bundgaard is also producing a work on the Parthenon)

P. Corbett, *The Sculpture of the Parthenon*, Harmondsworth 1959

Parthenos and Parthenon, Supplement to *Greece and Rome* 10, 1963;
essays on various aspects of cult and monuments, with bibliographies

F. Brommer, *Die Skulpturen der Parthenon-Giebel*, Mainz 1963
Die Metopen des Parthenon, Mainz 1967; these works, fully illustrated,
follow many articles by Brommer, and give a fundamental re-examination (Brommer is also producing a work on the frieze)

Rhys Carpenter, *The Architects of the Parthenon*, Pelican Books 1970
This remarkable book, not discussed above, is full of interest even if one
disagrees. Rhys Carpenter maintains persuasively that there was a distinct phase under Kimon, before the middle of the fifth century, with
Kallikrates as architect, when much was built, only to be discarded or
reorganized when under Perikles, with Iktinos as architect, a new plan
was adopted and a new beginning made. This idea has not been generally accepted (severe review by Dinsmoor in *AJA* 75, 1971, 339;
non-committal discussion by R. Meiggs in *The Athenian Empire*, Supplementary Bibliography 597). Unless more decisive archaeological
evidence is produced, it seems to me unlikely that such enormous additional expense would have been incurred; that such an important development would have left no record in our sources; and that the story
of the oath of Plataia, whether true or not, would have been current if
such massive building had taken place before the time of the Peace of
Kallias.

R. J. Hopper, *The Acropolis*, London 1971

Travlos *PDA* 148ff; 444ff; 482ff

T. Bowie and D. Thimme, *The Carrey Drawings of the Parthenon Sculpture*, Bloomington and London 1971

B. Ashmole, *Architect and Sculptor in Classical Greece*, London and New York 1972, Ch. 4 and 5

Martin Robertson (text) and Alison Frantz (photos), *The Parthenon Frieze*, London 1975

41. Erechtheion and Foundations of Old Temple as seen from Parthenon (Photo: Alison Frantz)

CHAPTER V

The Erechtheion and Its Cults

In contrast to the Doric grandeur and essential simplicity of the Parthenon the Erechtheion was curiously complex in plan and elaborate in ornamental detail. It represents the greatest refinement of Ionic architecture at the end of the fifth century. At the same time it was the successor of a series of earlier buildings and stood on a site long hallowed by a number of ancient traditions and cults, which had to be taken into account in designing the new temple. The palace of Mycenean Athens, the House of Erechtheus, occupied this northern part of the Acropolis; slight remains have been attributed to it, including two column bases of soft, yellow-gray poros, badly damaged, which stand, carefully enclosed now by small fences, a little to the southeast of the Caryatid porch of the Erechtheion, within the east cella of the great archaic temple. Each comprises a round element and a square plinth below. These bases, however, are highly problematical. When first discovered they were thought to be post-classical, Byzantine, or even Frankish; then Dörpfeld associated them with the undoubtedly Mycenean walls which came to light on this part of the Acropolis, and they have been commonly assigned to the porch of a megaron (hall). But there have been skeptics, and recently C. Nylander, after careful reconsideration of the context in which they were found, and their material and form, has come to the conclusion that they are early archaic rather than Mycenean.[1] Admittedly none of these criteria is decisive in itself, but the use of poros is certainly more appropriate to the later date. With due caution Nylander suggests that the bases are *in situ*, or only slightly shifted when the sixth-century temple was built; and that they belong to the eastward facing porch of a temple about 8m broad, built in the first half or middle of the seventh century B.C. Nothing has been found of the walls. One can imagine that it was at the statue in the temple that Kylon took refuge about 635 B.C. after his abortive attempt to seize power.[2] Of course it was not necessarily the very first shrine built on the site.

[1] *Opuscula Atheniensia* 4, 1962, 31–77.
[2] Herodotus 5.71; cf. Thucydides 1.126.

The late archaic Acropolis, in the time of the Peisistratids, must have given an impression of considerable splendor. Within the precinct still defined by the massive prehistoric wall, entered no doubt by a simple predecessor of the early fifth-century propylon on the west, stood a great peripteral Doric temple; possibly there was a second major temple to the south on the site of the Parthenon, though this is open to dispute; certainly there were a number of small temple-like buildings or "treasuries," whose existence is attested by architectural members and a series of curious pedimental sculptures, though their sites are highly conjectural. The numerous dedications, notably the long series of *korai* or maidens, gave life and color to the scene. In all this the only building of which our knowledge rests, quite literally, upon secure foundations is the great temple whose massive remains, clearly revealing the complex form of the building, can be seen north of the Parthenon, with their northern side underlying the south porch of the Erechtheion. Even here the earlier architectural history of the site and the fate of the temple after the Persian destruction are much disputed.

The great foundation comprises an outer and an inner rectangle. Within the latter, which measures about 34m by 13m, are cross walls which indicate that the building was divided into two main sections, a smaller eastern and a larger western, each with a narrow porch in front. The eastern room was divided into three by two foundations running east and west, which presumably carried interior colonnades. In the western part another cross wall separated a spacious forechamber from two smallish cellas standing side by side. All these inner foundations are of roughly shaped and fitted blocks of Acropolis limestone. The outer rectangle, clearly the foundation of the peristyle, is of the finer limestone of Kara, with blocks somewhat larger and more carefully worked. The upper structure was of poros, with details of marble, at least in the ultimate phase. The overall dimensions are about 43m by 21m.

Thus the general form of the temple is plain to see; but how it attained this form, and when the foundations were laid, are questions to which the architectural experts have given various answers. Dates range far up and down the sixth century. Among other difficulties, the character of the material used and the style of the masonry provide hazardous criteria. There have been three main views. Dörpfeld, followed by Wiegand and others, believed that the inner structure was built separately early in the sixth century and that the temple was rebuilt, with a colon-

nade, in the time of the Peisistratids.[3] Dinsmoor gave his great authority
to the view that there was only a primitive temple of very early date on
this site, and the great foundations and the building they carried were
wholly due to the Peisistratids;[4] he gives the name Hekatompedon
(hundred foot), and assigns the remarkable poros pediments which include a three-bodied giant ("Bluebeard") and Herakles wrestling with a
Triton, to a hypothetical temple on the northern part of the site of the
Parthenon. Plommer, after a lengthy re-examination of the remains,
places the original construction of the great archaic temple, colonnades
and all, in the early sixth century, attributing to the Peisistratids extensive rebuilding, and the substitution of pediments in marble.[5]

Dörpfeld believed that after the Persian destruction the temple was
restored, without its colonnade, the northern foundation of which was
ultimately built over by the Caryatid porch; and furthermore that it still
stood in Pausanias' time and has to be taken into account in his description. Probably no one would now support this view; more acceptable is
Dinsmoor's idea that the western part of the building was repaired and
served as a treasury, standing perhaps for a century or more. This
truncated building would still be awkwardly placed in relation to the
Erechtheion, but at least it was just clear of the south porch; and a
curious retention of the old beside the new was characteristic of the
Athenians.

This is not the place to discuss yet again the problems raised by the
various archaic sculptural groups, or the indeterminate names used for
different buildings in inscriptions. Consideration of such evidence has
not led to any definite or agreed solutions of our problems; indeed it has
been interpreted in different ways by different writers with great subtlety
to support conflicting theories. As regards the sculpture, one can at least
see how, through the sixth century, Attic sculptors were working out
solutions to the difficult problem of pedimental composition, crudely at
first but with increasing ingenuity. The powerful gigantomachy in marble
in the pediment of the Peisistratid temple, the first completely safe and
agreed attribution, represents the culmination.

Even if with Dinsmoor one postulates a large archaic temple on the

---

[3] For the extensive bibliography of Dörpfeld's work see Judeich 261ff; Travlos
PDA 143; cf. Th. Wiegand, *Die archaische Poros-Architektur der Akropolis zu
Athen*, Cassel-Leipzig 1904.

[4] *Architecture* 71ff; cf. *AJA* 36, 1932, 143–72; 51, 1947, 109–40.

[5] "The Archaic Acropolis: Some Problems," *JHS* 80, 1960, 127–59.

site of the Parthenon, one still need not think in terms of two more or less distinct cults and shrines of Athena existing side by side.[6] The whole Acropolis was Athena's sacred hill; the whole summit was her precinct, and the building area was repeatedly prepared and enlarged by terracing. All the successive buildings formed part of the continued effort of the Athenians to do ever greater honor to their goddess. Athena like the other major Greek deities was a highly complex personage. She meant something different to her citizens in different periods and under changing regimes; and to different Athenians in the same period, and indeed to one and the same Athenian on different occasions, for example at the various festivals. The Parthenon represents a culmination, a supreme effort in the time of the city's greatest power and political prosperity. But even then the Athenians were not satisfied; they turned yet again to the older northern site, in spite of the great difficulties of the time, and to do justice to the ancient cults they replaced what must have been a somewhat makeshift arrangement with a building of peculiar design but great architectural sophistication, very different both from the archaic temple and from the Parthenon. There was an obvious antithesis between the Parthenon and the Erechtheion; but there was a link between them symbolized in the Parthenon frieze, in which is represented a rite which took place in the old temple and its successor.

The Erechtheion was probably begun just after the Peace of Nikias in 421 B.C. The work was interrupted for some years, but was resumed in 409 B.C. and completed within four years. We do not know who was the original architect,[7] but we hear of two who took part in the later phases, Philokles and Archilochos. The sculptor-architect Kallimachos, inventor of the Corinthian capital and designer of the golden lamp which stood in the temple, may have played some further part; the elaborate ornamentation of the building is in keeping with the known style of his art, which was described as "katatexitechnic" ("frittering away one's skill upon details").[8] The highly detailed building inscriptions relating to the final

---

[6] Cf. B. Bergquist, *The Archaic Greek Temenos*, Lund 1967, 23, modifying the view of Herington in *Athena Parthenos and Athena Polias*.

[7] I. M. Shear, *Hesperia* 32, 1963, 408–24, makes a case for Kallikrates. On the date see C. W. Clairmont, "Euripides' *Erechtheus* and the Erechtheion," *GRBS* 12, 1971, 485–95; cf. W. M. Calder, "The Date of Euripides' *Erechtheus*," *GRBS* 10, 1969, 147–56.

[8] Pliny 34.92; Pausanias 1.26.6.

On the Caryatids see M. Brouskaris, *AAA* 1, 1968, 61–64; Erika E. Schmidt, *Die Kopien des Erechtheion Koren*, Berlin 1973; *Deltion*, 26, 1974, B1, 27.

years tell us a good deal about the labor force which was employed.[9] Athens itself was far from able to supply all the necessary craftsmen. More than half were metics (resident aliens); of the remainder a little more than half were Athenian citizens, the rest were slaves.

The temple was built of Pentelic marble, with poros foundations and with dark Eleusinian stone in the frieze. The main body of the building is a rectangle measuring about 24m east to west by 13m north to south. The eastern facade is conventional enough, with a prostyle porch of six Ionic columns, just over 6.5m high. The wall behind was pierced by a door and by two windows. The complications and oddities of design are all in the western part. What the architects had in mind when they produced this eccentric plan we can never know, but we can assume that they were influenced both by the natural contours of the rock and the multiplicity of ancient cults which had to be accommodated both inside and outside.[10] The west end of the main building consisted not of the usual kind of porch but of a series of columns standing on a low wall. A great northward-facing porch was attached at the west end of the north side, projecting 3m farther westward. It was as if what might have been a splendid western porch had been swung round in the design through an angle of ninety degrees. In the corresponding position on the south side a much smaller decorative excrescence was added in the form of the Caryatid porch, with figures of six *korai* in place of columns, in the same arrangement as the great columns of the north porch. As one sees it from the west nowadays, the western end of the Erechtheion seems a peculiar and ill-balanced conglomeration; one should bear in mind that it was not intended to be seen like this, and that the west facade of the main building was also the east side of a sacred enclosure which extended westwards and contained several important cult spots.

It is not our purpose at present to deal fully with the minor complications in the structure of the building nor with all the refinements of its decorative detail. Designers and stone-carvers alike showed extreme virtuosity in the Ionic column bases and capitals and moldings of every kind. The elaboration of the capitals contrasts with the classic simplicity of the Ionic interior capitals of the Propylaia, and in addition beneath each of them at the top of the shaft is carved a band of palmettes. Most

[9] *IG* I² 372ff.

[10] Dörpfeld's idea that the building was originally planned to extend as far west as east of the north and south porches is not generally accepted; *AthMitt* 29, 1904, 101–7; cf. Judeich 273f.

42. Erechtheion, Caryatid Porch, and East Front of Propylaia (Photo: Alison Frantz)

striking of all is the decoration of the frame of the great door, nearly 5m high, which leads from the north porch into the interior.

The Caryatids are in the finest tradition of the Parthenon sculptors, and they have indeed been attributed by some to Alkamenes; they recall the maidens who walk so sedately in the procession on the Parthenon frieze. The frieze is much less distinguished in style, but is remarkable for its unusual technique, by which figures in white marble were attached to the dark stone of the background. It ran round the whole building; but inevitably the figures have fallen and only fragments have been found. Even the subject is uncertain. The building accounts show that the work was parceled out in small bits among a number of sculptors, who received a payment of 60 drachmas for each figure, a good wage for the time. A typical section runs:

To Phyromachos of Kephisia for the youth beside the breastplate	60 dr.
To Praxias, resident at Melite, for the horse and the man seen behind it who is turning it	120 dr.
To Antiphanes of Kerameis, for the chariot and the youth and the pair of horses being yoked	240 dr.
To Phyromachos of Kephisia, for the man leading the horse	60 dr.
To Mynnion, resident at Agryle, for the horse and the man striking it. He afterwards added the pillar	127 dr.
To Soklos, resident at Alopeke, for the man holding the bridle	60 dr.
To Phyromachos of Kephisia, for the man leaning upon his staff beside the altar	60 dr.
To Jason of Kollytos, for the woman whom the child has embraced	80 dr.

Mynnion and Soklos were presumably metics, not Athenians.

The interior arrangement of the temple remains to be considered, together with the use to which its different parts were put. Later destruction and construction have greatly obscured the arrangement of the main building. On the basis partly of slight indications in the remains, partly of analogy with the Old Temple which it replaced, most historians of architecture since Stevens and Paton have assumed that it was divided by a cross wall into a smaller eastern section and a large western section; that this western section was divided into three, comprising two westward-facing cellas side by side behind a large fore-chamber (as in the archaic temple); and further, that the eastern room was the shrine of Athena Polias, while the various other known cult spots were distributed among the western parts. Recently, after careful re-examination of the building and its problems, Travlos has come to the conclusion that the only dividing wall which belongs to the original construction is the eastern north-to-south wall; the western cross wall was inserted much later, presumably to provide additional support for the roof, perhaps in the time of Augustus, when modifications were introduced in the west facade too.[11] The shrine of Athena Polias, Travlos believes, was in the western part. This suits the sequence of Pausanias' description; and it would be most appropriate that the great north porch and doorway, the most splendid entrance to the building, should lead to the main shrine about which the lesser cult spots clustered.

Pausanias, as so often, though his account may have been satisfactory for contemporaries who could see everything for themselves, is not altogether clear for the modern archaeologist (1.26–27). After the Parthenon he takes note of certain monuments towards the east end of the Acropolis, and so approaches the Erechtheion presumably from that direction. Before the entrance stands an altar of Zeus Hypatos (Highest). When one goes in, one finds three altars, one of Poseidon, on which sacrifices are also offered to Erechtheus, a second of the hero Boutes, a third of Hephaistos. "On the walls are paintings of the family of the Boutadai, and—for the building is double—there is sea water within it in a cistern" (the salt spring which was the gift of Poseidon). The mention of the double character of the building presumably marks Pausanias' transition to the other, western section. Next Pausanias mentions the most holy image of Athena Goddess of the Polis,[12] and the ever-burning golden lamp, with a chimney in the form of a bronze palm, made by Kallimachos. Still in the temple of the Polias is a wooden Hermes, said to have been dedicated by Kekrops, a chair made by Daidalos, and spoils of the Persians, the breastplate of Masistios and the scimitar of Mardonios. This like some other ancient shrines had tended to become a kind of museum of curiosities. At the next step Pausanias has apparently emerged from the building, presumably to the west, since he speaks of the olive tree produced by Athena in the contest with Poseidon. Adjacent to the temple of Athena is the temple of Pandrosos, daughter of Kekrops. The maidens called Arrephoroi (bearers of the holy things) live not far from the temple of Athena Polias. Remains of their dwelling have been tentatively recog-

---

[11] *AAA* 4, 1971, 77–84; *PDA* 213ff; cf. *AAA* 5, 1972, C. Kardara, 119ff, and J. C. Overbeck, who disagrees, 127ff.

[12] Travlos postulates a small *adyton* for Athena and another for Erechtheus, to which he assigns the doors mentioned in *IG* i² 372; but this arrangement is even more hypothetical.

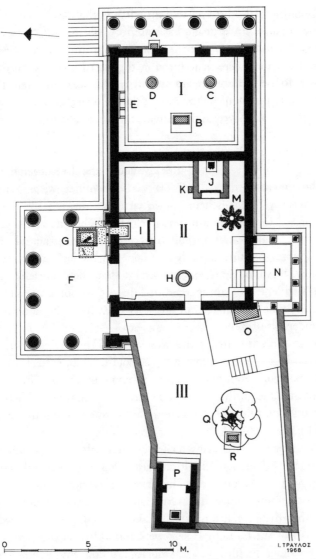

43. Erechtheion: Original Plan and Shrines as restored by Travlos (*PDA* 218
fig. 281)
  I. Eastern Section: A. Altar of Zeus Hypatos B. Altar of Poseidon and Erechtheus
    C. Altar of Boutes D. Altar of Hephaistos E. Thrones of Priests
  II. Western Section: F. North Porch G. Altar and marks of thunderbolt
    H. Salt spring and trident marks I. Tomb of Erechtheus J. Athena Polias
    K. Hermes L. Lamp of Kallimachos M. Persian spoil N. Caryatid Porch
  III. Pandroseion: O. Tomb of Kekrops P. Temple of Pandrosos Q. Olive tree
    R. Altar of Zeus Herkeios

(151)

nized in the foundations of a building northwest of the Erechtheion; and surely the "natural underground passage" by which they carried the unmentionable objects down from the Acropolis to the shrine of Aphrodite below must be the great cleft in the Acropolis rock to the northwest, in which was found a stairway leading first to an exit through a cave in the north face, probably sacred to Pandrosos' sister Aglauros, and then on downwards to a Mycenean spring, abandoned and forgotten in classical times.[13]

Thus numerous cult spots and objects, and shrines of gods and ancient heroes and heroines, clustered thickly about the Erechtheion; but not one of those mentioned by Pausanias can be identified with confidence or located precisely in the scheme. Two curious intrusions on the elegant architecture of the temple are indeed clearly visible, and obviously have some peculiar significance in cult. In the southeast corner of the north porch a square aperture is left in the floor, and holes can be seen in the rock below.[14] An obvious explanation is that these are the marks of Poseidon's trident; but an aperture is left in the roof and ceiling above too, and the whole arrangement suggests that this may be a spot struck by a thunderbolt of Zeus.

Again, in the structure of the west wall of the main building at its southern end, between the door and the south porch, special adjustments had to be made to accommodate a pre-existing monument. This is assumed to be the tomb and shrine of Kekrops, strangely omitted by Pausanias but mentioned in inscriptions which show that it was adjacent to the porch of the Maidens.[15]

In spite of lack of evidence which might identify the monuments listed by Pausanias, perhaps one should at least recognize a general east-to-west progression in his account and distribute the various cult spots accordingly. A portentous happening narrated by Philochoros tends to confirm the idea that the principal shrine, of Athena Polias, was indeed in the western part of the building. Dogs were forbidden on the Acropolis; but on one occasion, probably about 300 B.C., a dog entered the shrine of Athena Polias, slipped into the Pandroseion, jumped up on the altar of Zeus Herkeios, and finally was cornered beneath the sacred olive tree.[16]

---

[13] See p. 176 below.

[14] Judeich 279f; cf. M. H. McAllister, *Hesperia* 27, 1958, 161–62.

[15] *IG* I² 372 lines 9, 58, 62, 83; Judeich 282.

[16] In Dionysios of Halikarnassos *On Deinarchos* 3; Jacoby *FGH* IIIB 118 (no. 328, frag. 67).

44. Erechtheion, West Front, with foundations of Old Temple and Parthenon
on right (Photo: Alison Frantz)

One need not worry too much about precise locations. What is most
important is clear enough, that this most sophisticated specimen of late
fifth-century Attic architecture was inserted with much ingenuity into an
area of immemorial sanctity occupied by a multiplicity of ancient cults.[17]
Once again we have an example of the Athenian propensity for intro-
ducing new things without abandoning or destroying the old.

As regards the name Erechtheion—Athena "entered the house of
Erechtheus,"[18] who was closely associated with Poseidon, and the temple
was in some sense the successor of the royal house; as a distinctive name
for the new building, "Erechtheion" was as appropriate as any. In literature it occurs first in Pausanias,[19] but it may have been in popular use
before this time.

[17] In *Hesperia* 10, 1941, 113–24, G. W. Elderkin discusses "The Cults of the
Erechtheion," their origin and relation to one another, postulating besides those
mentioned an early cult of Aphrodite, whose mother Dione had an altar here. Note
also Kontoleon in Bibliography below.

[18] *Odyssey* 7.81; cf. *Iliad* 2.549.

[19] 1.26.5; cf. Ps. Plutarch *Lives of the Ten Orators* 843e; Judeich 271.

BIBLIOGRAPHY

G. P. Stevens and J. M. Paton, *The Erechtheum*, Cambridge, Mass. 1927

J. Dell, *Das Erechtheion in Athen*, Brunn 1934

W. Dörpfeld and H. Schleif, *Erechtheion*, Berlin 1942

N. Kontoleon, *The Erechtheion as a Building of Chthonic Cult* (in Greek) Athens 1949

C. J. Herington, *Athena Parthenos and Athena Polias*, Manchester 1955 (cf. "Athena in Athenian Literature and Cult," *Greece and Rome* Supplement to 10, 1963, 61–73)

W. H. Plommer, "The Archaic Acropolis, Some Problems," *JHS* 80, 1960, 127–59

J. Meliades, "The Acropolis in Archaic Times," *Greek Heritage (American Quarterly of Greek Culture)* Vol. 2 no. 6, 1965, 43ff

R. J. Hopper, *The Acropolis*, London 1971, 97ff (cf. "Athena and the Early Acropolis," *Greece and Rome* Supplement to 10, 1963, 1–16)

Travlos *PDA* 143ff, 213ff

CHAPTER VI

The Olympieion and
Southeast Athens

The southeast region of Athens, both within and without the city wall, was old in legend and in cult, second only to the Acropolis and its slopes in venerability, with many shrines, of which the most important, the Olympieion,[1] was singled out for great architectural splendor. The Arch of Hadrian, a massive gateway carrying an elegant superstructure of Corinthian columns, was built as an ornate approach to the area, and the inscriptions carved on its lower friezes, proclaiming, on the west side, "This is Athens, the ancient city of Theseus," and on the east side, "This is the city of Hadrian, not of Theseus," are somewhat inept.[2]

The shrine of Olympian Zeus was founded by Deukalion, according to tradition.[3] The great temple was begun by Peisistratos or his sons, and finished six and a half centuries later by Hadrian. In essentials it was the same building throughout; there was no drastic rebuilding, no change of site, scale, or basic design. The "great struggle with time"[4] was watched with interest by the ancient world, and each phase was noted by various writers. But their evidence remains highly problematical. What follows is an attempt to recapitulate the long and spasmodic history of the shrine, re-examining the value and meaning of the more significant pieces of evidence, and taking into account our increasing but still very limited archaeological knowledge of the whole site, including the numerous neighboring shrines.

Penrose first found evidence of a pre-Peisistratid temple on the site of the Olympieion, in the shape of a foundation which ran north to south across the cella of the later temple, with its southern end underlying a column of the southern inner colonnade.[5] Welter investigated the old

[1] For the name, Olympion, Olympieion etc., see *GRBS* 5, 1964, 161–162.

[2] *IG* II² 5185; Judeich 381–82; Travlos *PDA* 253.

[3] Pausanias 1.18.7–8; cf. the *Parian Marble*, Ep. 4.6–8 (Jacoby IIB.993 no. 239 A 4), and Strabo 9.4.2.

[4] Philostratos *Lives of Sophists* 1.25.6.

[5] *Principles* 82; fig. 11.

foundation further, established its northwest and southwest corners, and associated with it what Penrose had thought to be a continuous bedding for the individual substructures of the northern inner columns.[6] He interpreted these remains as the lowest course of the foundation of a peristyle, measuring 30.5m by probably ca. 60m. All the rest had been removed when the Peisistratid temple was built. The date of the early building is not clear.

Aristotle speaks of the "building of the Olympieion" by the Peisistratids;[7] Vitruvius says that the architects Antistates, Callaeschros, Antimachides, and Porinos laid the foundations for Pisistratus when he was building a temple for Jupiter Olympius, but after his death, since a republican regime intervened, they abandoned the attempt. Some writers have found a contradiction here. Welter maintained that Aristotle must be right and Vitruvius wrong. In fact, there is not necessarily any contradiction; the two accounts may be combined into a coherent whole. Peisistratos conceived the design in the closing years of his reign, in emulation of the great temples of Samos and Ephesos; appointed the architects, showing that he realized the magnitude and length of the task by naming four; and saw the site prepared and the first stones laid. A colossal task still remained for his sons. They may not have pursued it with all the energy which their father might have shown. Work may still have been going ahead on the Acropolis and elsewhere. The labor force in archaic Athens was no doubt limited. The transport and working of stone for the vast substructures, steps, and platform was a very laborious business, and we now know better than at the time when Welter wrote that work was by no means confined to these elements.

Just what was erected in the time of the Peisistratids is still an open question. Judeich took a surprisingly negative view, even for his day: "it never rose above the foundations (Grundmauern)."[8] The precise language of Aristotle calls for closer examination. "The building (*oikodomesis*) of the Olympieion by the Peisistratids" would not be a very happy phrase if used of mere foundations or little more. Aristotle gives the pyramids of Egypt, the offerings of the Kypselidai, the Olympieion, and

---

[6] *AthMitt* 47, 1922, 66.   [7] *Politics* 5.9.4; Vitruvius Preface to 7.15.

[8] Judeich 383; J. Boersma, *Building Policy of the Athenians*, Groningen 1970, 199. The building measured 107.7m x 42.9m. It probably had eight by twenty-one columns. The foundations naturally had to be deeper towards the south and west. The inner columns of the peristyle had individual foundations. The foundations were of Acropolis stone and Kara stone, the steps and columns of poros.

the works of Polykrates at Samos as examples of great projects by which despotic rulers kept their subjects out of mischief. Mere foundations are out of place in this company. There were other works of Peisistratos and his sons at Athens, not so vast of course, but carried to completion. Aristotle might have taken them all together as he does the works of Polykrates (the great aqueduct tunnel and the rest), but he chooses to single out the Olympieion as the most impressive example. He presumably knew what he was talking about; the days of Peisistratos were not so very distant and visible testimony was still before his eyes.

Penrose in 1886 noted the remains of a curious building adjoining the Hadrianic enclosing wall of the Olympieion on the north, built of segments of the drums of large unfluted columns of poros stone.[9] He assigned these, rightly of course, to the Peisistratid temple. He discovered also that "one of the isolated standing columns rests on a pile of complete drums of similar material and diameter"—Welter later confirmed this— "and probably some of the other columns were supported in the same way." More drums have come to light in recent excavations, and Travlos has demonstrated that the odd structure noted by Penrose was a large gateway in the Themistoklean city wall, which struck off in a southeasterly direction at this point so as to include the site of the Olympieion.[10] Column drums were apparently used extensively in this part of the fortification. One can assume that there were many others besides those which happen to have come to light. But the massive cylinders were awkward and intractable material. Some were left lying about, and some of these received deep diagonal cuts giving them the appearance of hot cross buns. Apparently the attempt to cut them up was abandoned when it was found that no more were needed or that more convenient material was available. One group found its way into the city moat which was dug outside the wall in the fourth century. Thus it has become increasingly clear that much material for the superstructure was at least assembled and prepared on the site. Whether any of the columns were actually erected one cannot say. It is not to be imagined that the archaic Olympieion ever looked like the unfinished temple at Segesta in Sicily. But it is not improbable that part of the colonnade stood to a considerable height before the work was abandoned, drums being placed in position as they became available.

[9] *JHS* 8, 1887, 273; *Principles* 88; cf. Welter 64. The columns had a lower diameter of 2.42m, nearly 8 feet.
[10] *AJA* 64, 1960, 267–68; J. Travlos *PEA* 45–46, 53; *PDA* 402.

45. Olympieion, Column drums of Peisistratid Temple (Photo: J. Travlos)

Until quite recently most writers have assumed that the temple was to have been in the Ionic order, like its rivals at Ephesos and Samos, but it is now generally agreed that it was planned as Doric. Bevier took this view on general grounds as long ago as 1885, arguing that "in that age a colossal temple of Zeus would be built in the severe Doric style rather than in the lighter Ionic."[11] Using more precise and reliable criteria, Dinsmoor says that the use of Ionic "is contradicted by the great diameter of the columns compared with their spacing, and also by the technical treatment of the bottom drums . . . which shows they were to rest directly on the stylobate without bases."

We can well believe that the task was abruptly abandoned in 510 B.C. "Probably the giant work was looked upon even then as a monument of tyranny," suggested Bevier (193), "and shared a part of the odium that was bestowed on the expelled tyrant." More important and decisive were the enormous scale and cost of the building—"its very size was its curse," as Bevier says (198)—though of course the two factors were closely con-

[11] 195; Bevier also points out that what Pliny (36. 45), says about strength rather than ornament suits Doric; cf. Dinsmoor *Architecture* 91.

nected. The Athenians would not have deliberately slighted Zeus, whom they assiduously worshiped as Soter and Eleutherios and under many other names. He was not the only deity associated with the tyrants; there were others too, notably Athena herself. The hard fact was that the Olympian project was beyond their powers. It had no doubt heavily taxed even the tyrants' resources, which were much more limited than those of an Antiochos or a Hadrian. Even in the time of Perikles the construction of the Olympieion could have been seriously resumed only by curtailing work on the Acropolis, which in any case faced difficulties and restrictions enough.

What happened to the temple when the Persians occupied Athens can only be conjectured. Since the site was already more or less derelict, it may have been spared further destruction. There would be little to pillage or burn. The crude and massive stones may have defied the invader.

No doubt the cult was carried on. An altar was indispensable. J. H. Jongkees maintains that a temple of some kind stood on the site in the fifth century, bridging the gap between Peisistratos and Antiochos; it may have been a comparatively small makeshift building, or alternatively it may have been the Peisistratid cella.[12] That this last was ever fully built is hard to believe; it would have been in itself a colossal and notable work. The evidence is very thin, being based on an interpretation of Aristophanes, *Clouds* 401f. "Zeus," says Sokrates there, "strikes his own temple and Sounion, headland of Athens, and the great oaks."[13] The lines certainly have more point if the allusion is Athenian, though one cannot be sure even of that. But there may have been a modest temple in one of the lesser shrines; and even if the Olympieion is meant, surely the impressive Peisistratid substructures, column stumps, and debris could naturally and legitimately be called "temple of Zeus."

In the absence of evidence it is safest to assume that no major work was done on the site between the archaic and Hellenistic periods. For the maintenance of the cult of Zeus Olympios evidence is provided by an early fourth-century boundary stone found, curiously enough, in the agora,

[12] *Mnemosyne* 10 (1957) 154ff.

[13] The bronze Zeus counted by Pausanias among the *archaia* 1.18.7 may possibly have survived from the archaic shrine; and it may have been the Zeus Kataibates to whom a dedication of the first century A.D. has been found in a house north of the Olympieion *IG* II² 4998. It should be noted that a cult of Zeus Kataibates may indicate a spot where lightning had struck. Zeus Kataibates is found elsewhere at Athens too; see A. B. Cook, *Zeus* III, Cambridge (Eng.) 1940, 20ff; *GRBS* 5, 1964, 167, 176.

by a treasure list and an inscription which mentions a sacrifice,[14] and by the existence of a festival called Olympieia.

We find an interesting reference to the temple in the famous description of Athens by Herakleides (the "pseudo-Dikaiarchos").[15] Among the wonders of Athens he includes, along with the theater, the Parthenon, and the gymnasia, "an Olympion half-finished, but astonishing in its architectural design (*hypographe*)—it would have been an excellent building if it had been completed." The use of the term "half-finished" is one of the reasons why it was formerly assumed that the author wrote after the time of Antiochos; one would hardly so describe the Peisistratid substructures, it was said. But his most recent editor, carefully reviewing all the chronological evidence, pushes the writer back into the third century. "Half-finished" is in fact a very vague and elastic term. It could well have been used of the Peisistratid remains if they were as we have envisaged them; it would have been less appropriate of a makeshift but usable temple.

A more meaningful word used by Herakleides is *hypographe*. This means a sketch or outline which suggests to the mind the finished product. The Olympieion apparently made on Herakleides the impression of a grandeur which might have been, which was not visible to the eye. *Hypographe* would be an appropriate word to use of the gigantic unformed Peisistratid remains, hardly of brand new Corinthian colonnades. If we attach more significance to this word than to the ambiguous *hemiteles*, "half-finished," we shall have further reason for placing the writer before rather than after Antiochos.

The rest of the story is well known and can be briefly told. Most historians of architecture assume, no doubt rightly, that the main structure, including most of what is still standing, was due to the munificence of King Antiochos of Syria (175–164 B.C.) and the work of his Roman architect Cossutius (why Antiochos employed a Roman is still a mystery). Vitruvius implies that the main structural elements, the great cella walls, and the columns and their epistyles, or at least a major part of them, were due to Cossutius; and he says that the temple as he knew it gave an impression of great splendor.[16] He takes it as an example of the hypaethral

[14] Agora I 6373, *Hesperia* 21, 1952, 113; 26, 1957, 91; for the festival see L. Deubner, *Attische Feste*, Berlin 1932, 177.

[15] *On the Cities of Greece* 1.1; see F. Pfister, *Die Reisebilder des Herakleides*, Wien 1951, 72; see Introduction 44ff for date.

[16] 3.2.8; cf. *Preface* to 7.15; Livy 41.20.8; Velleius Paterculus 1.10; Athenaeus 5.194a, quoting Polybios (the Olympieion is mentioned as evidence of the surpassing

temple, with cella open to the sky; and being an experienced architect he presumably knew that it was planned as such, and was not misled by the fact that the roof was still incomplete. The temple measured 107.75m by 41.10m on the top step, with a cella about 75m by 19m. It was dipteral, with a third row of columns at either end, and twenty (instead of twenty-one as in the archaic plan) by eight columns in the outer row. The interior arrangement is even less certain than in the final, Hadrianic form.

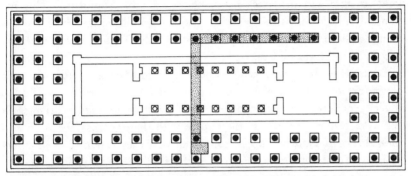

46. Olympieion; dotted area shows pre-Peisistratid foundation (Boersma, *Athenian Building Policy* 199)

However much was built, the work of Antiochos was in a real sense a continuation of that of Peisistratos. The Corinthian order was now used, and Pentelic marble; but the scale and proportions, the general design and character were the same, and the old substructures were incorporated with some adjustment.[17] The steps were replaced in marble, except the lower steps at the west end.

According to Pliny (36.45) Sulla took columns from the temple to Rome for the Capitoline temple (86 B.C.). It is difficult to believe that he dismantled colossal Corinthian columns which had been built up to their full height—an operation of great technical difficulty—and transshipped them. He may have helped himself to architectural members, possibly capitals only, which had not yet been incorporated when the work was broken off. Perhaps these belonged to the inner colonnade. In their new abode, the columns played an important part in the development of the Corinthian order at Rome.

---

generosity of the king). The question how much was built is discussed further in *GRBS* 5, 1964, 169–70.

[17] In architectural style, H. Plommer, *Simpson's History of Architectural Development* I: *Ancient and Classical Architecture*, London 1956, 264, sees a reaction against the "impurity" of some Hellenistic developments.

There is no good reason to think that there were any major building operations other than the three which so impressed themselves on the minds of the ancients. Any comparable attempt to complete the temple would probably not have gone unrecorded. As for minor attempts, this was not a task with which one would toy ineffectively: it required a bold spirit and immense resources. Suetonius tells us that a number of friendly and allied kings determined (*destinaverunt*) to finish the temple at their joint expense and to dedicate it to the Genius of Augustus.[18] This has sometimes been taken to signify an Augustan building phase; but if the plan had been even partially carried out, surely Suetonius, and probably others, would have said so.

Attempts to draw conclusions about the successive stages from the style of the extant columns have been singularly inconclusive and confusing. It has generally been assumed that these columns are not Hadrianic. "It is only necessary to compare the temple with these works (the Arch and the Library of Hadrian) to be convinced that they cannot be contemporaneous. The temple retains much of the simplicity of the earlier Greek taste, in contrast with the excessive ornamentation and effeminacy of the later time."[19] One might allow, however, that this superiority may have been due to careful and conscientious imitation of good earlier models, comparable to the fidelity and technical excellence with which works of sculpture were sometimes reproduced.

Whatever remained to be done was done by Hadrian.[20] Even if it was only a question of upper structures and interior arrangements, in such a vast building this would be a big and expensive task. The emperor finally dedicated the whole temple, the great gold and ivory statue, and his own statue in A.D. 131/2. The final arrangement of the interior is still not clear. Penrose reasonably conjectured that there were two rows of eight interior columns, and assigned a fragment of marble flute to one of them. Presumably a roof protected the statue, even if the major part of the cella remained hypaethral.

The great rectangular peribolos was built in the time of Hadrian, but

---

[18] *Augustus* 60.

[19] Bevier 201; cf. Penrose 76; M. Gutschow, "Untersuchungen zum korinthischen Kapitel," *Jahrbuch* 36, 1921, 60ff; Welter, *AthMitt* 48, 1923, 183–84; Dinsmoor, *Architecture* 281.

[20] Dio Cassius 69.16; Pausanias 1.18.6; Philostratos *Lives of Sophists* 1.25.6; Spartianus *Life of Hadrian* 13.6. Dinsmoor notes, 281, that even now pieces of sima are left unfinished, but that these may be rejected blocks.

it too may well have been part of the Hellenistic design. With its modest propylon placed towards the east end of the north side, and no great entrance gateway axially arranged, it is earlier Greek rather than Roman in character. Even so the formality of the plan must have contrasted and at some points conflicted with the modest old shrines clustered round the Olympieion. Yet the ancient cults were still maintained, as we see both in Pausanias and in the remains, and attention was not confined in this epoch to the Olympieion itself and its grandiose completion.

47. Olympieion from East, Arch of Hadrian on right (Photo: Alison Frantz)

Fifteen of the great Corinthian columns still stand, and one lies prostrate, wrecked by a storm in 1852. When Cyriacus of Ancona saw the temple in 1436, twenty-one columns were standing.[21] How and when the gigantic structure had disintegrated we do not know, but a later incident (between 1753 and 1765), recorded by Dodwell, shows the kind of thing that happened. When there were seventeen columns left, a Turkish governor pulled one of them down to make lime for a mosque; for this he was heavily fined by higher authority. Cyriacus and many after him called the building the Palace of Hadrian. J. G. Transfeldt in 1674 was the first in modern times to recognize it as the Olympieion,[22] and its identity was not fully established till the great work of Stuart and Revett a century later.[23] The title "Palace of Hadrian" was not entirely a misnomer or a flight of popular fancy. The temple was in a sense the abode of the divinized emperor.

But one cannot agree with Bevier when he concludes, "The galvanic revival at Athens was even a far worse mockery [than the continued worship of Zeus at Olympia], being little more than a half-concealed servile adulation of the Roman emperor himself by the Athenians."[24] Surely one need not take so cynical a view. Genuine ancient piety, expressed in worship of the old gods, was not dead in Attica. Pausanias and the monuments and inscriptions provide evidence. Hadrian had a deep love of Athens, and the Athenian response, shown by innumerable dedications on this site and elsewhere, was not mere sycophancy. Many Athenians must have felt a truly pious pride and pleasure in seeing their debt to Zeus, after more than six centuries, so fully and handsomely paid.[25]

"There are antiquities within the enclosure," says Pausanias (1.18.7)

[21] C. Wachsmuth, *Die Stadt Athen* I, Leipzig 1874, 727; E. W. Bodnar, *Cyriacus of Ancona and Athens*, Brussels 1960, 39. Cf. E. Dodwell, *Tour through Greece* I 390.

[22] His work was not made widely known until much later, *AthMitt* 1,1876, 102ff; Bevier 187.

[23] *Antiquities of Athens* III, London 1794, 11–17.

[24] 205; cf. 198, "it was the fate of the temple of Zeus to be a monument, not of the liberty of Athens, but of her slavery and degradation"—a statement unfair to all concerned. One should bear in mind, too, the humbler offerings which were still being made at the lesser shrines of Zeus, in large numbers for example at the shrine of Zeus Hypsistos on the Pnyx, p. 197 below.

[25] See *Hesperia* 32, 1963, 57ff; A. S. Benjamin here remarks, "Under Hadrian the cult of the emperor in the Greek world was closely associated with the emperor's program of Panhellenism . . . Hadrian's willingness to accept divine honors and his encouragement of Panhellenism have, among more complex motives, the common purpose of the consolidation of the empire."

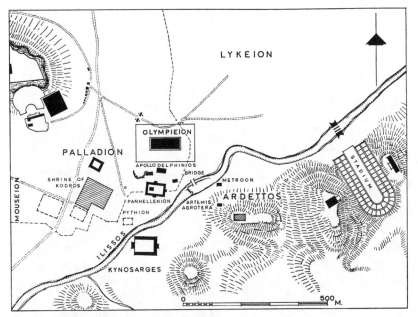

48. Southeastern Athens (J. Travlos, *Hesperia* 43, 1974, 510)

"a bronze Zeus and a temple of Kronos and Rhea and a precinct of Ge surnamed Olympia"; and nearby are the "plug-hole" of the flood and Deukalion's grave. *Peribolos* here can hardly mean anything but the rectangular Hadrianic enclosure (as it certainly does in 18.6). Such an identification creates an apparent difficulty since certain other writers seem to indicate that both Ge and Kronos were outside the enclosure to the south. The monument of Antiope the Amazon, seen earlier by Pausanias on entering the city from Phaleron (2.1), is said by Plutarch to be "beside the shrine of Olympia,"[26] i.e. Ge. This statement would seem to place Ge to the southwest of the Olympieion, perhaps on the rocky outcrop in this region. As for Kronos, his precinct, we are told, was "beside the Olympion as far as the Metroon in Agra," which was to the southeastward across the river. But the contradiction is only apparent. Both deities may have had precincts partly outside and partly inside the line of the Hadrianic enclosing wall; the *Kronion temenos* might then stretch down towards the river from the northwest, to be confronted by the Metroon on the other bank. The imperial architects, laying out a strictly rectangular enclosure, with more regard for formal planning methods

[26] *Theseus* 27.4; cf. Bekker, *Anecdota Graeca*, 1.273.20; see *Agora* III 153.

49. Southeastern Athens (Photo: German Archaeological Institute)

than their predecessors in earlier ages at Athens, may have cut across these areas, though they still left the ancient deities a place within the splendid new scheme.

"After the temple of Zeus Olympios, near at hand there is a statue of Apollo Pythios. There is also another shrine of Apollo, bearing the title Delphinios" (19.1). This passage is taken to mean that Pausanias has gone on a little farther south towards the Ilissos. Excavations south of the Olympieion have now gone a long way towards clearing up the topography of the area though, as so often happens, the correlation of the finds with Pausanias and the other written evidence is not simple and obvious. At least the antiquity and religious importance of the site are further confirmed. Mycenean pottery has been found, and pottery and walls of the geometric period. Foundations of a Doric temple, of mid fifth-century date, peristyle (6 by 13; over 15m by 33m), have come to light just below the middle of the south side of the Hadrianic enclosure of the Olympieion. Adjacent to this temple on the southwest is a curious complex consisting of a rectangular building divided into several rooms attached to an enclosure of irregular shape, built probably in the late sixth century B.C. The suggestion that here we have the Delphinion with its associated law court is convincing.[27]

The Delphinion more than any other monument illustrates the immemorial sanctity of the site. Pausanias knew of its association with Theseus. In this context he tells how the youthful Theseus to show his manliness hurled a yoke of oxen higher than the roof, which was just then being placed on the temple. Later (28.10) he reverts to the Delphinion in his list of Athenian law courts appended to the Areopagus and says that Theseus was tried there for justifiable homicide. Plutarch (12.3; 14.1; 18.1) adds other stories, and places the scene of Medea's attempt to poison Theseus "where now the fenced enclosure in the Delphinion is . . . for Aigeus was living there." Apparently he knew of some tradition of a royal residence hereabouts.

A little to the south of the Delphinion have been found the scanty remains of a peristyle court, apparently of Hadrianic date, with its entrance on the east and a small temple towards its west end. At first sight one might be inclined to associate this too with the Delphinion, and to assume that the shrine took this more regular form in the Hadrianic reconstruction; but now Travlos has made a good case for identifying it with the Panhellenion, Pausanias' "temple of Hera and Zeus Panhellenios," established by Hadrian in connection with a festival called the Panhellenia.[28] One should note however that Pausanias does not give it a place in his itinerary but merely includes it in a supplementary list of the many benefactions of Hadrian which he inserts at this point.

Though the Pythion, the shrine of Apollo Pythios, must have been near at hand, its precise location remains problematical. Part of the altar, with the inscription mentioned by Thucydides,[29] which says that it was dedicated by the younger Peisistratos, son of Hippias, was found long ago at a point southwest of the monuments we have been examining, near the river; and other inscriptions associated with the cult have been found in the same area. However, if the shrine was right here, it is odd

---

[27] *Deltion* 17B, 1963, 9–14 *GRBS* 4, 1963, 167; Travlos *PDA* 83ff.

[28] *PDA* 429ff.

[29] 6.54.6; *IG* I² 761; Judeich 386; *GRBS* 4, 166ff; Travlos *PDA* 100ff. I think that the altar of Zeus Astrapaios, which Strabo says, 9.2.11, was "between the Pythion and the Olympion," was in this region, not on the northwest slope of the Acropolis as some have said; see *AJA* 63, 1959, 69ff; 67, 1963, 75ff; p. 177 below.

that Pausanias mentions the Pythion first, before the Delphinion, describing it as *near* the Olympieion. A little to the southeast of the Delphinion are slight remains of a much smaller temple of Roman date (probably about the middle of the 2d century A.D.) peristyle and of the Doric order, within a rectangular enclosure. It is tempting to pair it with its neighbor and call it the Pythion, but again there are difficulties. We have no good evidence of a temple in the Pythion; indeed Pausanias' mention of a statue only, in contrast with the Delphinion, would seem to imply that there was none. If on the other hand one accepts Travlos' identification of the building as the temple of Kronos and Rhea,[30] one contradicts Pausanias' clear statement that this was within the *peribolos*; Pausanias is usually right, and to contradict him is very hazardous. As on so many topographical points, we must suspend judgment and await some decisive find.

In any case we realize more and more the complexity of the site and its cults. There was more than even the tireless Pausanias recorded. Of the heroic last king of Athens, Kodros, who sacrificed himself for the safety of the city, all he tells us (19.5) is that the place where he fell was pointed out down by the river. But we know from an inscription that he had an extensive precinct, which he shared with two obscure personages called Neleus and Basile, who were perhaps originally underworld deities.[31] The stone was found many years ago some distance southwest of the Olympieion. The finding place in itself means very little, but topographical indications in the inscription make it very probable that the precinct was indeed in this quarter; and when more recently a fifth-century boundary stone was found *in situ* a short distance to the east, even though in the tantalizing manner of many of these stones the inscription read merely HOROS TO HIERO (boundary of the shrine), the discoverers reasonably assumed that it belonged to Kodros and his companions, possibly marking the southeast corner of the precinct. The decree, passed by the Boule and the Demos in 418/417 B.C., makes provision for the enclosure of the *hieron*; it is not clear whether there was a temple, but mention is made of *ikria*, wooden stands such as we shall find in the

---

[30] *PDA* 335.

[31] *IG* i² 94; Judeich 387f; R. E. Wycherley, *BSA* 55, 1960, 60–66; G.T.W. Hooker, *JHS* 80, 1960, 115; *Deltion* 20B, 1967, 68–70; Travlos *PDA* 332ff. Just north are remains of a stoa (late 4th century) which Travlos assigns to the Palladion, another homicide court attached to a shrine of Athena and Zeus; *PDA* 412ff; *Hesperia* 43, 1974, 500ff.

theater, perhaps for persons witnessing the rites. The *temenos*, apparently a piece of ground attached to the *hieron*, is to be leased, on condition that the lessee will plant therein not less than 200 olive shoots; presumably the rent would assist in the maintenance of the cult. The actual burial place of Kodros may have been some distance farther north, since a base found near the monument of Lysikrates records in elegiacs that the Athenian people buried him "beneath the Acropolis." In any case the king was remembered and greatly honored in southeastern Athens.

In Plato's *Phaidros* Sokrates meets his young friends as he leaves the house of Epikrates near the Olympieion, probably on the north side where remains of houses have in fact been found. They walk down to the Ilissos, paddle in the stream for a short way, and finally recline on the bank, perhaps at the foot of the hill Ardettos. For this region we can take Plato as our guide along with Pausanias.[32] They are an oddly assorted couple—Plato is no periegete and his topographical indications are naturally more picturesque than precise—but between them they give a vivid impression of the scene and in particular its cult spots. Plato mentions Acheloos the river god, the Nymphs, whose worship is attested by the presence of *korai* or statues of young girls, and Pan; the Muses (whose messengers are the cicadas); and Boreas, whose altar, he says, stands a couple of stades downstream, at the place where the wind god carried off Oreithyia as she played with Pharmakeia.

One might linger in this once delightful suburb as long as Sokrates and Phaidros; for the sake of brevity we will merely place the shrines in sequence, as one walks downstream from northeast to southwest, even if one can locate very few precisely.

First we may note a very curious shrine which stands somewhat detached from the rest, beyond the purview of Plato and Pausanias, about a quarter of a mile upstream from the stadium.[33] Here in 1952, finds were made, as so often at Athens, by chance in the course of constructional work, and continued in more systematic excavation. Numerous dedications were found, ranging in date from the fourth century B.C. to the third century A.D.; some were decorated with reliefs, and most were set up in honor of a personage called Pankrates. Structural remains are very slight, and give little indication of the form of the shrine, except that a reclining figure of Herakles, of the fourth century B.C., may come

[32] *Phoenix* 17, 1963, 88–98; Travlos *PDA* 290ff.
[33] *Praktika* (Greek Archaeological Society), 1953, 47–59; *Ergon* 1955, 5; *AJA* 57, 1953, 281; Travlos *PEA* 91ff; *SEG* 16, 1959, 63; 22, 1967, 58; Travlos *PDA* 278ff.

from the pediment of a temple. This Pankrates seems to be a chthonian (underworld) deity, with healing powers, associated with Herakles, or even occasionally identified with him (the name then being treated as an epithet). One dedication is made to yet another personage called Palaimon. Clearly we have here a cult of considerable local importance and popularity, which persisted for many centuries. Before these finds were made neither literature nor inscriptions gave a hint of its existence; yet somehow the name of the deity has been preserved in the name of the district of modern Athens which extends northeastward from this point, Pankrati.

In looking for some of the much better known shrines downstream, one would be glad to find even this slight evidence. A curious relief was found many years ago near the stadium by the river.[34] It is divided into two registers: in the upper are Acheloos, Hermes, three nymphs, and Pan; in the lower, a man leading a horse on the left, and Demeter and Persephone on the right, with an altar in the middle. A horizontal band separating the groups bears an inscription, of the fourth century B.C., giving a dedication by certain cleaners (*plunes*) to the Nymphs and all the gods. It is rash to make any precise topographical deductions either from the finding place of the stone or the design of its decoration. The question arises, but cannot be answered, whether it indicates a second shrine of Pan besides the one we shall find lower down.

Before continuing farther downstream, we may scan the hills on the left bank, between which the stadium was constructed. Slight remains on the top of the northeastern hill have been tentatively assigned to the grave of Herodes Atticus, who rebuilt the stadium in the second century A.D.;[35] in a similar position on the southwestern hill, Ardettos, are the remains of what may well be the temple of Tyche, the Fortune of the City, yet another work owed to the munificence of Herodes, containing, according to Philostratos *Lives* (2.1.5) a gold and ivory statue. This hilly southeastern region was once called Helikon and somewhere on the ridge was an altar of Poseidon Helikonios, whose cult, Pausanias tells us (7.24.5), was imported by the Ionians of Helike in Achaia when they passed through Athens on their way to Asia. A possible site is farther to the west, near the modern windmill.

[34] *IG* II² 2934; G. Rodenwaldt, *AthMitt* 37, 1912, 141–50; Harrison, *Mythology and Monuments of Ancient Athens*, London 1890, 226f; R. E. Wycherley, *Phoenix* 17, 1963, 97; Travlos *PDA* 294.
[35] Judeich 419; Travlos *PDA* 498.

Lower down the hillside, but still well up above the riverbed, is the spot where a small temple, transformed into a church, stood until 1778, when it was demolished by Hadji Ali Khasseki to help build his new wall.[36] Nothing is on view now, and nothing was left for the modern investigators except slight remains of the foundations, measuring 14.6m by 7.8m, with a terrace wall below, and bits of the superstructure including slabs of a frieze. Fortunately the building was fully and finely recorded by Stuart and Revett before the destruction. It was an Ionic amphiprostyle structure, of great beauty, built soon after the middle of the fifth century B.C.; we have already noted that the plan was probably intended in the first place for the temple of Athena Nike on the Acropolis. As to the occupant, opinion has been divided between two notable shrines known to have stood in the district of Agrai, on the south bank of the river—the "Metroon in Agrai" and the temple of Artemis Agrotera. Travlos has now come out firmly on the side of Artemis, and found another site for the Metroon just below, immediately beside the river, where cuttings and a few blocks which may belong to the foundation have come to light. This site suits the Metroon in view of its relation to the precinct of Kronos on the opposite bank. Here the Mother and Demeter were apparently identified, and the Lesser Mysteries were celebrated.

We are now back on the river side. The altar of the Ilissian Muses cannot be precisely located,[37] but we have to assume that this cult was something distinct from whatever gave its name to the Mouseion Hill, some distance farther west, where, Pausanias tells us (1.25.8), Mousaios sang and was buried, and in the second century A.D. a showy and unsightly monument was erected to C. Julius Antiochus Philopappus, an Eastern prince who ended his days as an honored citizen of Athens.[38] A likely place for the altar of Boreas is at a point south of the east end of the Olympieion, where the spring Kallirrhoe debouches and great rocks stand in the river bed.

On the south bank nearby, immediately beside the Church of Hagia Photeine, we turn with infinite gratitude to something which we can

---

[36] Stuart and Revett, *Antiquities of Athens* I, London 1762, Chap. 2; Judeich 420–21; H. Möbius, *AthMitt* 60–61, 1935–1936, 234–68; Dinsmoor, *Greek Architecture*, 185–87; *GRBS* 4, 1963, 174f; Travlos *PDA* 112ff.

[37] Pausanias 1.19.5; cf. Plato *Phaidros* 237a, 259b, 262d; Judeich 419, 424; *GRBS* 4, 1963, 173f.

[38] Cf. 1.26.2; 3.6.6; Plutarch *Theseus* 27.1 and 3. For Philopappus see Judeich 388–89; Travlos *PDA* 462ff.

identify outright, as a modest shrine of Pan.[39] The rock is cut into a right-angled recess, and on the southern face is carved a relief of the god, standing with a syrinx in his right hand and a stick in his left. The figure is now so indistinct that one needs the eye of faith to see it except in the most favorable of cross lights, and its date is naturally very uncertain, possibly fifth century B.C.

Continuing our way downstream, we immediately find ourselves groping in an uncertain light again. "The Gardens" (*kepoi*) must have been on the bank or banks in this region; but we cannot locate precisely the shrine of Aphrodite in the Gardens, in which Pausanias (19.2) saw two contrasting figures of the goddess, one a primitive square Herm-like figure, inscribed as Aphrodite Ourania, oldest of the Fates, the other a masterpiece by Alkamenes—a characteristically Athenian combination of old and new.[40]

The Dionysion in Limnai (Marshes), included in Thucydides' list of ancient shrines,[41] still remains an insoluble riddle. It was most probably in southeastern Athens. One would expect to find a district called Limnai in the neighborhood of the river, but the shrine may have been somewhat to the north in the direction of the theater.

Kynosarges and its shrine of Herakles we may leave for consideration in connection with the gymnasium.

Ilissos himself is shown in the northern angle of the west pediment of the Parthenon, a sinuous powerful figure, a true river god, balanced in the southern angle by the graceful nymph Kallirrhoe, representing no doubt the southeastern spring, not the Kallirrhoe in the agora which later became Enneakrounos. We are not told that the river god had a shrine of his own on the bank. Yet there were times when his neighbors needed to placate him. The delightful rivulet, appropriate for girls to play nearby and for Sokrates and Phaidros to paddle on a hot summer day, after torrential rains could rise (as it did in 1961) with devastating effect.

Since leaving the Olympieion and while wandering around this southeastern quarter, we have met with uncertainty and obscurity at almost every point and precious little to help the imagination. Yet the picture

[39] G. Rodenwaldt, *AthMitt* 37, 1912, 141–50; Judeich 416; *Phoenix* 17, 1963, 95f; Travlos *PDA* 296.

[40] Judeich 424; E. Langlotz, *Aphrodite in den Gärten*, Heidelberg 1954; *GRBS* 4, 1963, 168–70.

[41] 2.15.4 (with Gomme's note); Judeich 290ff; A. W. Pickard-Cambridge, *Dramatic Festivals of Athens*, 2d edn. Oxford 1968, 19ff; G.T.W. Hooker, *JHS* 80, 1960, 112–17; *GRBS* 4, 1963, 170f; p. 195 below.

50. Rock-cut Relief of Pan (Photo: German Archaeological Institute)

which we can form of the local shrines is vivid and colorful. When Sokrates at the end of his talk with Phaidros concludes with the prayer, "Dear Pan, and all you gods in this place, grant that I may be beautiful within," he is addressing a large and varied company.

(173)

BIBLIOGRAPHY

L. Bevier, *Papers of the American School at Athens* 1, 1882–83, 183–212

F. C. Penrose, *Principles of Athenian Architecture*, London 1888, 74–87

G. Welter, "Das Olympieion in Athen," *AthMitt* 47, 1922, 61–71; 48, 1923, 182–201

P. Graindor, *Athènes sous Hadrien*, Cairo 1934

R. E. Wycherley, "The Olympieion at Athens," *GRBS* 5, 1964, 161–79 (The present chapter is based on this article and two others: "Pausanias at Athens II," *GRBS* 4, 1963, 157–75; "The Scene of Plato's *Phaidros*," *Phoenix* 17, 1963, 88–98; the reader is referred to these for further details, bibliography, and discussion of problems.)

CHAPTER VII

Other Shrines

O rich and renowned and with violets crowned, bulwark of Hellas, city of gods.

(Pindar frag. 76)

Paul's spirit was stirred within him when he saw the city full of idols; . . . standing in the midst of the Areopagus he said, "Men of Athens, I find you in all things excessively *daimon*-fearing."

(Acts 17: 16 & 22)

The Athenians more than all others show piety towards the gods . . . I have already said that they more than all others show an excess of zeal in the cults of the gods.

(Pausanias 1.7.1; 24.3)

When Pindar calls Athens *daimonion*, he does not mean, vaguely, divine, but rather possessed and inhabited by many *daimones*, divine beings of various kinds; the violet crown signifies the vernal festivals of the gods. Paul found a veritable forest of "idols" at Athens; this is the meaning of the adjective *kateidolos*, as one may see by analogy with such words as *katadendros* (covered with trees).[1] Pausanias found shrines of a remarkable variety of deities wherever he went in his extensive tour of the city. The all-pervading *deisidaimonia* or religiosity observed by these men is illustrated not only in the literature of all periods and in the copious epigraphical records but also in monuments found *in situ*.

The multiplicity of cults and the variety and complexity of religious life were naturally reflected in the visible architectural aspect of the city. The shrines were scattered throughout the city and suburbs. Many of them would consist of a simple *temenos*, a piece of ground set apart for the gods, marked off and enclosed in some way, with an altar for sacrifice and modest dedicatory monuments; some might have a small temple, some a stoa or colonnade.[2] Many, but not all, had a cult statue, a venerable ancient image, or a masterpiece by a famous sculptor of later times, or occasionally both. Some were maintained by the *polis* as a whole, some by a particular section or a family.

[1] See *Journal of Theological Studies* 19, 1968, 619–20.
[2] See B. Berquist, *The Archaic Greek Temenos*, Lund 1967.

We have already noted the greatest concentrations. On the Acropolis each of the major buildings was the nucleus of a complicated pattern of cult spots, scattered around or even clinging like limpets. The temple of Olympian Zeus was another such nucleus. The agora and the surrounding regions were full of shrines. But in addition to these obvious conglomerations, at Athens even more than in other Greek cities there were "gods everywhere." This can be illustrated by a rapid and extensive survey of other parts of the city, with a more detailed account of a particularly notable sector.

Many shrines clung to the upper slopes of the Acropolis, below the cliffs, or even penetrated into the rock itself, in the caves. Some are known only from literary or epigraphical references. To begin on the north side, one which can be securely located is the shrine of Aphrodite and Eros her son.[3] If Athena was supreme on the top of the hill, Aphrodite was worshiped in a variety of forms on its slopes, and we shall find two more shrines, even though we cannot locate them precisely, on the west and southwest. The northern site, below the Erechtheion and a little to the east, near the Mycenean stairway and postern, is conspicuously marked by numerous niches cut in the rock to receive dedications. Rock-cut inscriptions fortunately identify the deities, and suitable dedications, including *phalloi*, have been found. The extent and contents of the shrines are not clear; and the suggested identification of this as a second cult of Aphrodite in the Gardens must remain open to doubt.[4]

A little farther to the east, carved on a large boulder, is another inscription,[5] which may be safely restored to read, "Length of the circuit (*peripatos*) five stades eighteen feet," with reference to the ancient road which encircled the hill at this high level, giving access to many of the shrines. We shall meet it again in the neighborhood of the theater.

Some distance to the west of the shrine of Aphrodite, below the point at which archaic architectural members are built into the Acropolis wall, a deep cave is conspicuous in the rock face. This is a likely site for the shrine of the heroine Aglauros, daughter of King Kekrops, who hurled herself down from the cliff. The cave forms an exit at this level from

---

[3] O. Broneer, *Hesperia* I, 1932, 31–55; II, 1933, 329–49; Travlos *PDA* 228ff; cf. A. B. Cook, *Zeus* III, Cambridge (Eng.) 1940, 169ff.

[4] Pausanias 1.27.3 is confusing; the underground passage does not go *through* this shrine. Broneer, *Hesperia* Suppl. 8, 1949, perhaps goes too far in making outright doublets of shrines on the north slope and in southeast Athens; see *AJA* 63, 1959, 69; and for the indubitable Aphrodite in the Gardens see p. 172 above.

[5] Travlos *PDA* 229; the path is now being reopened.

the great cleft which led on down to the Mycenean springhouse.[6] Pausanias' account shows that the spacious precinct of the Dioskouroi or Anakes, Kastor and Polydeukes, was nearby.[7]

As we move westward from this point, round the west end of the Acropolis and onto the southwest slope, we can assume that we are in the area of immemorial sanctity known as the Pelargikon or Pelasgikon, a name which we have already noted in connection with the ancient western defenses of the hill; this area, Thucydides tells us, had to be left *argon*, unworked, unoccupied by ordinary mortals.[8]

Some of the series of caves at the northwestern end of the Acropolis were certainly occupied by deities, but only one shrine can be identified outright. In the second cave from the west are many votive niches, and many tablets with dedications to Apollo "under the Long Rocks" or "under the Heights" have been found.[9] This spot was the very cradle of the Ionian people, including the Athenians, since here, according to Euripides in the *Ion* (283) Apollo met Kreousa, who subsequently gave birth to Ion, their ancestor. Pan too was worshiped beneath the rocks, perhaps at a point a little to the east, where there are two narrower holes, and where votive niches are again visible.[10] Pan was a comparatively late importation at Athens, after the Persian Wars. The spring Klepsydra, a little to the west of the caves, in a cleft in the rock precariously converted in the fifth century into a fountain house, had its own sacred character.[11] Its early name was Empedo, and Empedo was worshiped as a nymph.

[6] Judeich 303; O. Broneer, "A Mycenean Fountain," *Hesperia* 8, 1939, 317–429; Travlos *PDA* 72ff.

[7] 1.18.1; Judeich 304; *Agora* III 61–65. The shrine has not been found. Pausanias notes paintings by Polygnotos and Mikon.

[8] 2.17.1; p. 7 above.

[9] Judeich 301–2; *Agora* III 54, 179; Travlos *PDA* 91. In *AJA* 67, 1963, 75–79, I have given the view that although it had Pythian associations, as Euripides shows, this was hardly a second Pythion, *the* Pythion of Athens being the unquestionable shrine in southeastern Athens, p. 167 above; and in *AJA* 63, 1959, 68–72, on Strabo 9.2.11, that there is no good evidence, in Strabo or elsewhere, for a shrine of Zeus on the northwest slope. For the contrary view see A. D. Keramopoullos, *Deltion* 12, 1932, 86; O. Broneer, *Hesperia* Suppl. 8, 1949, 54; Travlos *PDA* 91.

[10] Judeich 301–2; Travlos *PDA* 417ff; P. J. Riis, *Acta Archaeologica* 45, 1974, 130ff.

[11] Judeich 191ff; A. W. Parsons, "Klepsydra and the Paved Court of the Pythion," *Hesperia* 12, 1943, 191–267 (this "paved court," H. A. Thompson has recently suggested to me, is in fact rather a large cistern); Travlos *PDA* 323ff; *Deltion* 25B, 1972, 26ff; *BCH* 96, 1972, 600.

On the wall of the bastion above are vestiges of an inscription of the fourth century B.C. referring to the Street of the Panathenaia;[12] the great processional way passed just below on its final stage.

Before we leave Pan and his neighbors, it will be worthwhile to look at a remarkable relief which illustrates our present subject nicely even if precise interpretation is uncertain.[13] It was found in a late Roman house on the north slope of the Areopagus, but it can be dated in the fourth century B.C. It shows an assemblage of deities in a rocky cave-like setting; and T. L. Shear, who publishes it, relates the figures to the cults of the northwest slope and suggests that the relief was originally set up in the shrine of Pan. The deities seem to be present at a ceremony performed by Hermes at an altar in the center. To the right are Pan, in the far corner, and three of the nymphs. To the left are three figures who can be interpreted as Apollo, Artemis, and Demeter. Above, but still in the rocky setting, is a seated Zeus. We have already met Apollo on the northwest slope, and also Pan, who is constantly accompanied by Nymphs. Demeter is perhaps Demeter Chloe whom we shall find at the western approach to the Acropolis. Zeus is more problematical. Some archaeologists have attempted to install him in one of the caves, but the evidence is by no means as solid as for Apollo and Pan; and if one insists on a topographical interpretation of all the figures, one may think of Zeus as having stepped down from his undoubted shrine on the top of the hill to participate. The question also arises whether the scene might be related to the cults on the Hill of the Nymphs in western Athens, where we shall find a shrine of Zeus, clearly marked, and another of the Nymphs, with a temple of Artemis just below. This temple belonged to the deme Melite, and Neoptolemos who dedicated the relief was a Melitean. Perhaps after all one should not look for great topographical precision or consistency in such a work of art; but even so one can consider it in a more general way as a symbol and an illustration of the manner in which the shrines clustered in many parts of Athens.

The shrines seen by Pausanias as he approached the Propylaia from the west or southwest may well be associated with the hypothetical primitive agora west of the Acropolis. They were Aphrodite Pandemos, so called, according to Apollodoros, because "all the Demos gathered there of

[12] *Hesperia* 8, 1939, 207; 18, 1949, 135; *Agora* III 224.
[13] T. L. Shear, *Hesperia* 42, 1973, 168–70; *Opuscula Romana* 9, 1973, 191. H. A. Thompson tells me he interprets the scene as the presentation of Dionysos to the Nymphs as a baby.

51. Relief of Zeus, Hermes, and Other Deities (Photo: Agora Excavations)

old in their assemblies";[14] Ge Kourotrophos (Nurse of Youth); and Demeter Chloe (Green). Inscriptions relating to these cults have been found in the region, mentioning in addition an obscure personage called Blaute.

Before continuing the circuit we may glance westward to the Areopagus, the Hill of Ares, joined to the Acropolis by a saddle. The Areopagus was second only to the Acropolis itself in venerability, but the vestiges on its bare rocky summit and flanks consist of little more than cuttings; an ancient rock-cut stair leads up from the southeast corner. Ares was associated with the hill because he appeared as the first defendant before the ancient homicide court, the Boule of the Areopagus; whether he had a shrine is not clear. Athena was worshiped under the title of Areia. Pausanias (1.28.6) saw on the hill statues of Pluto, Hermes, and Ge, and a monument to Oedipus. But the most remarkable shrine was that of the Semnai, the implacable Furies now converted into "friends of the beloved Maiden," as Aeschylus calls them in the *Eumenides* (999),

[14] Frag. 113, Jacoby II B 1075; Pausanias 1.22.3; Judeich 285–86; *Agora* III 224f; F. Sokolowski, *Harvard Theological Review* 57, 1964, 1ff; p. 27 above.

deities benign but still august. A favored site for their shrine is below the great broken crags on the northeast side of the hill, where later stood the church of Paul's convert Dionysios the Areopagite.[15]

Passing on to the southwest slope, at the higher level, we still look in vain among the slight and confused remains for anything clearly identifiable. Aigeus had a shrine here, where he threw himself down in the belief that his son Theseus had not returned from Crete alive.[16] Finds in this area, below the south face of the Nike bastion, were made several years ago;[17] and because they include material appropriate to a cult of Aphrodite Dontas would place Aphrodite Pandemos here rather than immediately west of the Propylaia, and Demeter Chloe too, possibly in two small *sekoi* or shrines which have been found side by side. It is possible, however, that the material may have made its way down from a higher site. Dontas believes that the Pandemos shrine and the Hippolytos shrine were one and the same; but the literary references and inscriptions give the impression of distinct cults. On his way from the Asklepieion westward towards the shrine of Aigeus, Pausanias noted a temple of Themis and a monument to Hippolytos son of Theseus. With the latter we may reasonably associate the temple of Aphrodite originally founded, according to Euripides, by Phaidra for love of her stepson; here the goddess was worshipped as "Aphrodite for Hippolytos."[18]

The most striking feature among the remains on this part of the slope tells us nothing about the local shrines. It is a large pit of the kind used in bronze-casting (Fig. 58);[19] a major statue must have been fashioned here, but where it was destined to stand we cannot say, most probably on the Acropolis. As at the workshop of Pheidias at Olympia, one is brought tantalizingly near to an irretrievably lost masterpiece.

Some distance farther east, close under the cliff, is a spring in a shaft of polygonal masonry, probably of the sixth century, partly obliterated by a mediaeval cistern. Nearby are the foundations of a small temple of simple form (probably *in antis*) which may possibly have belonged to Pausanias' Themis, though some have suggested that it was the earliest temple of Asklepios. That the spring had a sacred character is shown

[15] For the cults of the Areopagus see Judeich 299ff; Hill 31, 190; there are no identifiable remains.

[16] Pausanias 1.22.5; Judeich 216.

[17] *Ergon* 1961 (for 1960) 10ff and *BCH* 85, 1961, 607.

[18] *Hippolytos* 29–33; Pausanias 1.22.1–2; Judeich 324f.

[19] *Deltion* 19, 1964, B1, 32–34; one is tempted to associate it with Athena Promachos, but the date is not clear.

by the fact that in the wall which ran east to west below, built of good polygonal masonry of a similar date to the shaft, is cut an inscription, in letters of the fifth century, reading HOROS KRENES (boundary of the fountain).[20] This wall, which a little farther east makes a northward return, may mark the limit of the Pelargikon at this point. The *peripatos* runs along its south side.

When we reach the Asklepieion we at last find ourselves on ground archaeologically safe, with buildings which are identifiable and can be securely reconstructed. Asklepios was a comparatively late comer at Athens; the shrine was established in 420/419 B.C., and singled out for architectural embellishment in the course of the succeeding century. The Athenians, with their extraordinary mixture of sophistication and superstition, were very much addicted to healing cults, and a number of simpler shrines to which the sick and disabled resorted were distributed about the city. We find two in western Athens, one of an obscure hero, one, on the Pnyx, of Zeus himself. Then there was the Hero Doctor, a neighbor of Theseus.[21] In the same way as Christian saints, a hero or a god became a healer by healing, just as one becomes a carpenter by carpentering or a just man by doing just acts. Lucian in his *Toxaris* tells an illuminating story, how a Scythian came to be honored as the Xenos Iatros, the Guest Doctor, and his tomb on the road to the Academy became a healing shrine, because at the time of the great plague he appeared in a dream to one Deimainete and revealed to her a cure. Athena was represented as Hygieia (goddess of health, a name commonly given to Asklepios' daughter) just inside the Propylaia; and Amphiaraos, who performed cures at his shrine at Oropos on the northern border of Attica, had a statue in the agora;[22] but it does not seem that either of these places was a regular resort for invalids.

Asklepios quickly established himself as the Great Healer, and his shrine became the most favored resort, as the abundance of material found on the site clearly shows (not to speak of the merciless parody in Aristophanes' *Plutus*). An inscription gives curious details of the early days of the cult.[23] The god came up from Zea, in Peiraeus (no doubt

[20] *IG* I² 874, 875; Judeich 190, 324; Hill 125; Travlos *PDA* 138ff.

[21] See p. 193 below; cf. F. Kutsch, *Attische Heilgötter und Heilheroen*, Giessen 1913, 2ff.

[22] Pausanias 1.8.2; 1.34; *Agora* III 49. Note also Pankrates, see p. 170 above.

[23] *IG* II² 4960–63; Judeich 320ff; R. Martin, *BCH* 73, 1949, 316–50; J. Travlos, *ArchEph* 1948 (1939–41) 35; *PDA* 127ff; R. A. Tomlinson, *JHS* 89, 1969, 112–17 (West Building). On the cult of Asklepios see E. J. and L. Edelstein, *Asklepios*,

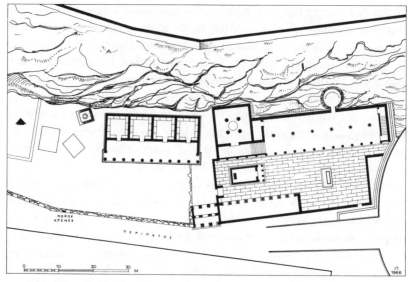

52. Asklepieion (J. Travlos *PDA* 129 fig. 171)

having come in the first place from Epidauros) and was lodged at first in the Eleusinion (elsewhere we hear that Sophokles received him in his house). The shrine on the south slope was established in the archonship of Astyphilos, 420 B.C.; a reference in the inscription to a dispute with the priestly family called the Kerykes or Heralds seems to indicate that there was some sort of difficulty concerning demarcation; one can imagine that as cults multiplied and grew in a restricted area a certain amount of jostling would take place from time to time, and a compromise would be necessary. The basic plan of the shrine was simple, being a special varia-tion of a common form—a temple with the altar to the east and a stoa forming a continuous background. The temple itself was quite small, 10.4m by 6m including a porch of four columns. The principal building was the stoa, nearly 50m long by 10m deep, built probably in the time of Lycurgus (338–326 B.C.); it had an upper story, and thus is a compara-tively early example of a type which became common in Hellenistic times. No doubt it was intended to make generous provision for the suppliants. Behind the back wall is a grotto in the rock of the Acropolis containing a spring; and at the northwest corner, in the middle of a raised platform, is a pit lined with polygonal masonry, which may well

Baltimore 1945; C. Kerenyi, *Asklepios*, London 1960. For Sophokles see *Ety-mologicum Magnum s.v.* "Dexion"; Marinos *Life of Proclus* 29.

have antedated the stoa; this presumably served some sacrificial purpose, or it may have housed the sacred snakes. The boundary on the south was a wall which continued the line of the old polygonal wall; the small stoa on this side was added in Roman times. The entrance to the precinct was a simple gateway in the west wall, approached from the south, from the *peripatos*, by a columnar propylon; the remains of this are mainly of Roman date, but it seems to have had a predecessor. Extending westward from the big stoa is an Ionic colonnade, with four square rooms behind, which to judge by their plan were dining rooms; though it stands somewhat detached, this building may reasonably be associated with the Asklepieion, the rooms being for the use of priests and perhaps important suppliants; it may well have been the cause of the dispute, since it straddles the old wall and encroaches on the presumed area of the Pelargikon.

In the inscriptions Asklepios is entitled Soter, Xenios, Epekoos (he who gives ear); he is commonly coupled with Hygieia, sometimes with other deities including Hypnos (Sleep) and Sarapis. Great numbers of dedications and records of dedications have been found, bearing witness to the popularity of the god, and his efficacy.[24] They range from the fourth century B.C. to the third century A.D. In the fifth century a greater Healer inherited the site, and a basilica was erected on the very foundations of the old stoas.

We shall spend some time in the precinct of Dionysos Eleuthereus when we examine the great theater. Here we need consider only briefly the general character of the shrine and its place in the pattern. This Dionysos came down from Eleutherai on the northern border in the form of an old wooden image, establishing another temple near the Academy on the way.[25] At first the shrine on the south slope was as simple as most of the others which we have seen. In the middle of the sixth century B.C. a small temple was built, probably with two columns *in antis*, represented now by scanty remains of the foundations. As the dramatic performances developed the theater spread itself far up the slope above, and the precinct remained as an adjunct on the south, with an enclosing wall of irregular plan. In the fourth century it took the shape of another variation on the temple-altar-stoa formula. A larger temple, but still modest, 21m by 9.6m,

---

[24] Besides inscriptions as given in *IG* note R. O. Hubbe, "Decrees from the Precinct of Asklepios at Athens," *Hesperia* 28, 1959, 169–201. Note the hymns and prayers, *IG* II² 4473, 4509, 4510 (Sophokles' paean), 4514, 4533; see Edelstein *Asklepios* 428, 587, 593.

[25] Pausanias 1.20.3, 1.29.2; for the theater temples see pp. 206ff below.

was added just south of the old one, and a long stoa was built on the north side with its back to the theater. Pausanias saw both the temples, the old containing the *xoanon* or wooden image, the later the splendid Dionysos made of gold and ivory by Alkamenes.

The monuments associated with the cult and the festivals stretched far beyond the confines of the precinct into the neighboring quarters of Athens. Pausanias' "Street called Tripods"[26] swung round the eastern end of the Acropolis, at a lower level than the *peripatos*, and no doubt entered the shrine through a propylon which is mentioned by Andokides, *On the Mysteries* (38, a passage of special interest for the topography of the theater quarter); along this street *choregoi* set up tripods to commemorate the victories of their choruses. A wealthy *choregos* might give his monument the form of a minor work of architecture, with the tripod itself as a mere adjunct. The foundations of several such choregic monuments have been excavated on the street, and by an extremely rare miracle of survival what must have been one of the finest still stands almost intact, having been incorporated in the structure of a Capucin monastery. This is the dedication of Lysikrates, set up in 335/334 B.C., a circular structure with Corinthian columns of a curious experimental form and curved slabs in the interstices, standing on a square base. The tripod itself stood on the floral ornament which crowns the roof. The choregic dedications extended to the west of the theater too; in 320/319 B.C. a *choregos* called Nikias erected a temple-like building with an imposing facade of six Doric columns;[27] this undoubtedly stood on a foundation just south of the east end of the Stoa of Eumenes, but many architectural members belonging to it can be seen in the so-called Beulé Gate (named after a French archaeologist) at the west end of the Acropolis; they were incorporated when this gate was built in the third century A.D. as an outer defense. Another successful *choregos* of 320/319 B.C., Thrasyllos, chose to give the cave above the theater, now the shrine of the Panagia Speliotissa, a handsome architectural facade.

Vitruvius says that stoas were attached to theaters to provide a promenade and shelter for the theatergoers and storage space for equipment; and he takes as an example the Stoa of Eumenes of Pergamon (197–159

[26] I.20.I; Judeich 183, 305; Travlos *PDA* 348 (Lysikrates), 566; S. Miller, *Hesperia* 39, 1970, 223ff (another choregic monument on the street); P. Amandry, *BCH* 100, 1976, 15ff, "Trépieds d'Athènes" (71ff Lysikrates).

[27] *IG* II² 3055; Judeich 319; Travlos *PDA* 357. For Thrasyllos see *IG* II² 3056, 3083; Judeich 315; Travlos *PDA* 562; P. Amandry, *BCH* 100, 1976, 53ff. The two Corinthian columns, of Roman date, standing above, also supported tripods.

B.C.), though no doubt it was used for more general purposes too.[28] This building, extending 163m westward, and eventually linking the old theater with the Odeion of Herodes, resembled the Stoa of Attalos in material—conglomerate, Peiraeus limestone, and marble both Pentelic and Hymettian—and in construction and design, with double colonnades in two stories, but no rooms behind, and with Doric and Pergamene columns. The massive arched buttresses, which are now so conspicuous, strengthened the back of the stoa so that it could serve as a retaining wall; immediately behind ran the *peripatos*. In this building, as in the theater itself and the adjacent shrine, we see a contrast between Hellenistic grandiosity and fifth-century simplicity.

So far, we have been treading on holy ground, for the most part. Even the Street of Tripods was in some degree a sacred festal way. And the area which we have covered, close under the Acropolis, belongs mostly to what Thucydides (2.15.3–6) recognized as the old original city, the most venerable part of Athens. As the city grew, the shrines spread and multiplied; some were imported from the country demes, from other cities, and ultimately even from non-Greek sources, to enrich and diversify the pattern of Athenian religious life. Descending from the north slope into the streets of the lower town, Pausanias saw a curious group of cult spots—first the Sarapieion, the chief center of the worship of the Egyptian gods at Athens, established by a Ptolemy in the third century; next a spot sanctified by the oath of loyalty taken by Theseus and Peirithous, probably what was called the Horkomosion; then a temple of a very ancient deity from Crete, Eileithyia, goddess of childbirth.[29] Epigraphical evidence, admittedly very uncertain, points to a region in northeast Athens near the present Metropolis Church.

Though we have surveyed a number of concentrations, series and groups, stretching diagonally right across the city and beyond, from the Ilissos and the Olympieion in the southeast to the Kerameikos and ultimately the Academy in the northwest, our list of sacred places is far from closed. Others were distributed about the city in odd places, many

[28] 5.9.1; cf. Judeich 325f; Travlos *PDA* 523ff.

[29] 1.18.4–5; Judeich 380; R. E. Wycherley, *GRBS* 4, 1963, 161f; on the Egyptian gods see S. Dow, *Harvard Theological Review* 30, 1937, 187ff; P. M. Fraser, *Opuscula Atheniensia* 3, 1960, 1–54; on Eileithyia, who also had a cult in Agrai in the southeast, see R. F. Willetts, *CQ* NS 8, 221ff. Plutarch, *Theseus* 27.5, gives a different account of the Horkomosion and places it "beside the Theseion." Sophokles, *Oedipus at Kolonos* 1594, puts the scene of the "loyal bond" of Theseus and Peirithous at Kolonos.

in residential quarters of no special sanctity. At Athens gods and heroes could be met, one might almost say, "in twos and threes in every street."

In the streets of course there were always the ubiquitous Herms, square pillars surmounted by a head of Hermes, who among other things was the great god of streets and gateways. The Athenians, we are told, invented this form of image, and set Herms everywhere, at the doors of both shrines and private houses.[30] There must have been hundreds in the city; many Herms and Herm bases have been found in the agora excavations. No more significant bit of stone has been unearthed at Athens than the fine but battered head of Hermes shown in Fig. 14a; set up at the time of the victories of Kimon, mutilated (no doubt) in the time of Alkibiades, and crudely patched up, it epitomizes the destiny of Athens, her glory and her humiliation. Though regarded with veneration, as is shown by the wrath of the pious when in 415 B.C. a group of young hooligans mutilated many of them, the ordinary simple Herms hardly constituted shrines in themselves; but passers-by, in somewhat casual fashion, paid their respect. Apollo too was a street god, with the title Agyieus;[31] he was represented in truly aniconic form as a tapering pillar or elongated half-egg, and these objects too, we are told, were set up at Athens in front of doors. None has been found, and they were presumably much less common than Herms. More like a true shrine was the Hekataion, sacred to Hekate, a goddess who was worshiped particularly at crossroads or places where three roads met.[32] She was shown with three heads and three bodies, facing three ways. Many small dedications to her in this form have been found, illustrating the popularity of her worship; and the aspect of her little shrines can perhaps be illustrated by reference to remains which have been found to the southeast of the agora, on the way up to the Acropolis. The Hekataion, if such it is, was set characteristically in a corner at a crossroads, where the processional way of the Panathenaia was crossed by an east to west street. In the middle was a circular socket, probably for a base on which the triple figure stood; around this were four square sockets as if for posts supporting an enclosing fence; but apparently this was not thought sufficient protection in view of the exposure of the shrine to traffic on the roads, for a wall of

---

[30] Pausanias 1.24.3; Thucydides 6.27.1. See E. B. Harrison, *Agora* xi 108ff; *Agora* xiv 94–96, 169; p. 38 above. For another mutilated Herm see *Hesperia* 42, 1973, 164f. See also H. Herter, "Hermes," *Rheinisches Museum*, 119, 1976, 193ff.

[31] Cf. Aristophanes *Wasps* 875, and commentators; *Agora* xiv 169.

[32] Harrison, *Agora* xi 86ff; *Hesperia* 28, 1959, 95ff; 29, 1960, 333; *Agora* xiv 169; p. 132 above.

rubble masonry, with an entrance at the east end of the north side, was next built around it. The whole square structure measured no more than 3m each way. It was not built as we have it until Roman times, but there may well have been a simpler earlier Hekataion on the spot; and in any case there must have been many such at crossroads in Athens in earlier periods.

These were deities of the streets by nature and function. Others simply happened to have their shrines on ordinary city streets among the houses and shops. Before dealing with remains found *in situ*, one might look at one or two inscriptions which mention shrines not yet located and which throw a little light on their distribution. Like other ancient cities Athens did not have a systematic method of naming streets and numbering houses. In documents concerned with the disposal of house property the site is commonly defined by reference to the neighbors; and one's neighbor might be a god. On one of the marble stelai which record the sale of the property of Alkibiades and his associates, confiscated because of their sacrilege in 415 B.C., we read, "Property of Diodoros: a house in Kydathenaion, which has a porch with two pillars"—and surely a Herm —"to which is adjacent the shrine of Artemis Amarysia from Athmonon."[33] Kydathenaion was a deme and populous residential district on the north side of the Acropolis. Athmonon was a country deme a few miles northeast of Athens (the modern name of the place, Amarousion or Marousi, is a relic of the ancient cult). Such cults of the Attic demes not infrequently had counterparts established within the metropolis. Artemis Amarysia came originally from Amarynthos in Euboia.

Another inscription dealing with the sale of confiscated property, dated in the fourth century, mentions "two workshops in Melite, to which are adjacent on the east a house of Philokrates of Hagnous, on the west a workshop of Hierokleides of Hermos, on the north a house of Philokrates of Hagnous, on the south the road leading from the shrine of Herakles Alexikakos [Averter of Evil] to the agora."[34] This shrine was probably in the extreme western part of the city, between the Hill of the Nymphs and the Pnyx hill.

The region southwest of the agora and west of the Areopagus provides

---

[33] *Hesperia* 22, 1953, 272 (Stele VI, lines 78–79). Note also Andokides 1.62, from which we gather that Andokides' house was adjacent to the shrine of the hero Phorbas. For the cults of a deme, Erchia, and counterparts in the city, see the important inscription published by G. Daux, *BCH* 87, 1963, 603ff.

[34] *Hesperia* 5, 1936, 400; cf. *AJA* 63, 1959, 67. On Herakles Alexikakos see S. Woodford, *AJA* 80, 1976, 291ff.

the best illustration and some of its many peculiar monuments repay more detailed examination. Western Athens comprised a series of rocky hills, strung out north to south, with valleys adjacent and saddles between. The district was residential, with an industrial element, and included two of the more populous city demes, Melite and Kollytos. Shrines on the Hill of the Nymphs above have long been attested by inscriptions carved in the rock. One of these, near the top and the Old Observatory, marks the place as sacred to the Nymphs.[35] These particular Nymphs were probably the daughters of Hyakinthos, sacrificed according to legend for the good of the city. Hyakinthos himself, as we learn from an inscription, had a shrine at Athens, and this may have been in association with his daughters; indeed the hill may be what was known in antiquity as the Hill of Hyakinthos (the present name is modern). If the identification is correct, these Nymphs were also known as *genethliai*, i.e., concerned with childbirth; and it is worth noting that St. Marina, to whom is dedicated the church which stands just below and a little to the east, is also concerned with birth and children, and may well be a true successor to the Nymphs.

A little farther down the hill, just below the church, if one searches hard one can still find an inscription in letters about three inches high cut deeply in the hard rock. It runs right to left and reads *horos Dios*, boundary of Zeus; nearby is another reading *horos* only. They may be dated in the sixth century. Presumably a portion of the hillside was marked off as sacred to Zeus. One imagines that the sanctuary consisted simply of *temenos* (sacred plot) and altar; a temple, even a small one, or other substantial building would have left some trace. Nothing is known from literature of a shrine of Zeus on this spot. But a boundary stone has more recently been found in the valley just below to the east, bearing an inscription which shows that it was a boundary of a shrine of Zeus with a cult epithet which might possibly be Exopsios (the inscription is unfortunately incomplete and open to doubt: Fig. 59.5). Exopsios means "looking out," and certainly from the hillside Zeus could look out and view the agora and the city as a whole. The stone is dated in the fourth century B.C., and so would belong to a later demarcation.[36] On the north-

---

[35] M. Ervin, in *Platon* 11, 1959, 146ff; cf. Judeich 398.

[36] Judeich 398; B. D. Meritt, *Hesperia* 26, 1957, 90; E. Vanderpool, *Hesperia* 35, 1966, 274f, suggests Exousios, but I still prefer Exopsios; see *Hesperia* 37, 1968, 121f. The problem is whether the last inscribed letter is psi or upsilon, whether the mark at the top of the vertical is purely accidental.

ern slope of the Hill of the Nymphs dedications to Zeus Meilichios have been found; whether they came from the same shrine or another one cannot say.[37]

At the northern foot of the Hill, about half way along the street which leads from the southwest corner of the agora to the Peiraeus Gate, a small temple of peculiar interest in Athenian cult and history was found by chance during building operations in 1958.[38] An inscription reveals that it belonged to the men of Melite, and that the deity was Artemis; and the shrine may well be one which was associated with the name of the most distinguished Melitean, Themistokles. Pottery shows that the site was occupied from the eighth century at least, but there is no definite evidence for a cult till the fifth. The plan of a small temple, facing west, was clearly revealed, though the remains are scanty. In front of it, placed obliquely, was an altar, and just beyond this a short section of an enclosing wall was found; the full extent of the enclosure is not known. The temple consisted of a cella about 3.6m square, with a porch between antae or projecting walls 1.85m deep. Thus the building represents the Greek temple in its basic, almost irreducible form, with the minimum elaboration of plan or architectural adornment.

About 3m west of the facade of the temple were found, *in situ*, two blocks of poros which must have been the foundation of the altar. The altar itself, another poros block, with a molding at the bottom, was found lying nearby. It was not placed on the axis of the temple, nor indeed did it have the same orientation; it was placed obliquely on almost the same line as the adjacent peribolos wall. The latter was built of rough polygonal masonry; outside was a street, its course marked by a late drain.

The finds show that the cult was maintained throughout the rest of classical antiquity. The inscription mentioned above, cut about 330 B.C., gives at the top a dedication by Neoptolemos son of Antikles to Artemis, made "when Chairylle was priestess." Below is a decree of the demesmen of Melite honoring this man for services rendered in connection with the cult. The relevant section of the inscription is almost obliterated;

[37] For Zeus Meilichios see Thucydides 1.126.6; Pausanias 1.37.4 (across the Kephisos); Cook, *Zeus* II, 1091ff; R. E. Wycherley, *GRBS* 5, 1964, 177; E. Mitropoulou, *AAA* 8, 1975, 120-23.

[38] J. Threpsiades and E. Vanderpool, *Deltion* 19, 1965, 26ff; Travlos *PDA* 121ff; P. Amandry, in *Charisterion for A.K. Orlandos*, Athens 1967, 265ff, thinks that the building excavated was a treasury, and the main temple was elsewhere; but this building is sufficient, and it is not very likely that such a local shrine and cult would have required two temple-like buildings.

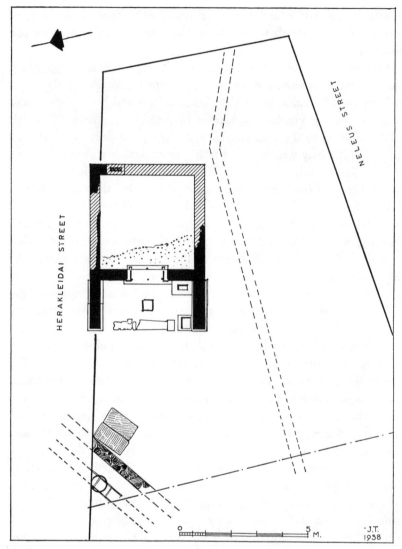

53. Shrine of Artemis Aristoboule (J. Travlos, *PDA* 122 fig. 104)

but one may naturally assume that the rebuilding of the temple was due
to him.

"Themistokles himself gave offense to the majority," says Plutarch in
his *Life* (22.1), "by founding the shrine of Artemis. He called the goddess
Aristoboule, on the ground that he had given the best advice to the city
and to Greece, and he built the shrine near his house in Melite. A por-

54. Triangular Shrine Southwest of Agora (Photo: M. Vernardos)

trait of Themistokles stood in the temple of Aristoboule even in my day, and it is clear that he was a man heroic not only in spirit but also in appearance." It is hardly rash to identify the remains with the shrine of Plutarch's story. When Themistokles fell into disfavor and disgrace, it would not be surprising if for a time the shrine was neglected and disowned. In the following century he was permanently installed as one of the glorious heroes of Athenian history; the temple was naturally restored, and perhaps the shrine also became a kind of *heroon* of Themistokles.

The valley which runs southwards from the agora, with the Hill of the Nymphs and the Pnyx on the west and the Areopagus on the east, presents a much more coherent picture; and a number of interesting shrines are interspersed among the houses.

A little to the southwest of the agora, across the important street which bordered its south side, and at a point where several streets converged, the excavators found in 1966 a curious triangular structure which in any case could hardly be anything but a small shrine, and which was fortunately identified as such by a boundary marker.[39] The triangle is equi-

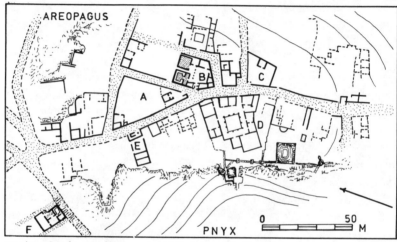

55. Area Southwest of Areopagus (J. E. Jones, after Judeich)

A. Enclosure with temple
B. House with mosaics
C. Amyneion

D. Late house and water system
E. Miniature temple and lesche
F. House on Pnyx Hill

lateral (ca. 8.6m), with the northern side running approximately east to west along the street. The wall was solidly built of blocks of Acropolis limestone in polygonal style. There is no sign of an entrance, and the triangle was probably an *abaton*, an "untrodden" area normally inaccessible to worshipers. An open *temenos* would also be required of course, and this probably consisted of ground to the east, west, and south, entered by a gateway in a wall which ran eastward from the corner of the triangle.

[39] *Hesperia* 37, 1968, 58ff and 123; compare the shrine of the Tritopatreis, p. 259 below.

Other Shrines

The boundary stone, of Pentelic marble, stands *in situ* against the east end of the north side of the triangle (Fig. 59.2); at the west end of the same side is a socket for a similar marker. With brevity and economy infuriating to the modern investigator the stonecutter carved nothing more than TOHIERO, meaning "[this belongs to] the shrine," and omitted the name of the occupant. The fine letter forms indicate a date not long after the middle of the fifth century, and this is probably the time when the triangular structure was built. The cult, however, may have been much older. A massive rectangular foundation discovered at a lower level in the middle of the triangle, and dated probably in the sixth century, may well belong to an earlier altar.

No dedications have been found to give a clue to the character of the deity. The form of the sanctuary is very appropriate for a *heroon*, the shrine of a hero rather than an Olympian god. The Athenians were much given to the cult of the heroized dead, and there were many hero shrines in the city, some of great men like Theseus, some of obscure and shadowy figures whose character was mysterious even to the ancients.[40] Beneath the triangular enclosure two small circular pits cut in bedrock may well mark the place occupied by ash urns; and in the surrounding area a number of burials of the Geometric period were found, notably one of a lady of wealth and rank, buried about 850 B.C., with her fine gold ornaments which included an exquisitely worked pair of earrings. A little to the south of the triangle a curious elliptical structure, comparable in size and shape to the peribolos of Nymphe, had already been found many years ago.[41] It may be dated in the eighth century B.C.; at first it was thought to be an oval house, but it now seems more probable that it was a sacred enclosure; above its ruins was found a votive deposit of the seventh century, containing figurines, vases, and plaques. There is, however, no evidence to show a direct continuity between this ancient cult and that of the triangular shrine.

The identity of the hero is purely conjectural. Not far to the west of the site a little marble plaque was found, carved with an eye in relief, and bearing an inscribed dedication, which may be dated in the third or second century B.C., to the Heros Iatros, but the healing shrine of this Doctor Hero was probably near the shrine of Theseus, which was prob-

[40] For the cults probably connected with ancient burials see *Hesperia* 22, 1953, 47; 24, 1955, 195, 202; 27, 1958, 148ff; 35, 1966, 48; p. 62 above.
[41] *Hesperia* 2, 1933, 614ff, 636ff; *The Athenian Agora: A Guide*, 2d edn 1962, 154f.

ably to the east of the agora.[42] There was also a certain Heros Strategos, Hero General; a dedication to him has been found in the agora, and his cult may have been associated with the Strategeion, which was in the region southwest of the agora;[43] but again it would be rash to place him in the triangular shrine.

Continuing southward one traverses the "industrial district," with its workshops and houses. There were Mycenean chamber tombs cut in the hillside to the west, but these were apparently forgotten in classical times. The main street continues to climb and curve around the southwestern foot of the Areopagus; and at this point, on the western side, to the right as one ascends, one can see the foundations of a *naiskos* or miniature temple, with a circular altar base in front of it.[44] The little building is only about 2m wide east to west and 2.5m deep north to south, but the socle is well built of solid masonry. The south end is open, and there is no porch; thus it represents an even simpler form of shrine than the temple of Artemis. Presumably it stood in a small precinct and housed a cult statue, but there is no evidence to show who the occupant was. There were no doubt many tiny temples like this in Athens, and another has in fact been found more recently on the hillside to the southwest, on the saddle between the Pnyx and the Hill of Philopappos. A little of the superstructure has survived, including the upper part of a small pediment. The little shrine in the valley below, originally built in the sixth century, was encroached upon in the fourth by a rectangular building identified by two inscribed boundary stones as a *lesche*, a kind of lounge or club room. Whether this had any connection with the ancient cult we cannot say; but the use of boundary markers would seem to indicate that it was on sacred ground.

On the opposite side of the street was a much larger precinct, triangular in form, measuring about 45m on its longest side, and enclosed by a good solid wall.[45] A cross wall cut off a much smaller triangle at the south end, and in this was a small temple—small, but not minute like those we have just been examining; it measured 3.96m by 5.2m and had a porch

---

[42] *Hesperia* 17, 1948, 39. For the Heros Iatros see Demosthenes 18.129; 19.249; cf. *Agora* III 115; *Agora* XIV 121, 125; C. Kerenyi, *Asklepios*, London 1960, 72ff.

[43] *Agora* III 176; p. 46 above.

[44] Judeich 299. Judeich suggests that there was also a shrine of Zeus Xenios (god of strangers or guests) hereabouts; it is attested by a boundary stone found built into the wall of the *lesche* mentioned above, *IG* I² 886, which shows that the shrine belonged to a particular *phratria* or clan, called Thymaitis.

[45] Judeich 291ff; Hill 192f.

56. Miniature Temple and Altar Base Southwest of Areopagus (Photo: M. Vernardos)

facing south. The occupant of this shrine has been the subject of much dispute; it now seems unlikely that it was the ancient and famous shrine of Dionysos in Limnai (in the Marshes),[46] but there is evidence of a

[46] See p. 172 above. Travlos *PDA* 274 places here Herakles Alexikakos, following A. Frickenhaus, *AthMitt* 36, 1911, 113-44, who drew attention to a base for a four-

Dionysiac cult. At the moment we are concerned only with its general form and its setting and place in the scheme of this quarter of Athens. Streets bordered it on all sides, the main thoroughfare on one side and side streets on the other two. Across the streets to east and west are remains of houses, except where the tiny temple stood.

Still farther south and still on the east side of the main street, at a point opposite a small fountain house, which probably served this locality, was another precinct which is fortunately identified by a number of inscribed dedications as belonging to one Amynos, the Helper, a hero who had powers of healing.[47] The sanctuary was an irregular quadrilateral, narrowing towards the south, enclosed by a wall of blocks of various shapes. On the west was the main street, on the north a narrow street which led up towards the Acropolis; on the other side houses seem to have been adjacent. One notes again how the shape of the precinct was determined by peculiar local circumstances, in contrast with the neat rectangular enclosure which one finds in well-planned cities. The total area was about 250 sq.m. The entrance was at the north end of the west side, and was later provided with a porch of two marble columns. A healing shrine needed water, and in the middle of the area was a well, whose water was augmented by a conduit leading from the great aqueduct built by the tyrants in the sixth century to supply southern Athens. The first excavators thought that they detected remains of a small covered shrine or chapel set against the eastern precinct wall; but further examination seems to have shown that there was nothing more than a retaining wall for a terrace. At this point part of a marble table for offerings was found, decorated with snakes.

Among the dedications were several of the type customary in healing shrines, representations of parts of the human body. The inscriptions, mostly of the fourth century B.C. but extending down to the second, show that one of the religious corporations which called themselves *orgeones* was concerned with the maintenance of the shrine, and that Amynos was closely associated in cult with Asklepios, and with one Dexion, who

---

columned structure such as is found on votive reliefs of this hero; but such a structure was not necessarily confined to Herakles shrines; and the identification seems to me to be incompatible with the inscription cited above, p. 187. For *tetrastyla* cf. D. W. Rupp, *AJA* 78, 1974, 176.

[47] Judeich 289; Hill 193; Travlos *PDA* 76ff. I am grateful to Professor Walter Graham, who has re-examined the area in connection with the houses, for additional information sent by letter. For inscriptions see *IG* II² 1252, 1253, 4365, 4385 (probably also 4386 and 4387), 4422, 4424, 4435, 4457.

was said to be the poet Sophokles sanctified after his death and added to the list of healing heroes at Athens.[48]

Finally, if after reaching the head of the valley one bends round eastward, south of the Areopagus, and reaches the southwestern slopes of the Acropolis, one finds yet another curious little shrine, discovered a few years ago when the area was being cleared and investigated before the construction of a more convenient and handsome approach for modern playgoers to the theater of Herodes.[49] It comprises an elliptical enclosure, happily identified by dedications and an inscribed boundary marker as belonging to an obscure personage known as Nymphe, the Nymph or Bride. The site is nearly 180m from the southwestern cliffs, and the shrine is not one of those which were immediately dependent on the Acropolis. Indeed it stood in an area occupied mainly by houses in the fifth century and in Hellenistic and Roman times, and these have left remains in the form of wall socles, wells, cisterns, and waterpipes. In the fourth century the house immediately above the shrine to the north was abandoned, and the space was used as a small open square, supported by a retaining wall strongly built of large blocks of poros. Thus we have a situation not unlike that of the shrines southwest of the Areopagus.

The *peribolos* measured about 12m north to south by about 8m east to west. The wall is best preserved on the west and south, and reaches a height of 1.10m; it is made of irregular blocks of limestone of various sizes, which no doubt originally carried an upper structure of unbaked brick. When it was built is not clear, perhaps towards the end of the sixth century. Even this simple enclosure does not represent the most primitive form of the shrine. The masses of pottery found on the site show that the cult went back to an earlier date, when presumably the shrine was marked off by some less solid means. The enclosure contained an altar, of which traces of the foundations have been found, and votive stelai or squared upright pillars of marble, which must have carried offerings to the deity. One of these was found standing in its place on a base, another fallen (it has now been set up again). A marble fragment which was found nearby represents the draped left leg of a woman. It is of excellent work-

[48] See p. 182 above. O. Walter, in *Geras A. Keramopoullou*, Athens 1953, dissociates Sophokles-Dexion from the Amyneion and would have his shrine on the south slope of the Acropolis. Note that there was yet another healing shrine, of Zeus Hypsistos, on the Pnyx up above; see Judeich 393, 396; *Agora* III 124; *GRBS* 5, 1964, 176; Travlos *PDA* 569ff.

[49] *Ergon* 1957 (for 1956) 9ff; 1958 (for 1957) 5ff; 1960 (for 1959) 157ff; *AJA* 62, 1958, 321. M. Ervin, in *Archeion Pontou* 22, 1958, 129–66; Travlos *PDA* 361ff.

57. Shrine of Nymphe; behind, wall of Roman house; above, Odeion of Herodes (Photo: M. Vernardos)

manship of the late fifth century; and if, as is quite probable, it belonged to the cult statue, the little shrine received a notable embellishment at this time.

The name of the deity was first revealed by graffiti on some of the dedicatory vases, and then confirmed by a stone marker, found not actually *in situ* but undoubtedly belonging to the shrine. It bears an inscription which shows that it was a Boundary of the Shrine of Nymphe, cut in fine letters which may be dated late in the fifth century B.C. The provision of such markers commonly indicates some clearing up or reorganization of a sacred spot, and this evidence, possibly combined with the new statue, seems to show that the old shrine was the object of some attention in this period. The cult continued, to judge by the dedications, until the second century B.C., and then it ceased, at least on this spot. It may be that the shrine suffered badly in the destruction wrought at Athens by Sulla in 86 B.C. In general, as we know from archaeological (especially epigraphical) and literary sources, the Athenians showed remarkable piety and pertinacity in maintaining ancient cults in late Hellenistic and Roman times. In this case the cult may have been transferred

58. View from Acropolis down Southwest Slope; bronze-casting pit; behind, Odeion of Herodes, with shrine of Nymphe to left (Photo: M. Vernardos)

to one of the shrines higher up on the Acropolis slope, perhaps that of Aphrodite Pandemos (Goddess of all the People); this is suggested by one of the late inscriptions on the theater seats, which reads, "(This is the seat of) the priestess of Aphrodite Pandemos and Nymphe."[50] In the old *temenos* there was no temple or other buildings to restore when prosperity returned in the time of Augustus; the site was forgotten and built over.

It is by no means clear who this Nymphe was, or what name one should attach to her, if indeed one should give her a particular name at all. Suggestions have been put forward—that she was Oreithyia, who was carried off by Boreas the North Wind, or Aglauros, daughter of Kekrops, or Kreousa, daughter of Erechtheus and mother of Ion, the eponymous ancestor of the Ionian race; or the Bride of Zeus Meilichios, the "gentle" god[51]—this title was a euphemism for Zeus in the character of chthonian or underworld deity, who had several shrines at Athens. For this last identification a little evidence is provided by the discovery

[50] *IG* ii² 5149; cf. A. N. Oikonomides, *The Two Agoras in Ancient Athens*, Chicago 1964, 7, 16, 22.

[51] By G. Daux, *BCH* 82, 1958, 367; cf. n. 37 above.

in the shrine of a marble stele of the late fourth century, carved in relief with a bearded snake (a creature commonly associated with this god and indicative of his chthonian nature), and inscribed with a dedication to Zeus Meilichios. Perhaps one might call the deity Hera Meilichia; but for cult purposes she was known simply as Nymphe, and one cannot go safely beyond that. The masses of votive debris comprise vases of various types, painted plaques, masks, and figurines; particularly characteristic is the *loutrophoros*, a tall-necked water jar used for the bridal bath, and the discovery of large numbers of these shows that the deity was intimately connected with marriage.

Raising one's eyes from the little *peribolos* to the exquisite Doric forms of the Parthenon towering above, one encompasses the whole range of Athenian religious architecture from the simplest to the most sophisticated. In between are the small temples of which examples have been noted above. It might be said that plain walls and stone slabs hardly merit the name of architecture; but in fact these simple structures were an essential part of the architectural pattern of Athens; and they were scattered about the city.

Aristotle in the *Politics* (7.11.1) recommends that for dwellings of the gods a suitable place should be chosen, the same for all. Pausanias (9.22.2) praises the people of Tanagra in Boiotia because they have their houses in one place, their shrines in a separate place, up above, "a pure and holy spot away from men." At Athens such segregation was obviously not achieved or even desired. There is no reason why one should not accept the district which we have been examining as fairly typical. Some cities possessed what was called an Agora of the Gods, a closely packed assemblage of important cults.[52] At Athens the Acropolis was an elevated place, pure and holy and aloof from common human affairs; and several different spots might be considered in some sense Agoras of the Gods. But gods and heroes also lived in many modest or even humble abodes on ordinary streets as next door neighbors to ordinary citizens. If one wishes to understand the character of Athenian *deisidaimonia*, one must look at the whole city, with even more thoroughness than Pausanias, and at the many unpretentious shrines set in diverse places.

---

[52] R. Martin, *L'Agora Grecque*, Paris 1951, 169–74.

General Note. This chapter is partly based on an article "Minor Shrines in Ancient Athens," *Phoenix* 24, 1970, 283–95, where further details and references will be found.

1. "Of the Pool of Athena"

2. "Of the Shrine"

3. "Of Kerameikos"

4. "Of the Garden of the Muses"

59. Sacred Boundary Stones, 1-4 (See 5 on overleaf) Photos: 1) German Archaeological Institute; 2, 3, 5) Agora Excavations; 4) Eugene Vanderpool

59.5. "Of Zeus Exops . . ." (?)

CHAPTER VIII

Theaters

In modern times the great theater of fifth-century Athens, the theater of Dionysos, the scene of the productions of Aeschylus and Sophokles, Euripides, and Aristophanes, has almost vanished from before our eyes. At one time its form seemed sufficiently clear and substantial, though architecturally simple. Now, after repeated down-dating of the scanty remains, only faint outlines or vestiges are left, seeming to mock the earnest student of this most vital time and place in theatrical history. But one need not despair. This same elusiveness, this negative character of the evidence, may in the end provide an essential clue to the nature of the theater in its greatest days.

"The subject is one from which the boldest may recoil," says D. S. Robertson in his *Greek and Roman Architecture* (164); yet a long series of ingenious scholars have attempted it, with varying results. The difficulty is due in part to the fact that the south slope of the Acropolis was investigated in the extensive excavations of the last century, when in a great wave of archaeological activity, inspired by a determination to disinter the principal monuments of the ancient city from later and especially Turkish accretions, enthusiasm outran technical skill and method, and the material was not handled with the scrupulous care of the modern archaeologist. A fairly satisfactory sequence of monuments was established, from crude archaic retaining walls to the elaborate theatrical architecture and sculpture of the Roman theater; precise dating was much more difficult and has remained throughout a subject of dispute.

Before looking further at problems and solutions, one should consider the word *theatron* and see what it meant to the Greeks and to the Athenians in particular. A *theatron* was any place where people gathered to witness a *thea* or spectacle. The most convenient site was on a slope where the spectators could sit or stand above a flat area where the performance could take place. Athens, like most Greek cities, had several *theatra*. Such spectacles always had a certain religious character and included dances, processions, and other religious rites. The plays were performed in the worship of Dionysos. Athletic games were held in honor

(203)

of various gods and heroes. And wherever a group of people, large or small, assembled to see anything of this kind, there was a *theatron*. We hear of *ikria*, the wooden seating used in primitive theaters to improve the natural site, in the hero shrine of King Kodros in southeastern Athens.[1] The huge stadium was a specialized form of theater, elongated to adapt it to the 180m long racetrack. Xenophon speaks of a *theatron* in the Lyceum, the famous gymnasium to the east of the city, attached to the shrine of Apollo Lykeios, where cavalry displays were held;[2] we know approximately where this *theatron* was—in the region of the present Syntagma Square; the rising ground to the east, where the Old Palace stands, would be a convenient place for the watching crowds. One would call the great assembly place on the Pnyx hill a "theater" and describe the two successive council chambers in the agora, the city center, as small roofed "theaters," seating the Council of 500; but this would be a metaphorical usage, since these places were used for serious political assemblies, not festal gatherings and spectacles.

Strictly speaking, *theatron* means the auditorium, where the *theatai* sat (oddly, the Greek word lays the emphasis on seeing, the Latin on hearing); but since this was by far the greater part, the word came to be used of the whole arrangement. In a *theatron* used for plays, the only other essential element was the *orchestra*, the flat "dancing-place" used by the performers, which might be backed by a *skene*—the very name, meaning "tent" or "booth" (including the flimsy structures used by small traders in the agora) proclaims its originally light construction and simple form.

The theater in the agora, northwest of the Acropolis, is even more evanescent than the early theater of Dionysos on the southeast slope. Certainly in the wider Greek sense the agora or part of it was indeed a *theatron* on occasion. Various rites took place there, watched by the citizens; processions passed through, choruses sang and danced, the cavalry gave displays, and possibly athletic games were held there before a specialized stadium was constructed.[3] The ground had a natural gentle slope down from south to north; but to give spectators a better view of the shows *ikria* were erected, structures consisting of wooden planks set on wooden uprights. There is clear evidence for an *orchestra* or dancing place somewhere in the middle of the agora, possibly on the site where in a much later and architecturally more sophisticated age, Agrippa, Au-

[1] *IG* I² 94; p. 168 above.   [2] *Hipparch.* 3.7; p. 228 below.
[3] Xenophon *Hipparch.* 3.2; *Agora* XIV 95, 121, 150; H. A. Thompson, "The Panathenaic Festival," *AA* 1961, 224–31; p. 38 above (Anthippasia).

gustus' great minister, built an Odeion or covered theater. Pindar probably has this *orchestra* in mind when in his dithyramb in honor of the
Athenians he invites the Olympian gods to "come to the dance, in holy
Athens, approaching the navel stone (*omphalos*) of the city and the famous richly adorned agora";[4] the *omphalos* is very probably the Altar of
the Twelve Gods, of which identifiable remains have been found, in the
middle of the northern part of the agora. Whether we can assume a regular theater, and fully dramatic performances in it, is more problematical,
and involves the disputed interpretation of obscure notes in ancient commentators. Several years ago N.G.L. Hammond carefully reconsidered
the question;[5] accepting the theater in the agora, he tentatively recon-
structs it in the middle of the west side, showing how certain simple
archaic buildings may have contributed to the scenic background, with
the *ikria* facing them from the east. This is an ingenious and acceptable
arrangement, but like other suggestions it must remain hypothetical. Another area which seems to have had a certain theatral character is the
northwestern sector, backed by the Stoa Basileios; this was certainly the
scene of civic ceremonies and may have been used on more festal occasions.[6] Indeed one has to admit the possibility that the theater in the
agora, since it had no permanent and purpose-built structure and since
there was no identifiable shrine of Dionysos to which it might attach
itself,[7] may not always have been fitted out in the same place. In any
case we may think of this primitive theater, in which the plays of Thespis and perhaps the young Aeschylus may have been produced, as a
suitable segment of the agora, adapted for the occasion by very simple
means.

Postholes suitable for *ikria* have been found,[8] but they are mainly on

[4] Sandys, Loeb ed. 1927, 552; *Agora* III 122; XIV 127, 133.

[5] "The Conditions of Dramatic Production to the Death of Aeschylus," *GRBS* 13,
1972, 387–450.

[6] I owe this suggestion to H. A. Thompson.

[7] The Lenaion, the shrine of Dionysos Lenaios, with its "big enclosure," remains
elusive. Judeich 293ff placed it in the region southwest of the agora; so did C. Anti,
Teatri Greci Arcaici, Padua 1947, 202ff, associating an early theater with it. A. W.
Pickard-Cambridge, *Dramatic Festivals*, Oxford 1968, 37ff, places it in the agora,
but the evidence depends on very obscure scholia. It remains possible that the
Lenaion was associated with the other shrines of Dionysos in southeast Athens;
I have discussed the problem, inconclusively, in *Hesperia* 34, 1965, 72–76 and *Agora*
XIV 128.

[8] *Agora* XIV 126; on *ikria* see R. Martin, *Revue de Philologie* 31, 1957, 72ff; cf.
D. Ohly, *AA* 1965, 309.

the line of the great Panathenaic Way, which cuts diagonally across the agora from northwest to southeast, and are probably to be associated with the Panathenaic procession depicted in the Parthenon frieze. The steps in front of various buildings, and a broad set of steps built into the hillside on the west, below the temple of Hephaistos, were no doubt used as vantage points for viewing spectacles in the agora; and also, on a grander scale, the broad terraces raised in front of the long stoas built in the Hellenistic period on east and south.[9] Thus the agora retained in successive ages and in different ways its theatral character.

There is no good reason to assume that any of the plays which we have, beginning with the *Persians* of Aeschylus (472 B.C.) was produced anywhere but in the theater on the south slope of the Acropolis, attached to the ancient shrine of Dionysos Eleuthereus. The site was excellent, because of its contours and the shelter which the Acropolis provided against cold north winds. For a long time this theater too was nothing more than a very simple adaptation of the natural terrain, namely the moderately steep slope which lies below the abrupt rocks. As the modern visitor sits in the seat of the priest of Dionysos and views the great stone auditorium, the elaborately paved orchestra, the sculptured stagefront, and the complicated remains of the successive scenebuildings, he has to bear in mind that almost nothing of all this was there when, for example, Aeschylus produced the *Oresteia* in 458 B.C.; the question now is whether there was much more even when Aristophanes produced the *Frogs* in 405 B.C. On almost every point in the interpretation of the remains there has been long and brisk controversy. Archaeologists have at least arrived at a generally acceptable series of phases in the architectural development of the theater; but absolute dating has been subject to a kind of sliding scale, with a general tendency to slide downwards, i.e. in the direction of later dates. What follows gives in very sketchy outline the principal stages, as attested by the remains, in the growth of the theater down to the fourth century B.C.

A. A little to the northeast of the small archaic temple which housed the ancient statue of Dionysos Eleuthereus, a curved wall was built to create a terrace and provide a flat space for the orchestra. This is the commonly accepted interpretation of certain segments of masonry which survive, the most significant being a curving line of six polygonal limestone blocks on the southeast side. The slope above provided the auditorium, and we can assume that it began to be molded into its characteristic

[9] *Agora* XIV 67, 71, 104, 126, 149; pp. 78f above.

shape and to be provided with wood seating. Early scene structures must have been light and ephemeral.

B. A solid foundation of large blocks of red conglomerate stone (HH) was built, running more than 60m. east to west, to carry a kind of dual and double-purpose wall. On the south the wall was the back of a long colonnade, facing southwards and forming the north side of the large irregular enclosure of the shrine of Dionysos, which in this period received a second, larger temple, standing a little to the south of the old one.[10] The western end of the colonnade was made into a separate chamber, crowded awkwardly against the north wall of the old temple. On the north side, besides acting as a retaining wall for the orchestra terrace, the long wall provided support for wooden structures used for scenic purposes, as is shown by a series of slots cut into the blocks in the central section, clearly for the insertion of the upright timbers. How extensive these structures were, and what form they took, is anything but clear, and many different restorations have been offered. From a point somewhat west of center a solid foundation of conglomerate blocks, about 7m long and 3m deep, projects forward onto the terrace. It may have supported a central feature of the *skene*, or a platform to provide additional height when required by the action, or indeed both; or again it may have carried the *bema* or speakers' platform used when the Ekklesia met in the theater instead of on the Pnyx.[11] It is generally agreed that a high stage, difficult of access from the orchestra, would have been out of place but, as Arnott shows, a lower platform, easily accessible from orchestra level, was scenically effective. The orchestra seems to have been pushed northward a little, and there must have been some remodeling of the auditorium.

C. At last a permanent and substantial stone *skene* was built, in the form of a building over 46m long, with its back to the old *skene* wall and the stoa, and columnar structures called *paraskenia* projecting forwards towards the auditorium at a short distance from either end. Details of the plan are not altogether clear, but in general it may be thought of as a well-built, enlarged, and sophisticated reproduction of a typical and serviceable form of its wooden predecessor. There was still no permanent raised stage, though a wooden platform may have been set between the paraskenia. The orchestra was still simply an area of hard earth, but its circular form was defined, except on the south, and at the same time

[10] See p. 183 above.
[11] See p. 62 above; I owe this suggestion also to H. A. Thompson.

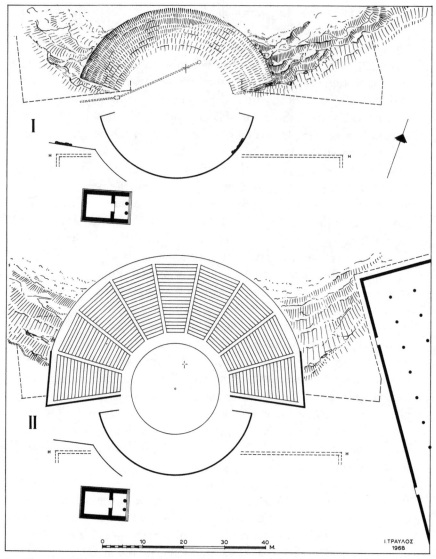

60. Theater of Dionysos, Restored Plans, I) late 6th c.; II) 5th c. (Travlos *PDA* 540 fig. 667)

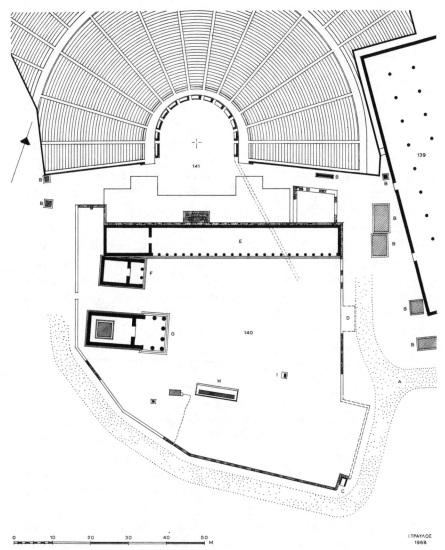

61. Theater of Dionysos, Restored Plan, 4th c. (Travlos *PDA* 541 fig. 678)

the drainage of the theater was improved, by a well-constructed stone channel. The auditorium, repeatedly remodeled and perhaps already provided with a limited range of stone seating, was now given more definite and permanent shape, with embankments and solid retaining walls at the ends, and stone seating on a vast scale. Divided by horizontal passages or *diazomata*, of which the upper was made continuous with the *peripatos*, an ancient path encircling the whole Acropolis, and by stairways which divided it into "wedges," it stretched far up towards the cliffs of the Acropolis, and could hold an audience of 14,000.

There was a time when weighty authorities placed Phase A well back in the sixth century, B in the first part of the fifth; on this hypothesis one might call A the theater of Thespis, B the theater of Aeschylus. More recent writers have generally agreed that A should be dated at the end of the sixth century, B in the latter part of the fifth. Pickard-Cambridge, whose great trilogy established itself as the bible of students of the Greek theater, calls B the Periklean theater, C being the fourth century theater, built after the great days of tragedy were over, and completed by Lycurgus, who played a leading role in Athenian affairs in the third quarter of the fourth century, and was highly honored by the Athenians for his notable public works.[12]

But a few years ago Greek archaeologists carefully re-examined the site and, on the basis of archaeological evidence, such as the pottery associated with the remains, came to the conclusion that the second temple of Dionysos, hitherto dated towards the end of the fifth century, was in fact built not before the middle of the fourth.[13] This in itself is surprising. We are told that the splendid gold and ivory statue of the god which stood in the temple was made by the most distinguished of Pheidias' pupils, Alkamenes, who worked in the latter part of the fifth century; and as in the case of the Parthenon, if one was making an expensive and elaborate statue of this kind, it was advisable and normal to have a worthy temple waiting to receive it. However, we have to accept the archaeological evidence and assume that during the interval the statue was housed in some makeshift manner; it cannot have stood in the smaller older temple with the primitive statue. The archaeologists go further, and though the evidence is not so precise (as far as it has been published in brief reports) and seems to be based mainly on construction and orienta-

[12] *Theatre of Dionysus* 15ff, 134ff.

[13] J. Travlos, *Praktika* (Greek Archaeological Society) 1951, 41–52; *PDA* 537ff; P. Kalligas, *Deltion* 18, 1965, B1, 12–18.

tion, they maintain that along with the temple the stoa and the supporting wall and foundation for the scene building (B) must also be down-dated into the fourth century. Much use was made in these structures of a red conglomerate stone, which was not used on a large scale before the fourth century, but from then onwards was a favorite material.[14] Travlos now attributes the *skene* of Phase B to Lycurgus, and regards C as a reconstruction carried out later in the century, though in his plan he seems to credit Lycurgus with a well-built auditorium.[15] However, it is still possible within narrower limits to push things up and down a little on the sliding scale; and one might prefer to place B somewhat earlier and assign C mainly to Lycurgus, assuming that under his guidance the Athenians at long last built a theater which was a deliberate and satisfying architectural creation. No doubt the process of construction was spread out over a long period. Lycurgus, we know, was a kind of Minister of Works, and he sought to provide the city with worthy public buildings to match its fine temples.

The down-dating to the fourth century of even the earliest and simplest permanent building on the site makes a notable new contribution to theater history. Among other things it strengthens one's conviction that the temporary scene structures of the fifth century were not so elaborate and imposing in fact as in certain imaginative reconstructions (one should bear in mind that timber was in great demand and limited supply). It may seem astonishing nowadays that when tragedy and comedy had reached the level of supreme art the Athenians still did not take the trouble to design and construct a comparably fine setting. This is because we think in terms of later theaters, ancient and modern, substantial works of architecture; we must heed Hammond's warning and "dismiss from mind all preconceptions and in particular the physical image of the later theater." While recognizing important differences, we should think rather in terms of outdoor shows—plays, pageants, *son et lumière*, and such like —in which the production makes the best use it can of a given natural and historical setting, with modest adaptation and temporary aids, rather than a purpose-built theater. The slope between the Acropolis wall and the shrine of Dionysos was very appropriate. The crucial fact is that in the Periklean Age the Athenians still concentrated their artistic efforts and their financial resources in the temples of the gods and were content not

[14] See p. 273 below.

[15] *PDA* 541, 548. Erika Simon, *Das Antike Theater*, Heidelberg 1972, 11ff, takes a view similar to the one given above.

only with modest houses but with comparatively simple public buildings. The law courts provide an interesting parallel example. The great
democratic courts were a characteristic and dominant feature of Athenian
life; yet their real-life dramas, which in fact had a great influence on the
theater, were played, before an audience consisting of a jury of many
hundreds, not in splendid halls of justice but in simple unroofed enclosures with meager furnishings, as far as we can make out from the
equally exiguous and problematical remains.

Of course one has to admit that the stones may not tell the whole
story, even in outline, that there may have been phases in the development which are not represented by them. To go back to the beginning,
Webster has assumed that from the very first tragedy was performed on
the south slope, and that there must have been an elementally simple
theater, in front of the old temple of Dionysos, even before the rough
stones of Phase A were laid.[16] Again, Hammond draws attention to the
fact that the old terrace wall is represented by short sections towards
either end, with a gap of about 18m between. This might be thought to
suggest that most of the wall was pulled down to make way for a new
structure, perhaps a *skene* which was comparatively solid and permanent,
even though it has vanished without trace; and Aeschylus, who is said
to have improved the *skene*, may have had such a structure available for
the *Oresteia* in 458 B.C.[17] This must remain a hypothesis unless more positive evidence appears; and in any case such a *skene* must have been comparatively small and simple in form and construction.

Another very ingenious suggestion made by Hammond calls for consideration; indeed it may give a clue to the essential character of the early
Athenian theater. He notes that on the eastern side of the orchestra in the
theater of Dionysos there appears at one time to have been a rocky outcrop, which was later cut away to level the ground. This rocky platform,
he suggests, was brought into service for scenic effects by Aeschylus and
his contemporaries, supplementing the simple *skene* of the day; it was
used by actors and even chorus as occasion arose, and in fact is the *pagos*
or hill which repeatedly figures in certain plays, namely the *Persians*, the
Seven against Thebes, the *Suppliants*, and the *Prometheus*. This again is
a hypothesis, but an ingenious and attractive one.

The account given above is admittedly sketchy and incomplete. Many
interesting and disputable points have been evaded or passed over lightly.

[16] "Le Théâtre grec et son décor," *L'Antiquité Classique*, 32, 1963, 562–70.
[17] See Hammond, *GRBS* 13, 1972, 413ff.

The perplexing literary and archaeological evidence will no doubt long continue to be the subject of constant reinterpretation. But one central fact can be stated with greater conviction than before—the theater of the great Athenian dramatists of the fifth century was amazingly simple in form; it was not so much a great work of architecture as a modest adaptation of a fine natural site.[18] Even in its most sophisticated later form the theater still bore the stamp of its simple origins.

This is not the place to give anything more than a brief mention of the curious contrivances by means of which the meager structural elements were supplemented for purposes of production—scene painting on panels (no doubt suggestive and symbolical rather than realistic, and leaving the poet plenty of scope for effective word pictures); the *theologeion* on which gods appeared aloft; the crane or flying machine; the *ekkuklema* or rolling platform. Just what these were and how and when they were used has been the subject of further long and inconclusive dispute; but we can assume that such devices were quite simple, sometimes even crude in their effect—Aristophanes saw in some of them possibilities of comic caricature no less than in the peculiarities of tragic diction.

Even in its Lycurgan form the theater of Dionysos, though impressive, did not attain the completeness, elegance, and symmetry of the great theater of Epidauros, built by Polykleitos in the fourth century to a single harmonious design. It remained slightly irregular in outline and odd in arrangement to the end. In particular the northwest angle of the Odeion, the large rectangular hall built by Perikles to house musical contests and the preliminaries of the dramatic festivals, cut in deeply and prevented the semicircle of the auditorium from being completed on the east. Architecturally, the most important theater in Greece, the home of the greatest drama, was far from being the finest.

The element of spectacle was provided largely by the costuming and equipment of actors and chorus; in particular the presentation of the chorus was one of the "liturgies" or jobs entrusted to wealthy and—some-

---

[18] C. Anti, in *Teatri Greci Arcaici*, and with L. Polacco in *Nuovi Ricerche sui Teatri Greci Arcaici*, Padua 1969, argues that through the 5th century a rectilinear arrangement of seating was found in Greek theaters, including those in Athens. This problem is difficult and the evidence obscure, but in any case our view of the essential simplicity of the 5th century theater is not affected. Anti and Polacco even deny the relevance of the curved wall for the old orchestra, but do not say for what else it could have been built. Note also R. Ginouvès, *Le Théâtre à Gradins Droits et l'Odéon d'Argos*, Paris 1972; and E. Gebhard, *Hesperia* 44, 1975, 428ff.

62. Theater from Acropolis (Photo: Alison Frantz)

times—public-spirited citizens, who vied with one another in putting on a good show.

The later history of the theater can be summarized with even greater brevity, though in every phase difficulties of precise dating and detailed interpretation of the complicated and superimposed remains continue to proliferate. At some time in the Hellenistic period, a *proskenion* was built, a row of columns between the *paraskenia*, supporting a platform which was no doubt used as a high stage in a time when except in revivals of old plays the chorus was no longer important and contact between stage and orchestra not essential.

In Roman times a stage building was erected in the ornate architectural style of the period, the orchestra was elaborately paved with marble slabs, and a stage lower and much deeper than the *proskenion* cut off a segment of the orchestra. These features were alien to the character of the old theater, and even more so was a stone barrier several feet high, erected between auditorium and orchestra probably to provide some protection when gladiatorial contests were exhibited. In the Hellenistic and Roman periods the theater of Dionysos had superseded the Pnyx, the political

(214)

"theater" in western Athens, which was itself a simple nonarchitectural adaptation of a convenient hillside, as the usual assembly place of the Athenian people; and the philosopher Apollonios of Tyana,[19] who lived in the first century after Christ, invited to address the Athenians, is said to have refused to appear in a place polluted by the shedding of real blood.

Meanwhile the city had acquired several other buildings of theatral type. The construction of the stadium of Athens, to the southeast of the city, in a convenient trough between the hill Ardettos and a neighboring hill, was credited to Lycurgus, probably about 330 B.C.[20] In the second century A.D. the wealthy Herodes Atticus provided marble seating throughout, sufficient for a crowd of 50,000, stretching in a very slight curve along both sides, open at the northwest end towards the city, joined by a semicircle at the southeast end to form a vast "theater." The stadium which one now sees, built on the occasion of the first modern Olympic games in 1896, represents a fairly successful attempt to reproduce Herodes' building. We must imagine Lycurgus' stadium as something very much simpler, less impressive in fact than his theater; probably what he did was to level the floor of the valley, and build terraces and embankments where required, providing stone seating only for a privileged few.

Athens had three buildings known by the name of Odeion or Music Hall. First by several centuries came the Periklean building mentioned above, adjoining the theater of Dionysos.[21] The scanty remains, still not fully investigated, show that it was nearly square (just over 62 by 68m)

[19] Philostratos *Life of Apollonios* 4.22.

[20] *IG* ii[2] 457; Ps. Plutarch *Lives* 841d, 852c; Pausanias 1.19.6 (Herodes); P. Graindor, *Hérode Atticus*, Cairo 1930, 181–84; Judeich 417–19; H. A. Harris, *Greek Athletes and Athletics*, London 1964, 136ff; Travlos *PDA* 498ff.

The stadium was used occasionally by the Boule and possibly the Ekklesia; see B. D. Meritt, on *IG* ii[2] 893; *AJP* 78, 1957, 377ff; O. W. Reinmuth, *Hesperia* 43, 1974, 246 and 254.

The Hippodromos, presumably a kind of large stadium for horseraces, has commonly been located near Phaleron, Judeich 456; but S. Benton, "Echelos' Hippodrome," *BSA* 67, 1972, 13–19, locates it near the Kolonos Hippios northwest of Athens.

[21] Plutarch *Perikles* 13.5–6 says that the Odeion was built in imitation of the tent of the Persian King, under the supervision of Perikles; but Vitruvius 5.9.1 ascribes it to Themistokles, who used timber from the Persian ships for the roof; cf. J. A. Davison, "Notes on the Panathenaia," *JHS* 78, 1958, 33–36. See also Judeich 306–8; O. Broneer, "The Tent of Xerxes and the Greek Theater," University of California, i, no. 12, 1944, 305–11; Travlos *PDA* 387.

with a forest of internal columns, which must have impaired visibility of the performance—till Roman times Greek architects were very limited in their methods of roofing very large halls.

The Odeion seen by Pausanias in the agora can be safely identified with the theater called Agrippeion after Augustus' great minister, built about 15 B.C.[22] Its nucleus was a roofed auditorium with curved seating for about 1,000, surrounded by two-storied galleries on three sides—east, south, and west—with a porch and foyer on the north and another foyer on the south, all built in elaborate architectural style. We know that it was used also as a lecture hall for sophists.

Finally, the same Herodes Atticus in the middle of the second century A.D. built a great Odeion at the west end of the south slope of the Acropolis as a memorial to his wife Regilla.[23] This had one important feature in common with the old theater—the auditorium was formed mainly by reshaping the natural hillside, not by erecting huge substructures in the Roman manner. Otherwise it was typical of the Roman imperial theater, with a lofty and ornate scene building, united into a single structure with the auditorium, the orchestra being cut down to a semicircle in the process. Since it is much better preserved and better suited to modern requirements, it is this theater which has been reconstituted, with extensive replacement of the marble seating, to accommodate modern productions. The auditorium holds more than 5000, and sitting in the packed audience, under the Attic sky, spellbound by the words of Oedipus or Electra, spoken with rare clarity and power, one catches something of the spirit of the original Athenian theater; but it still calls for an effort of the imagination to think away the fine architectural frame, and to put oneself in the position of a spectator at a Sophoklean "first night," sitting on a bench on the open hillside, looking across an orchestra of beaten earth to a veritable *skene*, with the Acropolis rock above and the temple of Dionysos below, and beyond it the plain of Attica stretching up to Hymettos and down to the sea. The whole setting was drawn into the dramatic scene rather than shut out or obliterated, and it was the proper setting for Attic drama, tragedy and comedy alike, which was an intimate part of the life of the whole Athenian people.

[22] H. A. Thompson, *Hesperia* 19, 1950, 31–141; *Agora* III 161f; *Agora* XIV 111–14. In the middle of the 2d century A.D. the north side was given an elaborate facade adorned with the figures of giants (eventually incorporated in the late gymnasium), and the auditorium was greatly reduced in size.

[23] P. Graindor, *Hérode Atticus*, Cairo 1930, 218–25; Judeich 326–28; Travlos *PDA* 378ff.

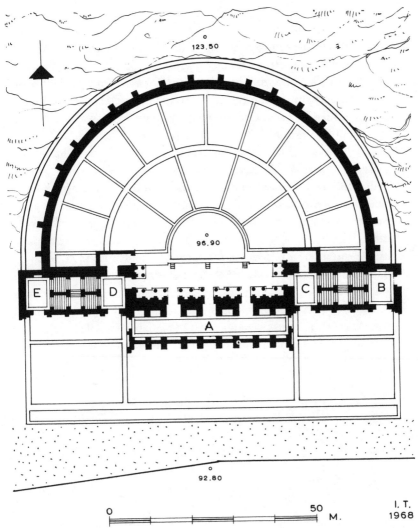

63. Odeion of Herodes Atticus, Restored Plan (J. Travlos, *PDA* 379, fig. 492)

BIBLIOGRAPHY

E. Fiechter, *Antike Theaterbauten, Das Dionysos-Theater in Athen*, Stuttgart 1935–36 (with supplement, 1950)

A. W. Pickard-Cambridge, *The Theatre of Dionysus in Athens*, Oxford 1946 (bibliography 272ff) (cf. *Dithyramb, Tragedy and Comedy*, 2d edn, ed. T.B.L. Webster, Oxford 1962; *Dramatic Festivals of Athens*, 2d edn, ed. D. Lewis and J. Gould, Oxford 1968)

W. B. Dinsmoor, "The Athenian Theater of the Fifth Century," in *Studies Presented to D. M. Robinson*, St. Louis 1951, 309–330

P. D. Arnott, *An Introduction to the Greek Theatre*, London 1959 *Greek Scenic Conventions*, Oxford 1962

M. Bieber, *History of the Greek and Roman Theater*, 2d edn Princeton 1961

T.B.L. Webster, *Greek Theatre Production*, 2d edn, London 1970

A. D. Trendall and T.B.L. Webster, *Illustrations of Greek Drama*, London 1971

Travlos, *PDA* 365ff, 537ff

Agora XIV, 111–14, 126–29

S. Melchinger, *Das Theater der Tragödie*, München 1974

CHAPTER IX

Gymnasia and Philosophical Schools

The three ancient and famous gymnasia of Athens were all attached to old suburban shrines. We are not particularly concerned with their obscure names or their cults at the moment. One may note, however, that the Academy was founded by or was the shrine of Akademos or Hekademos;[1] but it was sacred to Athena, and Zeus Morios or Kataibates, Prometheus, Hephaistos, Hermes, and Herakles were worshiped there, and an altar of Eros was set up at the entrance by a friend of the tyrants.[2] The use of the name in later writers is very flexible; it meant primarily the shrine, but by a natural extension it was used of the gymnasium, the school of Plato, of course, or of the district; and sometimes, improperly, of the cemetery on the way to the Academy, or of the Kerameikos.[3] The original cults on all three sites were no doubt very ancient, and perhaps one can reasonably assume that the gymnasia were archaic in origin, and that from early times the young men of Athens went out to the open spaces around these suburban shrines for military and athletic exercise. The Athenians themselves thought of the gymnasia as pre-Solonian. Demosthenes (24.114) says that Solon made a law that if anyone stole clothes from any of the three gymnasia he should be liable to the death penalty. Hipparchos, we are told, built a wall at the Academy, which became proverbial for an expensive job;[4] and archaic remains thought to belong to the gymnasium have been found. About the Lyceum authorities differ: Theopompos says it was founded by Peisistratos, Philochoros by Perikles, Pausanias and the author of the *Lives of the Ten Orators*, wrongly of course, by Lycurgus.[5] The third gymnasium, Kynosarges, was at least earlier than the time of Themistokles.

In the fifth century Kimon, as part of his program for increasing the amenities of Athens, made the Academy a kind of suburban park; it was

---

[1] This personage—man, hero, or god—may well be an artificial eponym derived from the old name; see Judeich 413; cf. J. Coldstream, *JHS* 96, 1976, 16.

[2] For the cults see Judeich 413; cf. Frazer on Pausanias 1.30; Travlos *PDA* 42.

[3] *Agora* III 221.

[4] Judeich 66, 413; below, p. 224.

[5] Harpokration, Hesychios, s.v.; Pausanias 1.29.16; Ps. Plutarch *Lives*, 841c.

formerly waterless and dry, says Plutarch (13.7), but Kimon made it a well-watered grove, equipped with running tracks and shady walks. Aristophanes gives a delightful picture of life in the gymnasium. The young man of healthy body and mind, he says in the *Clouds* (1005ff), will go down to the Academy, and beside the sacred olives will run off races with his modest friends, fragrant with bryony and *apragmosyne* (leisure), delighting in the springtime when the plane whispers to the elm. For Aristophanes all this healthy activity of clean-limbed young men makes a contrast with the clever chatter of the pale, weedy, sophisticated *habitués* of the agora. But the antithesis is artificial and unsound. No doubt in the fifth century the Academy was already making its contribution to the intellectual and philosophic development of Athens. Sophists, as we see in Plato, found promising material among the young men of the palaestra and the gymnasium no less than of the agora. Athletic exercises alternated with discussion on ethical and political themes. Sokrates himself made at least an occasional appearance in the Academy.[6]

When we come to the fourth century and Plato's school, we find that very little is known of the practical arrangement of the establishment. Diogenes says (3.5) that "he pursued philosophy at first in the Academy, then in the garden by the Kolonos," the nearby hill, and it is generally assumed that he set up school in the gymnasium, and then moved to his own house and garden.[7] Elsewhere (3.7) Diogenes simply says that after returning to Athens Plato "spent his time in the Academy, which is a suburban gymnasium." In any case there is evidence that the school continued to use the neighboring gymnasium as well as the private house and garden. In a fragment of the Middle Comedy poet Epikrates someone asks, "What are Plato and Speusippos and Menedemos up to now?"; and the answer is, "I saw a crowd of young men in the gymnasia of the Academy, earnestly trying to define whether a pumpkin is a vegetable, a grass, or a tree, while Plato stood benevolently by encouraging them."[8] One might say that Epikrates is no more evidence for Plato than Aristophanes for Sokrates; but it is inevitably implied that Plato with his pupils was a familiar figure in the gymnasium. Aelian (3.19) tells an illuminat-

---

[6] Plato *Lysis* 203 a; cf. Aelian *Varia Historia* 9.29. See R. G. Hoerber, *Phronesis* 4, 1959, 17ff on the scene of *Lysis*.

[7] Cf. *CP* 43, 1948, 130ff, a very critical review of H. Herter's *Platons Akademie*, Bonn, 1946. Here, as in *The Riddle of the Early Academy*, Berkeley and Los Angeles, 1945, 2, H. Cherniss gives salutary warnings to those who with slight evidence profess to know all about the arrangement and teaching of the school.

[8] J. W. Edmonds, *FAC* II, Leiden 1959, 355, Frag. 11.

ing story (one may assume in dealing with such anecdotal material that the stories are dubious but the setting may well contain authentic details). When Plato was old, on one occasion when Speusippos was ill and Xenokrates was away, Aristotle made himself so unpleasant that Plato left the outer *peripatos* and walked within with his companions. Xenokrates returned and was told that Plato was not ill but that Aristotle had made him leave the *peripatos* and he had withdrawn and was philosophizing in his own garden; Xenokrates turned Aristotle out and restored to Plato his customary place. This *peripatos* (walk) may have been in the gymnasium. In any case we appear to have a distinction between a more open and a more intimate place of instruction and study. Plato's famous lecture on the Good was a public lecture, and one may well imagine that it was given in the gymnasium.[9] Later, says Diogenes (4.9. 63), Karneades lectured there; he had a very loud voice and the gymnasiarch remonstrated with him for making so much noise. Cicero and his friends are apparently in the gymnasium when they point out the academic landmarks to one another. Thus we should probably think of the school as operating both in the private property and in the gymnasium.

The shrine of the Muses which Plato established was apparently in the gymnasium. The life by Olympiodoros says, "He set up a school in the Academy, marking off a part of this gymnasium as a *temenos* for the Muses"; another life says, "Plato dedicated a *temenos* to the Muses *in front* of the School."[10] Of course in a sense the school itself was a Mouseion, as were all philosophical schools, and in fact all schools, as Aischines shows (1. 10) when, speaking of the duties of teachers, he says they are concerned "with shrines of the Muses in the schools and shrines of Hermes in the gymnasia." Plato's garden was adjacent to the Academy.[11] Diogenes says it was beside the Kolonos (3.5); now the Kolonos Hippios is some distance to the northeast of the Academy excavations, but perhaps not far enough to make these statements contradictory. Presumably the gymnasium was quite extensive and the garden was on the side of it towards Kolonos. One hopes that further excavations will clarify the relationship among gymnasium, school, and Mouseion.

What of the students? There is no evidence that the Academy was any-

[9] Cf. H. Cherniss, *Early Academy*, 12; though opinions have differed on this point.

[10] See A. Westermann, *Biographi Graeci*, Brunswick 1845, 387, 393; cf. Diogenes Laertius 3.25; 4.1.1; 4.3.19.

[11] Apuleius *On Plato* 1.4; cf. Diogenes 3.20; Plutarch *de Exilio* 10.

thing in the nature of a residential college, or the Lyceum for that matter, except perhaps for a select few. One presumes that most of the students normally lived at their homes or lodgings in and about Athens, and that the disciples of Polemon were exceptional when they made little huts for themselves and lived not far from the Mouseion and the *exedra* or lecture hall.[12]

Fortunately there has never been much doubt about the situation of the Academy, as in the case of the other gymnasia. We know the road on which it stood, and the direction that road took; and we are told fairly precisely how far it was from the gate.[13] It was about three-quarters of a mile away, near the river Kephisos, and not far from the Kolonos Hippios, the hill which is the scene of Sophokles' *Oedipus Coloneus*. Fifty or sixty years ago the spot must have had something of the character and spirit which Kimon gave it and which Aristophanes so vividly conveys. Frazer quotes a description by Mahaffy: "I have wandered whole days in these delightful woods, listening to the nightingales, which sing all day in the deep shade and solitude . . . and seeing the white poplar show its silvery leaves in the breeze, and wondering whether the huge old olive stems . . . could be the actual sacred trees. . . . Now and then through a vista the Acropolis shows itself in a framework of green foliage."[14] Now the squalid and monstrous urban spread of Athens in the twentieth century has overrun and engulfed it, and made investigation almost as difficult a job as in the agora.

Extensive excavations were carried out in the region of the Academy in the 1930s, and again in the post-war years,[15] but the topography of the area is still far from clear. In particular very little has been found which can be assigned to the gymnasium of the fifth century or the time of Plato; the most important buildings excavated belong to a great reconstruction of Roman imperial times. A further section of the tomb-lined road which led from the Dipylon to the Academy has been unearthed, near the Church of St. George; and most recently, on the east side of the area, at the corner of Tripolis and Haimon Streets, a stele of Pentelic marble 0.84m high has been found *in situ* on a base of poros, inscribed

---

[12] Diogenes Laertius 4.3.19.

[13] Cicero says it was six stades from the Dipylon, *de Finibus* 5.1; Livy makes it about a Roman mile, *mille ferme passus*, 31.24.9; but of course such distances are approximate.

[14] Pausanias Vol. II, 388; cf. Aristophanes *Clouds* 1005–8.

[15] Travlos *PDA* 44. *Megale Hellenike Enkyklopaideia*, Suppl. 22, gives a useful summary by Ph. Stavropoullos.

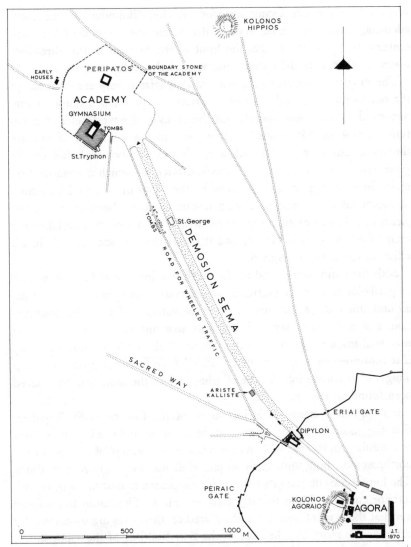

64. Northwest Suburbs of Athens, with Academy (J. Travlos)

(223)

vertically on the side facing towards the city, "Boundary of the Hek-ademeia," in letters which may be dated towards the end of the sixth century B.C.[16] The stone fixes the limit of the precinct in this direction; it stood rather more than 300m southwest of the Kolonos.

The district of the Academy was inhabited from very early times. To the northwest the foundations of a curious hairpin-shaped house of pre-historic date have been found, and the excavators have labeled it hope-fully "House of Akademos." A few yards to the southwest of this are the more extensive remains of a much more elaborate house of the geometric period, with walls of unbaked brick, of which a good deal re-mains in spite of great damage done by the floods in 1961, and a number of rooms on either side of a long narrow passage. Because it contains plentiful evidence of cults carried on within its rooms, this building has been called the Sacred House; and it shows that the spot already had a religious character of its own.

Both these buildings stood to the northwest just outside a long section of peribolos wall, with buttresses at intervals, which ran in a wide arc around this part of the precinct. It is of varied and irregular construc-tion, and one cannot say with certainty that any of it is archaic, but it may well mark the position of the famous Wall of Hipparchos. Certainly if it continued in a similar line around the whole site it must have been a big and expensive job. A little of what may be the same wall has indeed been found on the south side.

It is in this southern area, just north of the Church of St. Tryphon, that the most imposing remains have come to light. Here is a great rectangular courtyard, with its entrance and a group of rooms on the northeast side, built apparently in late Hellenistic or early Roman times. The long rooms on the other three sides appeared at first to be stoas with interior columns. More recently however H. A. Thompson has pointed out that the rows of square plinths placed on their axes are unsuitable for columns, are more like the slabs in the East Building of the south square of the agora, and probably supported book chests.[17] It may be that this building contained the library and study rooms of the Roman Academy. Nearby, to the northwest, a bathing establishment was built.[18]

We are still far from the Academy of Plato, but we approach nearer in another of these piecemeal areas of excavation, about 200m to the northeast

[16] *AAA* 1, 1968, 101; *Deltion* 22B, 1968, 46; Travlos *PDA* 47.
[17] *Hesperia* 35, 1966, 42 n. 7.
[18] Travlos *PDA* 43, 48.

in the direction of the Kolonos. Here a row of large and undoubted column bases is conspicuous; the plan of the building to which they belonged is not so clear, but it was probably a colonnaded court; the excavators have labeled it "peripatos," and Plato may indeed have walked here with his pupils. The building is dated to the fourth century B.C.; but architectural fragments, terracotta antefixes and the like, of the sixth century B.C., point to an earlier structure on the site or nearby. In this area too a number of inscriptions were found, some of which may be relevant to the gymnasium; they include a dedication to Hermes, who was regularly worshiped in the gymnasia, and a list of names of intriguingly Platonic character—Char(mides?), Aris(ton?), Menekr(ates?), Kriton.[19] Another set of curious inscriptions has been found to the northwest near the circuit wall. They are scratched or lightly inscribed on thin slate-like stones, and suggest that in the late fifth or early fourth century there was a much more elementary institution of learning in or near the Academy.[20]

Enough has been found to show how important it is to clear up the topography of the whole site and determine the character and history of its monuments. At present we still have to go elsewhere for a coherent picture of a gymnasium of Plato's age; to Delphi for instance, where the gymnasium with its open and covered running tracks, square palaestra, and round plunge bath, was laid out on the terraced slopes of Parnassos, a very different kind of site.[21] "Palaestra" needs a word of explanation before we proceed to the other two sites. The word means wrestling school; but the palaestra was in fact a general-purpose gymnastic building. In its developed architectural form it normally consisted of a colonnaded court with rooms suitably disposed around it for the various needs of the athletes. No doubt the three great Athenian gymnasia each had one, but no recognizable trace has been found. But in addition we know that by the end of the fifth century there were many palaestras at Athens which were independent units and did not form part of a greater gymnasium complex.[22] Some were public, some were privately owned. In either case they could be rented for both gymnastic and literary instruc-

---

[19] The date is probably Hellenistic, to judge by the letter forms; see *SEG* 13 no. 28; *SEG* 21 no. 638.

[20] *SEG* 19 no. 37; *SEG* 22 no. 61.

[21] J. Jannoray and H. Ducoux, *Fouilles de Delphes* II, Paris 1953, *Le Gymnase*.

[22] Ps. Xenophon *Ath. Pol.* 2.10. Note also the baths, which were sometimes associated with gymnasia, p. 251 below.

tion, and they were used by sophists and also by elementary schoolmasters to supplement the resources of their private houses. Once again there is a sad dearth of archaeological evidence at Athens; the literary evidence is both plentiful and colorful, especially in Plato. In the opening scene of the *Lysis* we are told how Sokrates was walking from the Academy to the Lyceum and skirting the city wall (i.e. in its northeastern sector). Here he was diverted by his friend Hippothales, who pointed out to him an enclosure, just opposite the wall, with an open gate in it, and explained that it was a newly built palaestra, where he and his friends went not so much for exercise as for discussion, in which they would like Sokrates to join them. A friend and admirer of Sokrates, Mikkos, a sophist, gave instruction there—whether by way of self-advertisement or because he had set up a regular school one cannot say. Sokrates of course cannot resist his young friends and enters the palaestra. There he finds some of the boys busy with a sacrifice, others engaged in games of dice. Most are playing in the courtyard, but one group is in the *apodyterion*, the changing room. Sokrates and his companions find a comparatively quiet spot to sit down, and presently Lysis and others gather round to listen. The scene of the *Charmides* is very similar; Sokrates describes how after his return from the campaign at Poteidaia he began to seek out his customary haunts and went to the palaestra of Taureas, opposite the shrine of Basile (in the southeastern part of Athens, near the Olympieion and not far from Kynosarges).

The Lyceum, the shrine of Apollo Lykeios ("wolf-god"), was to the east of the city, outside the gate of Diochares, and probably not far away. We know nothing of its early form. Presumably it had the usual running tracks and perhaps stoas.[23] Plato mentions an *apodyterion*, a covered running-track (*dromos*), and columns. The place was used as a parade ground. "We are worn out," say the chorus in the *Peace* (355ff), "wandering to the Lyceum and from the Lyceum with spear and shield."[24] In the fourth century the indefatigable Lycurgus planted trees and built a palaestra there.[25]

[23] Judeich 142, 415; Travlos *PDA* 345; Plato *Euthydemos*, 272e, 273a.

[24] *IG* I² 114 line 35 implies that the assembly also met there occasionally; see H. T Wade-Gery, *BSA* 32–33, 1932–33, 120.

[25] Ps. Plutarch *Lives* 841c–d; cf. *IG* II² 457 lines 7–8. Travlos *PDA* 291, 345, tentatively assigns conglomerate foundations discovered on Xenophon Street east of the Gate of Diochares to the palaestra, and one farther east in the garden to a small temple.

When Aristotle had left the Academy, the Lyceum was the obvious place in which to set up school.[26] There, we are told by Diogenes, quoting Hermippos (5.1.2), that he had found a *peripatos* (probably a colonnade) where he could walk up and down discussing philosophy with his pupils until it was time for them to anoint themselves with oil (presumably for athletic exercise). When they became more numerous, Diogenes adds, he sat down to the job. Perhaps this last remark contains a certain symbolic truth. The elementary and informal arrangements of an old gymnasium cannot altogether have sufficed for the encyclopedic program for the organization of knowledge on which the Peripatetic school presently embarked. We hear of its library,[27] perhaps the first truly great library and a forerunner of Alexandria and Pergamon; and there appears to have been something of a museum in the modern as well as the ancient sense; and there must have been *exedrae* and study rooms.

About Theophrastos we are told a little more. After Aristotle's death he acquired "a private garden too," i.e. in addition to the public or semipublic facilities associated with the gymnasium. Thus we find an arrangement similar to that of the Academy. Up to 2000 used to turn up for his lectures, says Diogenes (5.2.37), no doubt the less specialized evening lectures instituted by Aristotle. The number may well be exaggerated, but a large lecturing space would be needed, perhaps the old *peripatos* in the gymnasium.

The wills of the Peripatetics are informative (they are probably authentic; Diogenes quotes Straton's from a collection of Ariston of Keos). Theophrastos' will (5.2.51) gives instructions to place the image of Aristotle in the shrine, to restore the little stoa by the Mouseion, and to place in the lower stoa the tablets on which are the maps. "The garden and the *peripatos* and the buildings adjoining the garden I leave to my friends, named below, who wish to pursue the study of philosophy together . . . let me be buried in the garden wherever seems most fitting." This *peripatos* is a private one, not the original *peripatos* in the gymnasium. The school had a body of property which was handed on by each head to his successor or a representative group; such property would give substance and permanence to a school, though the Stoics apparently continued solidly enough without it. Straton leaves the school to Lykon, to-

---

[26] Cf. A. H. Chroust, "Did Aristotle Own a School at Athens?" *Rheinisches Museum* 115, 1972, 310–18. As an alien he probably rented a house. See also J. P. Lynch, *Aristotle's School*, University of California Press, 1972.

[27] Athenaeus 5.214d.

gether with the books, and the furniture in the dining hall (5.3.62). Lykon leaves the *peripatos*, presumably meaning the school in general, to a group of friends, who are to put a suitable person in charge; "and the rest of my friends are to cooperate for my sake and for the sake of the place" (5.4.70).

With all this we may have a tenuous archaeological and epigraphical link. In Syntagma Square there stands a stone (see Fig. 59) inscribed "Boundary of the Garden of the Muses,"[28] which was found (not *in situ*) at a short distance from this spot, i.e. not far outside the suggested site of the gate of Diochares. E. Vanderpool, submitting this stone to a fresh and careful scrutiny, has found that it bore another inscription on its other side, which, though it is not so well preserved, he would tentatively restore as "Boundary of the Temenos of the Muses." He assumes that this was an older marker of the same plot. One's thoughts naturally fly to Theophrastos and the Peripatetics, and the Mouseion and the Lyceum. A dedication to Apollo by an *epimeletes* (overseer) of the Lyceum was found only a little to the south, near the Russian church.[29]

As far as the literary evidence goes there is something to be said for bringing the Lyceum into Syntagma Square, not far from the wall—if we leave room for the *dromos* to the gate which Xenophon mentions[30]—in preference to placing it away to the east. Such a situation makes better sense of what Sokrates says in the *Lysis* at the beginning, that he was walking from the Academy straight to the Lyceum, right beneath the wall itself. He would not so naturally follow the line of the wall if the Lyceum were much farther east. Such a position would suit Sokrates' general habits too—he constantly frequented the Lyceum but he seldom went far outside the city.[31] Again, the commentators say that the gym-

[28] *IG* ii² 2613; a precisely similar marker, 2614, was found south of the Acropolis. In *ArchEph* for 1953–54 Part ii (published 1958) 126ff Vanderpool shows that 2613 and 2614 were originally one single block bearing the older inscription. Note also W. Peek, *AthMitt* 67, 1942, 33.

[29] *IG* ii² 2875; 1945, a dedication to Apollo found to the east in the gardens, may also be relevant. Lynch, *Aristotle's School* 20f, suggests that the name of the obscure saint to whom the Russian Church is dedicated, Lykodemos, preserves a reminiscence of the ancient name.

[30] *Hellenika* 2.4.27. Note also *Hipparch.* 3.6f, where a *dromos* in the Lyceum is mentioned, up which the cavalry are to ride "to the top of the facing theater" (p. 204 above). Perhaps these *dromoi* were continuous, forming a ceremonial street leading from the gate and on through the parade ground.

[31] *Euthyphron* 2 a, *Euthydemos* 271 a, *Symposium* 223 d. Note also the "sophists

nasium "lay beside the city,"[32] which one would hardly say of the Academy. On the other hand, it may have stretched some distance to the east, being used for extensive cavalry maneuvers; so that Strabo's statement (9.1.19,24), that the springs of the Eridanos, up on the slopes of Lykabettos, are outside the gate of Diochares near the Lyceum, is a little vague but not inept, even if we have Theophrastos and the Peripatetics in Syntagma Square.

The third gymnasium was at Kynosarges, a place sacred to Herakles and his friends and relations; its strange name was a mystery to the ancients and was explained by a story about a white dog.[33] Kynosarges is now generally located in the southern suburbs, "not far from the gates" according to Diogenes (6.1.13). At the end of the last century members of the British School at Athens unearthed, south of the Ilissos stream and southwest of the Olympieion, upstream from the church of Panteleimon, remains of an archaic building said to be suitable for a gymnasium, and of another possible gymnasium building a little farther east of Roman Imperial date, probably Hadrianic; one recalls that Pausanias (1.18.9) mentions a gymnasium of Hadrian at Athens. These discoveries were never fully published, the site was built over, and the identification remains uncertain.[34] Several years ago during building operations it proved possible to re-examine the foundations of the later building, and this proved to be a peristyle measuring 64m north to south and over 80m east to west—the east end was not recovered. In general the area is not unsuitable for a gymnasium. A chain of low hills rises from the Ilissos bed, but at this point there is a fairly extensive strip of level ground before the ascent. Travlos still places Kynosarges here, associating with the gymnasium the *"dromos* to Agrai" mentioned in an inscription;[35] Agrai extended upstream along the south bank.

---

of the common herd" who frequented the Lyceum, according to Isokrates, *Panathenaikos* 18.

[32] Schol. Aristophanes *Peace* 353; Suidas *s.v. Lykeion*; Lynch, *Aristotle's School*, 16ff, 209ff, re-examines the evidence, questions the relevance of *IG* ii^2 2613, and locates the shrine and the gymnasium south and southeast of Syntagma. Doubt must remain until definite archaeological evidence is found.

[33] See Frazer on Pausanias 1.19.3; Judeich 422.

[34] *BSA* 2, 1895–96, 23; 3, 1896–97, 89, 232; *JHS* 16, 1896, 337; *AthMitt* 21, 1896, 463. *IG* ii^2 1665 and possibly 1102 are relevant inscriptions found in the area. For recent work see Travlos *PDA* 579; *AAA* 3, 1970, 6–13; A. Kokkou, *Deltion* 25A, 1971, 165ff.

[35] *IG* ii^2, 2119, line 128.

But one still has to consider the possibility that the shrine of Herakles and the old original gymnasium of Kynosarges was somewhat farther downstream, to the southwest. Here the ground is more level and open, and the site commands the approach from Phaleron better—Kynosarges is known to have been a place of strategic importance on this side.[36] Recent epigraphical evidence too points to this quarter—a relief with a dedication to Herakles and several other inscribed stones which may be associated with the Herakleion, found a little to the south of the Fix brewery.[37] Even more interesting is an inscription which was found just south of the choregic monument of Lysikrates, but which must have stood originally on the bank of the Ilissos and near Kynosarges.[38] The inscription is of the late fifth century and the extant fragment is concerned with tanning; skins are not to be treated in the Ilissos above the *temenos* of Herakles; a stele inscribed with the decree is to be set up "on either side," i.e., no doubt, of the river at the point in question. Where this point was one cannot say; a likely place is just south of Athens, clear of the immediate suburbs and the shrines which stood along the Ilissos to the southeast of the city. The evidence though cumulative is still slight and indecisive. The old gymnasia, vital centers of the spiritual life of Athens, remain elusive and enigmatic. But one can think of them as distributed around the outer periphery, to northwest, east, and south, and associated each with one of the Athenian rivers.

We read that Kynosarges was used by young men of illegitimate or half foreign birth; but Themistokles, according to Plutarch (1.2), tried to raise the tone by inducing the wellborn to go there too. Antisthenes the Cynic taught at Kynosarges in the fourth century B.C. according to Diogenes (6.1.13), but for some of his followers Cynicism was not so much an academic philosophy as a way of life, which was not practiced in seclusion but carried into the streets and exhibited, sometimes very offensively, in public. We should hardly visualize at Kynosarges an establishment of anything like the scale and complexity of the Lyceum or the Academy. However, in the early third century Ariston of Chios lectured there and founded a sect of his own, a branch of Stoicism diverging in the direction of a return to Cynicism. On a lower intellectual plane, a

[36] Cf. Herodotus 6.116; Diodorus Siculus 28.7; Livy 31.24.18.

[37] *Hesperia* 17, 1948, 137ff; *Deltion* 8, 1923, 85ff; *SEG*, 3, 1929, no. 115–17. Note also *IG* II² 1665.

[38] *Deltion*, 8, 1923, 96; *SEG* 3, no. 18; Travlos *PDA* 341.

body of Athenians who prided themselves on their wit and called themselves The Sixty met at Kynosarges.[39]

The great philosophical schools of the Hellenistic age were identified with the Stoa of Zeno and the Garden of Epicurus, though they had associations with the gymnasia too. For some philosophers the garden had become the scene and the symbol of the philosophic way of life, and this was true not only of the Epicureans. "A philosopher and a great lover of gardens, and one who minded his own business," comments Antigonos of Karystos in Diogenes (9.12.112); and curiously he is speaking of Timon the skeptic, whom in another scene we find in the Agora of the Kerkopes, a den of thieves and tricksters, gibing at the Academic Arkesilaos who happens to pass by (9.12.114). The same words would of course have been a perfect description of Epicurus, the man of the garden *par excellence*, as an exponent of quiet withdrawal from the disturbing impact of public affairs. For Epicurus even the gymnasia, not to speak of the agora, did not provide the conditions he wanted.

Meanwhile the Stoics, like Sokrates, were able to face the hurly-burly of the agora. Their original meeting place was the Poikile. Presumably as the school developed more elaborate facilities would be needed than in the early days of Zeno. We hear of Stoic philosophers using the gymnasia both outside the city and inside.[40] Chrysippos was said to have been the first to conduct classes in the open air in the Lyceum,[41] and we shall find a Stoic giving lectures in the new Ptolemaion. The members of this school apparently tended to circulate rather than to develop a collegiate home. Diogenes, quoting Hermippos, says that Chrysippos also taught in the Odeion. Plutarch, listing the haunts of philosophy at Athens, mentions the Odeion and the Palladion, besides the Academy, the Lyceum, and the Stoa.

In the Hellenistic age greater provision was made at Athens for the more formal academic studies of the schools, and at the same time for athletic exercise. In this as in other developments the city owed much to

[39] Diogenes 7.2.161; Athenaeus 14.614 d.

Clement of Alexandria, *Protrepticus* 4.54, mentions a statue of Philip II of Macedon at Kynosarges; see H. S. Versnel, *Mnemosyne* Series 4, 26, 1973, 273–79.

[40] Decrees in Zeno's honor were set up at the Academy and the Lyceum; this may indicate that he was already associated with these gymnasia as well as with the stoa; see Diogenes Laertius 7.1. 6, 11, 15.

[41] Hardly the first philosopher of all; perhaps the first Stoic; see Diogenes 7.7. 184–85, cf. Plutarch *de Exilio* 14.

(231)

the patronage of foreign potentates who looked to Athens as a cultural center of Hellenism. One of the kings of Egypt, probably Ptolemy VI Philometor (181–145 B.C.), founded a new gymnasium, the Ptolemaion.[42] This differed radically from the Academy and the older gymnasia in that it was a building confined within the heart of the city, a fact which no doubt not only restricted its extent but also determined its form. Incidentally, a site within the walls meant greater safety in war. Plutarch, speaking of the grave of Theseus (36.2) says it was in the middle of the city beside the gymnasium; this gymnasium can hardly be other than the Ptolemaion. Pausanias (1.17.2) says that it was not far from the agora. One wonders how a gymnasium of Hellenistic type was inserted into the heart of the ancient city. One imagines that in form it was something like the gymnasia we know on other Hellenistic sites, Priene and Miletos for example: planned around a rectangular colonnaded court, with *exedrae* and rooms of various proportions for the use of athletes and scholars; perhaps with a certain emphasis on the northern, southward-facing side, which was apt to be made more imposing architecturally.

Another gymnasium was built in the city towards the end of the third century B.C., the Diogeneion, named after a Macedonian general whom the Athenians wished to honor for his good services. Diogenes later received a hero shrine, and games were held in his honor. Thus the old connection between hero shrine and gymnasium continued in historical times. The Diogeneion is known from only one literary allusion,[43] and from numerous inscriptions, found mainly at the church of Demetrios Katephores, in the eastern part of the late Roman fortification, i.e. some distance to the east of the Ptolemaion. These inscriptions are sometimes said to indicate the site of the Diogeneion, but they can only do so very approximately; stones were apt to be moved in batches some distance for incorporation in this fortification. The Diogeneion, like the Ptolemaion,

[42] *Agora* III 142–44; Travlos *PDA* 234; the idea that the complex of stoas on the south side of the agora was the Ptolemaion has been abandoned, see p. 80 above.

[43] Plutarch *Quaestiones Conviviales* 9.1.1; Ammonios, a contemporary and teacher of Plutarch, holds an examination in the Diogeneion of the ephebes learning letters, geometry, rhetoric, and music; cf. S. Dow, *HSCP* 63, 1958, 423ff; *TAPA* 91, 1960, 381ff; O. Reinmuth, *TAPA* 90, 1959, 209ff; 93, 1962, 374ff. For the site see Judeich 379; Travlos *PDA* 281; A. Papagiannopoulos-Palaios, *Polemon* 3, 1947, 22–24, prefers to associate with it certain remains in the extreme north of the city, including the column of Roman date round which the Church of St. John on Euripides Street is built.

was associated with the training of the ephebes, the corps of eighteen-year-olds. It may well have played some part in the activities of the philosophical schools, but we have no clear evidence.[44]

The Ptolemaion was to make a notable contribution to academic and philosophical life. The Antiochos whom Cicero mentions was the contemporary head of the Academy, who apparently came into the city to lecture in the Ptolemaion on occasion. A fragment of Apollodoros' verse history tells how a certain philosopher, whose name and sect are not preserved, came to Athens in 151/150 B.C., obtained Athenian citizenship, and opened a school in the Ptolemaion among the people anointing themselves, i.e. practicing athletics there.[45] Athletic and philosophical life were apparently still complementary. Inscriptions tell us a little more. It appears that at this time the ephebes were directed to attend philosophical lectures as part of their training. In one of the long rambling decrees in which they and their officers are commended for carrying out their various duties with diligence and decorum—mainly religious rites, dedications, and ceremonial processions—we also read: "They attended diligently the classes of Zenodotos too in both the Ptolemaion and the Lyceum, and similiarly those of all the other philosophers in the Lyceum and the Academy through the whole year."[46] The ephebes must have traversed Athens back and forth like Oxford or Cambridge undergraduates circulating from college to college. Many, no doubt, were not serious students of philosophy but were merely complying with the requirements. One notes the significant verb which means "they stuck it out." A more serious form of circulation may be implied by Diogenes (4.6.42) when he says that Arkesilaos, head of the Academy, recommended his pupils to hear other philosophers too. The inscription quoted above is dated 122/121 B.C. Zenodotos is probably the Stoic philosopher of that name. It may well be that the Stoic school transferred part at least of their operations to the Ptolemaion when the greater facilities of the gymnasium became available. Chrysippos, the most famous head of the school after Zeno, was honored with a statue there, seen by Pausanias (1.17.2).

---

[44] It has been sometimes suggested that by this time, perhaps after the sack by Sulla, the Academic school had moved to the urban gymnasium; but Cicero does not imply it, and Horace, *Epistles* 2.2.45, implies the contrary.

[45] Frag. 59, Jacoby *FGH* IIB 1036; *Agora* III 142; *Hesperia* 43, 1974, 246.

[46] *IG* II² 1006 lines 19f; cf. 1043 line 20, and *Hesperia* 43, 1974, 246 line 14. On the library in the Ptolemaion see *IG* II² 1029, lines 25f; *Agora* III 144. On the ephebes and the gymnasia see now Lynch, *Aristotle's School*, 132ff.

We learn from an inscription that the ephebes when passing out made gifts of books to the library in the Ptolemaion, which may have acquired the character of a state library, as contrasted with private collections, attested from at least the fifth century, and the libraries accumulated by the schools.

Cicero gives a pleasant glimpse of the gymnasia and the academic life of Athens in his time.[47] One day in 79 B.C., when he was studying at Athens, he and a group of friends took a walk along the same road as Lucian's Philosophia, but in the opposite direction.[48] They had listened, as usual, to a lecture by Antiochos, delivered in the Ptolemaion, and they resolved to take a quiet afternoon stroll in the Academy. Forgathering at Piso's they traversed the six stadia from the Dipylon, and reached the Academy. There Piso remarks, "When we set eyes on the very places frequented by great men, we are more deeply moved than when we merely hear of their deeds or read their writings. Plato used to hold discussions here; I can almost see him walking in those little gardens near by. Here taught Speusippos and Xenokrates and Polemon, who used to sit on the very seat which we can see over there. The power of suggestion which places possess is indeed great." Quintus Cicero is more attracted to the Kolonos near by, with its Sophoklean associations. "I of course am an Epicurean," says Pomponius (Atticus), "and I spend much time with my dear friend Phaidros in the garden of Epicurus, which we were passing just now."[49] M. Cicero fully agrees about the stimulating effect of places in one's studies of famous men; though all parts of Athens are full of reminders of the great, he is particularly moved by an *exedra*, a classroom or lecture hall, which he now sees—it was used by Karneades not so long ago. L. Cicero concludes, "There is no end to this in Athens; wherever we set foot, we tread upon some bit of history."

It is beyond our present scope to pursue the subject in detail into imperial times, when there was more than one period of Indian Summer.[50] Two further developments known from archaeological evidence can be

[47] *De Finibus* 5.1.

[48] *Piscator* 13; "we will wait for her in the Kerameikos; she will be there presently on her way back from the Academy, to take a stroll in the Poikile too."

[49] R. E. Wycherley, *Phoenix* 13, 1959, 73ff; M. L. Clarke, *Phoenix*, 27, 1973, 386ff.

[50] J.W.H. Walden, *The Universities of Ancient Greece*, New York, 1909; J. H. Oliver in *Hesperia* 3, 1934, 191ff shows that "Mouseion" probably refers not to Alexandria but to the local University, now with its complement of official "chairs."

briefly mentioned. We have already noted, among the theaters of Athens, the Odeion or Agrippeion in the agora. The remains have revealed that in the second century A.D. it was reconstructed with a smaller auditorium, seating about five hundred, and with space which was perhaps used for classrooms. Philostratos shows that at this time the theater was used to accommodate the large crowds who came to hear the discourses of leading sophists.[51] He describes an occasion when one of these displeased the audience and the meeting degenerated into an undignified shouting match.

Seated figures of philosophers were placed along the front of the building. One which has been discovered is tentatively identified as Epicurus.[52] One can imagine what Epicurus (or indeed Plato) would have thought of the ochlagogy of Herodes Atticus and his contemporaries, and the noisy demonstrations which it evoked. But he would have witnessed with even greater distress the violence and rioting between students of rival schools which disfigured academic life in the days of Libanios, two centuries later. By that time the Odeion and indeed most of the buildings of the agora, and no doubt of the suburban gymnasia too, lay in ruins after the destruction of the city by the Herulians. Eventually a large gymnasium, with several courtyards and numerous rooms of various kinds and sizes, was built on the same site and on the ground to the south.[53]

BIBLIOGRAPHY

J. Delorme, *Gymnasion*, Paris 1960

R. E. Wycherley, "Peripatos: the Athenian Philosophical Scene," *Greece and Rome* 8, 1961, 152–63; 9, 1962, 2–21 (the present chapter is based on the second of these articles)

Travlos, *PDA* 42ff, 233ff, 340ff, 345ff

On education see—H. I. Marrou, *History of Education in Antiquity*, London 1956 (in French, Paris 1948)

M. L. Clarke, *Higher Education in the Ancient World*, London 1971

---

[51] *Lives of Sophists* 2.5.4, 8.4; p. 216 above.

[52] *Hesperia* 19, 1950, 125.

[53] H. A. Thompson, "Athenian Twilight" *Journal of Roman Studies* 49, 1959, 62ff; *Agora* XIV 211ff; note also certain large houses, each with a large room ending in an apse, thought to be the establishments of contemporary sophists. On "The Last Days of the Academy at Athens" see A. Cameron, *Proceedings of Cambridge Philological Society* 195, 1969, 7–29, who believes that the schools did not come to a final end with the edict of Justinian in A.D. 529; cf. Lynch, *Aristotle's School*, 162ff.

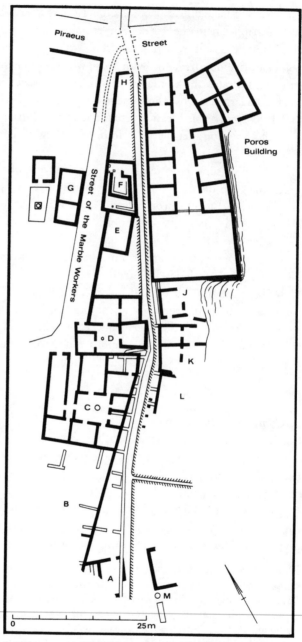

65. Houses and Workshops West of Areopagus, and Poros
Building (Boersma, *Athenian Building Policy* 253)

CHAPTER X

Houses, Streets, Water Supply

The excavation of Olynthos in the 1930's provided for the first time a complete and satisfactory picture of the residential quarters of a classical Greek city, of the fifth and fourth century B.C.; earlier work had been mainly on Hellenistic sites such as Delos and Priene. Even then it was difficult to estimate to what extent the evidence of Olynthos in northern Greece was applicable to Athens. One was curious to know what kind of houses accommodated the builders of the Parthenon and the other splendid public monuments of the age of Perikles and Pheidias. Archaeological material was scrappy and difficult to interpret; literary evidence was vague and could mislead. In the last few years more satisfactory material has come to light. Traces of houses have been found by the American excavators at several points on the fringe of the agora; in two groups in particular the remains are substantial enough to produce coherent plans, with the aid of which one can form a fairly clear idea of the form and construction of the Athenian house.

Southwestwards from the agora lies a deep trough, on the west side of the Areopagus. Rodney Young carefully excavated a large part of this area, and published the results in an article which he called "An Industrial District of Ancient Athens."[1] The site was extraordinarily complicated, with Mycenean tombs, an archaic burial ground and, from the fifth century B.C. to Roman imperial times, streets lined by houses and workshops. A narrow street left the agora at the southwest corner, near the *archeia* or public offices, following the line of the Great Drain which carried off the water of this part of Athens. Just at this point, adjacent to one of the boundary stones of the agora, are the remains of a modest house (see Fig. 68.1) which seems to have belonged to a cobbler, to judge by its contents, possibly Sokrates' friend Simon;[2] its courtyard had a well and a cesspool, a support for a workshed on the north and at least one room opening on the south. Crossing a broader east-to-west street which

[1] *Hesperia* 20, 1951, 135–288. Compare the "industrial quarter" at the south Attic deme Thorikos; see p. 262 below.

[2] *Hesperia* 23, 1954, 51ff; D. B. Thompson, *Archaeology* 13, 1960, 234–40; R. F. Hock, *GRBS* 17, 1976, 41–53.

led to the Peiraeus Gate, the street continued to ascend the valley and after a short distance turned west up the hillside. The remains of a number of houses were found along this street; according to the archaeological evidence they were built in the fifth century B.C. though some were considerably modified in the fourth. In some cases there is nothing more than fragments of wall or foundation, insufficient to give a clear picture; but in several the plan is clear enough. The best specimens are the two labeled C and D, situated just at the westward turn (see Fig. 68.3). In the fourth century they were combined into one establishment, and perhaps D served as workshop, C mainly as residence. These houses were irregular in size and shape, and so were the rooms; the corners were usually not right angles. A narrow passage led into a small courtyard, which as at Olynthos tended to be in the southern part of the house. There is no trace of colonnades of the Olynthian type, merely a single support, perhaps for a kind of workshed, in the court of D on the west side. The court of C was paved, in the later phase, with pebbles set in cement. Most floors were of hard earth topped with clay. There is little evidence for the character of individual rooms. The large rooms opening onto the north side of the courts may have been the *androngs* or principal dining and entertaining rooms. One of the small rooms on the east side of C had a drain and may have been a bathroom. What appears to have been a shop, opening independently onto the street, occupies the northwest corner of C; its floor level was higher and it had its own well. There are no signs of stairs in the court or of upper floors, but they may well have existed—the walls are thick and strong enough and space was precious. The stone socles, which are all that is preserved, no doubt carried walls of the ubiquitous unbaked brick; the roof was probably tiled. A neighboring house had an unusual feature, an external balcony, attested by a row of stone slabs.

There is plentiful evidence, in the form of chips and fragments and grinding tools, to show that at least some of the people who lived in these houses were marble-cutters. The courtyard of House D was apparently used as a workshop. This may indeed be the Marble-Carvers' Street mentioned by Plutarch.[3] There are signs of pottery-making and metalworking in the quarter too, including a leaden curse tablet on which someone calls down destruction upon the heads of certain bronzefounders.[4] The major trades of Athens seem to have extended sporadi-

[3] See p. 97 above.   [4] *Hesperia* 20, 1951, 223.

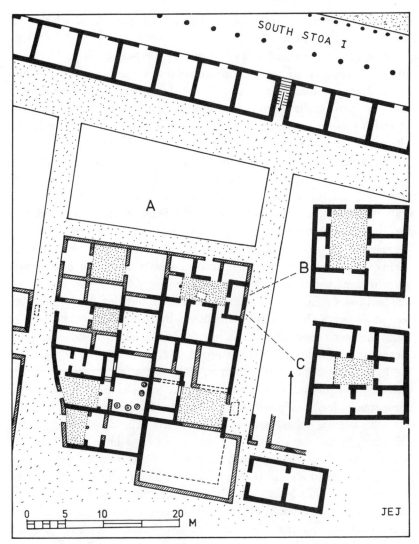

66. Houses North of Areopagus, with South Stoa I; inset on the right, for comparison with the northeastern house A), are B) a 4th c. house on the northeast slope of the Areopagus, and C) a Byzantine house of 12th c. A.D., showing continuity of type (J. E. Jones, after Travlos)

cally about the city, beyond the confines of the quarters in which they were especially concentrated.

These houses have an affinity in general type with those of Olynthos. But of course they are much more irregular and informal, as one would expect from the notorious irregularity of the Athenian streets; and they have no particularly distinctive features such as the characteristically Olynthian *pastas*, a colonnade on the north side of the court which usually extends across nearly the whole width of the house.

The other group was found on the south side of the agora and the north slope of the Areopagus (Fig. 68.4).[5] The houses with their small size, irregular form, and simple construction make an interesting contrast with the spacious architecture of the South Stoa. A comparatively broad street, continuing the one mentioned above as leading to the Peiraeus Gate, passed along the back of the Stoa. Narrower streets ran down the slope below the Areopagus to join it, and with cross streets formed small compact blocks.

The houses seem to have been built in the middle of the fifth century B.C., replacing archaic houses demolished by the Persians. The plan of even the best preserved block is not certain in all its details; nor is it clear just how many units it comprised. But at least it can be seen that we have a number of modest houses, each with a few rooms grouped in various ways around a tiny courtyard. The unit on the northeast is the most intelligible. It is approximately square, and smaller than a standard Olynthian house (about 11m as against 17m). The courtyard is *not* on the south in this case; in fact the largest and most important room was on that side. A single column on one side of the court apparently supported the roof of a small porch; a similar arrangement is tentatively restored in two other houses—this is the nearest approach to a colonnade. A large room in a house on the western side seems to have had a cement floor and may have been the *andron*. Beddings for large jars in a room farther south indicate that it was used for storage. In others terracotta grills and loom weights suggest the varied domestic activities.

The socles of the main walls are of surprisingly impressive construction, in a kind of polygonal masonry; those of the secondary walls are of rubble. The floors are mostly of hard-packed earth as usual. In the court of the northeastern house and out in the street near the entrances to two others were stone-lined pits which must have been cesspools.

[5] *Hesperia* 28, 1959, 98ff.

67. Socle of House Wall North of Areopagus (Photo: Agora Excavations)

This primitive mode of sanitation was common in the Athens of Perikles.

One need not think of this as a comparatively poor quarter—not that one has any reason to think that wealthier and poorer quarters at Athens were to any degree distinct. The situation, on the Areopagus slope overlooking the agora, was attractive and convenient. There were worse houses in the Athens of Perikles and Demosthenes than those we have been considering. One notes a small two-roomed structure to the southeast of the block, though this may have been merely a shop with storeroom.

A group of fifth- to fourth-century houses has more recently been investigated on the northeast slope of the Areopagus above.[6] The remains are confused by the superimposition of a large late Roman house, and the plans are not clear; but these houses too were built round central courts. The middle house of three was comparatively large, overall about 25m east to west and 19m north to south, with an *andron* on the southeast and a spacious court which in its late fourth-century form may have

[6] *Hesperia* 42, 1973 146ff; note also the "house of Mikion and Menon" (so called from names inscribed on certain objects) just southwest of agora, remodeled several times in 5th and 4th centuries; *Hesperia* 38, 1969, 383ff.

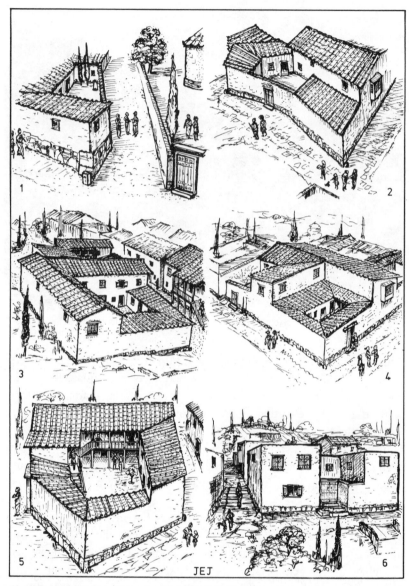

68. Athenian Houses (Reconstructions by J. E. Jones)

1. House of Simon, from Northeast
2. House of Mikion and Menon, from Southeast
3. Houses C and D in Industrial Quarter, from Southwest

4. Houses on North Slope of Aeropagus, from Northeast
5. House with Mosaics Southwest of Areopagus, from South
6. House on Northeast Slope of Pnyx Hill, from North

had a peristyle—there are foundations which may belong to two of the columns.

On the hills of western Athens, above the valley in which lies the "Industrial District," are numerous traces of houses, consisting largely of cuttings in the rock, seldom sufficient to give a clear plan. Recently German archaeologists have re-examined a number of these houses;[7] and in one example (see Fig. 68.6), on the eastern slope of the Pnyx hill, and less clearly in several others, they detect a convenient type of plan attained by adding to a primitive form of dwelling—merely a room with a small court in front—other rooms on either side, giving a Π-shaped arrangement. They suggest that houses of this general form may have been common in the city.

We know from literature that at Athens in the late fifth and fourth centuries there were better houses than any of these, more spacious, and with the addition of internal colonnades. A house of the late fourth century (see Fig. 68.5) situated southwest of the Areopagus, first excavated long ago and recently given a thorough re-examination by Professor Graham, now provides the best archaeological object lesson.[8] Like so many Athenian houses, it was irregular in shape, with overall dimensions nearly 23m north to south by 17m east to west. It was built round a courtyard provided with colonnades, though to what extent these belonged to the original plan is not clear. The rooms formed an odd mixture. Two on the north, obviously the most important part of the house, were large and rectangular. There were spacious rooms on the east side too. The southwestern part of the house was irregular, comprising small rooms of various shapes, with an entrance through a porch on the west. Construction was similar to what we have seen elsewhere; the main socles were of good solid limestone masonry. Though there is no clear evidence, one may assume that the house had an upper story, at least in the principal, northern part. The most interesting feature is the northwestern room, which with its vestibule forms an *andron* of the Olynthian type. On all four sides is a raised border of plaster to support the couches, and both the main room and the anteroom have floors decorated with pebble mosaics in simple but effective geometrical patterns.

An even more recent discovery, in a chance excavation in Menander Street, on the northern edge of the ancient city, confirms the existence of

---

[7] H. Lauter-Bufe and H. Lauter, *AthMitt* 86, 1971, 109ff. It is possible that some houses had flat roofs.

[8] *Hesperia* 35, 1966, 51ff; *Agora* xiv 180ff.

rooms of this type in Athenian houses of the fourth century.[9] Very little else was found, but fortunately this, the most important part of the house, survived. One room had a pebble mosaic with a circle in a square, and griffins filling the corners; of the adjoining room only a corner was uncovered, but it was clearly an *andron*, and it had a mosaic of two griffins attacking a stag. The size of these two rooms is impressive—each about 9m square; this must have been a remarkably handsome and commodious house, almost a mansion.

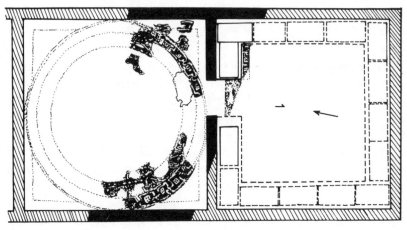

69. House on Menander Street, Andron (J. W. Graham, *Phoenix* 28, 1974, 50 fig. 3)

Bits of house walls are constantly coming to light in widely scattered quarters of Athens and are reported annually in *Deltion*. They are seldom sufficient to afford the reconstruction of a plan or to add substantially to our knowledge; but at least they tend to confirm the impression that most of the space within the city walls not required by the shrines, the agora, and public buildings was occupied by houses. Working on this hypothesis Travlos has calculated that there were probably up to 6000 houses within the upper city, with perhaps 36,000 occupants.[10] This figure would be supplemented by houses in the immediate suburbs, and would be at least duplicated in Peiraeus.

We now have a fairly wide range of classical Athenian domestic archi-

---

[9] *Deltion* 22, 1967, B1, 98–100; for other *androne*s at Athens see Graham, *Phoenix* 28, 1974, 47–50; Jones, "Town and Country Houses," 79, 132. (See Bibliography for Ch. X below.)

[10] *PEA* 72.

tecture, and the general impression derived from the accumulating evidence is that the standard of housing was higher than one used to think. The builders of the Parthenon did not live largely in slums; and there may be some rhetorical exaggeration in Demosthenes' statement that in the great days of the preceding century the houses of Miltiades and Aristeides were in no way out of the ordinary, in contrast with the imposing dwellings of some of his contemporaries.[11] We have seen evidence of handsome houses in the fourth century; one would like more material, especially from the fifth century, before generalizing with any confidence—some day perhaps the house of a Kallias, as described in the opening scene of Plato's *Protagoras*, will be found.

In the *Memorabilia* (3.8.10) Xenophon comments unfavorably on the use of elaborate painted decoration in private houses; one may imagine that most houses, especially in the fifth century, had little more than a color wash painted in a simple scheme on the plaster applied in the principal rooms. The evidence of the sale of the goods of Alkibiades and his friends suggests that the furniture of even the wealthy was simple and somewhat sparse in the late fifth century by modern standards.[12] One notable feature, found in several houses at Olynthos, has not yet been found at Athens—the altar in the courtyard, commonly dedicated to Zeus Herkeios; but we know from the opening scene of Plato's *Republic* that such domestic cults were maintained.

In the Roman period, though there were no doubt still many dwellings of the humbler type, there is also some evidence, for example in the "industrial district," of houses which were somewhat more spacious, more regularly planned, and with more elegant internal appointments such as a full peristyle in the courtyard.[13]

Thucydides says (2.65) that some of his wealthier contemporaries had handsome establishments out in the Attic countryside, which they were reluctant to leave when the land had to be abandoned to the Peloponnesian invaders. Since two notable examples of Attic farmhouses have recently been examined, we may for once permit ourselves an excursion outside the city, to eke out our material and to provide an interesting

---

[11] 3.26; the statement of Herakleides Kretikos, 1.1 (ed. Pfister p. 72) in the 2d century B.C., contrasting the meanness of Athenian houses with the temples, etc., is probably exaggerated.

[12] *Hesperia* 25, 1956, 210ff.

[13] *Hesperia* 20, 1951, 272ff; 35, 1966, 53; 37, 1968, 69; 42, 1973, 156ff; *Agora* xiv 183ff.

comparison.[14] Both are finely situated, one between Mount Parnes and Mount Aigaleos, adjacent to the "Dema" wall which guarded the pass, one on a southward spur of Hymettos, just below a well-known cave sanctuary of Pan, near Vari. The Dema house was built in the latter part of the fifth century, the Vari house a century later. In both the basis of the whole construction is a broad and solid main outer socle, rectangular in plan, stretching east to west, 20.05m by 16.10m in the Dema house, ca. 17.6m by 13.7m in the Vari house. In both, the entrance was in the middle of the south side, and led into the courtyard, which in the Vari house was paved, together with its colonnades, with large flagstones. In both, the principal range of rooms was on the north, and opened onto the court through a portico of wooden columns. In the Vari house the room in the southwest corner had exceptionally thick wall socles, no doubt designed to support a feature which we know to have been common in farmhouses—the tower (*pyrgos*), useful for storage and in emergency for defense. Both these houses, one observes, were not only more spacious than most of the townhouses which we know, but also more regular in plan—they were not subject to the vagaries of ancient city streets.

The streets of Athens were notoriously narrow and tortuous.[15] The residential parts of the ancient city were never thoroughly replanned on more regular and spacious lines. In this we shall find a strong contrast with the harbor town Peiraeus. Some of the streets were of great antiquity, going back to prehistoric times, fixed in their course by the natural lines of communication; indeed some have persisted through mediaeval into modern times. Even important streets were given a width of only 5 or 6m; many were mere alleys; exceptionally, the Panathenaic Way and its extension outside the city were given great width for ceremonial purposes. Surfaces consisted normally of hard earth reinforced by gravel. Since this had to be renewed from time to time, with the effect of raising the level, the stratification is often helpful to the archaeologist. Stone paving was confined to particular small areas and was very rare before the Roman period; a fine example, of the first century A.D., can be seen on the Panathenaic Way where it climbs up towards the Acropolis.

---

[14] C.W.J. Elliot, J. E. Jones and L. H. Sackett, *BSA* 57, 1962, 75–114; J. E. Jones, A. J. Graham and L. H. Sackett, *BSA* 68, 1973, 355–452; brief accounts by J. E. Jones in *Archaeology* 16, 1963, 276–83; 28, 1975, 6–15; *The Greeks*, in Young Archaeologist Series, London and New York 1971, 33–52; *AAA* 7, 1974, 293–313.

[15] Judeich 177–89; Travlos *PEA* 70, 120; *PDA* 585; *Agora* XIV 108ff, 192ff; on the Panathenaic Way see now *Hesperia* 42, 1973, 125ff, 370ff; for colonnaded streets in Roman times see pp. 88f.

70. Attic Houses (Reconstructions by J. E. Jones)

1. House in ancient village at Draphi, south of Mount Pentelikon (alternative versions)
2. "Priest's House" near Temple of Apollo at Zoster, Southwestern Attica
3. House near Dema Wall
4. House near Vari
5. Farmstead near Sounion, with detached round tower
6. House and Factory at Thorikos

Cobblestones were used here and there, and steep slopes were sometimes provided with rough stone steps.

For the provision of water,[16] wells were in use throughout antiquity; and since all kinds of material were dropped or dumped into them, some of them are archaeological goldmines. Solon in a special law quoted by Plutarch (23.5) encouraged the citizens to dig wells. In the classical period they were normally about 1m in diameter, lined at first with small stones, later (from the fourth century B.C.) with terracotta drums built up in segments. To augment the supply, rainwater was collected by means of pipes in bottle-shaped cement-lined cisterns, several of which were sometimes united by channels.

Like most Greek cities Athens relied mainly on water available on the spot. Lengthy aqueducts were both expensive and precarious. However the tyrants supplemented the supply by bringing water from sources to the northeast of the city by means of conduits cut in the rock and by pipes. One branch traversed the southern slopes of the Acropolis to feed southwestern Athens. Another fed a fountain house southeast of the agora, a structure 6.8m north to south by 18.2m east to west, with a water basin at either end and a columnar facade in the middle of the north side facing the agora.[17] It was built in the latter part of the sixth century, and it is now generally agreed that we have here the much disputed Enneakrounos (Nine-spouted), erected by the tyrants, where formerly there had been a simple spring called Kallirrhoe (Fair-flowing). However there are difficulties still in the identification. The water which rises on the spot now is by no means copious; and it is difficult to see how the "nine spouts" were arranged—perhaps the name has reference to something more than this simple building. The pipe which approached in a trench from the east was constructed of well-made and carefully jointed sections, some of which bear the name of the maker Charon.

Early in the fourth century, at a time when not much major building was going on in the agora or in Athens generally, the old fountain house was reconstructed, and the pipe line south of it was replaced by a massive stone-built conduit .5m wide and 1.2m high.[18] The water flowed along

[16] Judeich 189ff; *The Athenian Agora, A Guide*, 1st edn 1954, 91–96; *Waterworks in the Athenian Agora*, 1968 (Excavations of the Athenian Agora, Picture Book No. 11) 1968; *Agora* XIV 197–203. For a notable cistern (Menon's) see S. G. Miller, *Hesperia* 43, 1974, 194–245.

[17] *Hesperia* 22, 1953, 29–35. On Enneakrounos see *Agora* III 140; XIV 198f; *GRBS* 2, 1959, 33ff; Travlos *PDA* 204.

[18] *Hesperia* 24, 1955, 52f; 25, 1956, 52f; *Agora* XIV 200.

71. Pipeline to Southeast Fountain House (Photo: Agora Excavations)

a channel in the floor, but later pipes were inserted to carry a second stream at a higher level. The aqueduct was continued westwards along the line of the southern street, to feed the new southwest fountain house, which was built immediately west of the old court building. Although remains of this are very scanty indeed, enough is left to show that it was built on the common principle with capacious basins behind a columnar facade, but with two wings in the shape of a reversed L.

Pipe lines, mostly of terracotta, rarely of lead, took water from the main aqueduct and the fountain houses to serve public buildings and shrines of the agora, including the grove of the Twelve Gods. There was no question of piping water to ordinary private houses. Many public buildings required water, but the fountain houses attached to several of them are not earlier than the Hellenistic period. We have already noted the handsome addition to the system made in the time of Hadrian. In all periods care and ingenuity were shown in ensuring that the best use was made of the available water. Fountains were under the supervision of a special *epimeletes*.[19]

Drainage was needed both for the effluents of houses and other buildings and for rain water; after heavy rain veritable torrents could form, which, if not properly controlled, brought down quantities of silt into the low-lying regions. In much of the city drainage was primitive or left to nature. Along some streets there were gutters cut in stone blocks. Once again special provision was made for the agora region, by means of the "Great Drain" which runs down the west side, debouching eventually into the Eridanos stream.[20] The archaeological evidence shows that it was originally made early in the fifth century, rather than in the time of the tyrants. It was impressively constructed, with floor, walls, and roof of solid stone slabs, and in both depth and width it measured about 1m. The surviving covering slabs are mostly later replacements. In the early years of the fourth century two major branches were added, one southwestward up the valley in which the "industrial district" was situated, the other turning eastward and traversing the southern part of the agora. Side drains brought the effluents from various buildings and entered the main channel through apertures; in the case of the Tholos for example the original drain was made of terracotta pipes, but this was replaced at the end of the fourth century by a channel cut in stone blocks, covered partly

[19] Aristotle *Ath. Pol.*, 43.1.
[20] *Hesperia* 2, 1933, 103; 6, 1937, 3–4; 23, 1954, 65; 37, 1968, 61; *Agora* XIV 194ff.

72. Great Drain on West Side of Agora (Photo: Agora Excavations)

by stone slabs, partly by roof tiles.[21] The construction of such minor drains was variable and somewhat haphazard.

In the southwestern branch of the Great Drain, small drains brought in effluents from the houses on either side.[22] Though evidence is scrappy, we can be sure that sanitation (if that is the word) was primitive in classical Athens. Many houses must have depended on cesspools. Well-appointed public latrines do not occur till the early Roman period, when a particularly fine specimen was built just east of the Roman Market, with accommodation for more than sixty persons on the four sides of a large square, and a continuous water channel below; this was not so much a "privy" as a variety of that typically Athenian institution the *lesche* or communal lounge.[23]

Elaborate public baths of Roman type are characteristic of the imperial age, especially the time of Hadrian when the water supply was much improved. Remains have been found, notably hypocausts and marble

[21] *Hesperia* Suppl. 4, 1940, 75–76.
[22] *Hesperia* 20, 1951, 198ff; cf. 28, 1959, 102.
[23] Travlos *PDA* 342; *Agora* XIV 197.

(251)

and mosaic pavements, in many parts of the city.[24] Earlier and simpler *balaneia* are attested by literature and remains as far back as the fifth century B.C. A characteristic form was the tholos or round house, with tubs of terracotta or stone disposed radially around the wall, and simple arrangements for heating the water. Such a bath has been found just outside the Dipylon, built in the fifth century, with an interior diameter of 8.2m. Remains of a smaller establishment have been found outside the Peiraeus Gate, and inscriptions tell of others at the southern and eastern gates. These would be much appreciated by travelers. The baths too served as *leschai*, and Aristophanes reproves the gilded youth for idling in them.

BIBLIOGRAPHY

D. M. Robinson, J. W. Graham et al., *Excavations at Olynthus*, Baltimore 1929–46, especially Volumes VIII, x (on contents) and XII

R. E. Wycherley, "Houses in Ancient Athens," *Journal of Royal Institute of British Architects*, 68, 1961, 282–83 (the first part of the present chapter is based on this)

B. C. Rider, *Ancient Greek Houses*, 2d edn Cambridge (Eng.) 1965

J. W. Graham, "The Greek House and the Roman House," *Phoenix* 20, 1966, 3–31; "Houses of Classical Athens," *Phoenix* 28, 1974, 45–54

Waterworks in the Athenian Agora, 1968 (Excavations of the Athenian Agora, Picture Book No. 11)

Travlos, *PDA* 392ff

Agora XIV, 173–203

J. E. Jones, "Town and Country Houses in Attica in Classical Times," *Miscellanea Graeca* I, *Thorikos and Laurion in Archaic and Classical Times*, Ghent 1975, 63–141

[24] Travlos *PDA* 180f notes twenty-four; cf. T. L. Shear, *Hesperia* 38, 1969, 394ff. On the Dipylon bath see *AA* 1964, 417; at Peiraeus Gate, *Deltion* 21, 1968, B1 74; at other gates, *IG* I² 94, line 37; II² 2495, lines 6–8. For Aristophanes see *Clouds* 991, 1045, 1054, etc.; cf. Ps. Xenophon *Constitution of Athens* 2.10. R. Ginouvès, *Balaneutike*, Paris 1962, gives a detailed study of Greek baths.

CHAPTER XI

The Kerameikos and Other Cemeteries

At Athens as in all Greek cities the graves were outside, especially along the roads leading from the gates. To carry out can mean to bury, in Greek. Pollution was avoided and valuable space within the defenses was not lost. As the city of the living grew, the abodes of the dead were pushed farther outward, though traditions, cults, even pockets or plots of hallowed ground, might be left. We have seen what happened in the agora region, rich in Mycenean and geometric tombs. Some of the suburban cemeteries may have begun as the burial grounds of outlying early communities.

In historical times *sepultura intra urbem* was forbidden. When Marcus Marcellus died at Athens in 45 B.C., Cicero and Servius Sulpicius found that ancient *religio* still prevailed, and Marcellus was given an honorable resting-place at the Academy.[1] As Rodney Young has shown, a ban was imposed probably towards 500 B.C., though the custom may have prevailed from the beginning of the sixth century. The archaic cemetery at the western foot of the Areopagus, apparently a family plot enclosed by a wall, ceased to be used towards 500 B.C., but for about a hundred years longer it continued to exist as a kind of island.[2] Another family burial ground, at the southeast foot of the Kolonos Agoraios, used in the late eighth and early seventh century B.C., was similarly respected and not built over in later times though it was in a very busy area, just south of the Tholos.[3] Presumably the view was taken, as of the Pelargikon, that it was *argon ameinon*, better unworked.

This is not the place to give a complete history of Athenian burial

[1] Cicero *ad Fam.* 4.12.3; see R. Young, *Hesperia* 20, 1951, 131ff; Kurtz and Boardman, 70, 92, doubt whether there was an absolute ban from 500 B.C.; for possible burials *intra muros* they quote *Deltion* 23, 1969, B1, 65, 71ff, to the north of the agora; but if these are indeed adult burials (infants were sometimes buried within the city) they are exceptional.

[2] *Hesperia* 20, 1951, 72ff; *Agora* XIV 10–12.

[3] *Agora* XIV 10.

places and modes of burial—the material is overwhelming—nor to ana-
lyze in detail the form which the graves and the monuments erected
above them assumed in successive periods.[4] It will be sufficient to define
the place of the cemeteries in the scheme of the city, and to look in particular at the Kerameikos, according to Thucydides (2.34.5) the most
beautiful *proasteion* or suburb of Athens.

Graves have been found sporadically all around the periphery, and
near the sites, known or presumed, of a number of gates. Their discovery
has sometimes been helpful in fixing the formal limits of the city and
the line of the walls. Within the confines of the later city early graves,
Mycenean or geometric, are similarly helpful in marking or confirming
the course of age-old streets.

The greatest concentration was outside the northwestern gates. We
can imagine that as compared with the Kerameikos the other cemeteries
were simpler and less well organized, and in general less impressive in
the character of their monuments. In origin and basic form the Kerameikos cemetery was typical; but singled out as the burial place of those
whom the city wished to honor most highly, it attained unusual splendor
and elaboration. But there were notable cemeteries outside the northern
gate on the road to Acharnai, in the northeastern suburbs,[5] and outside
the Gate of Diochares on the east and the various southeastern gates.

The name Kerameikos calls for comment since it has a very flexible
connotation.[6] It means Potters' Quarter; and with certain concentrations
the potters were widely spread—their shops crowded in on the burial
plots as on the agora. "Kerameikos" can be used, properly and literally,
of an extensive northwestern area, both inside and outside the Themistoklean wall; but it also developed certain special meanings, different in different contexts (just as one can say "Covent Garden," meaning neither the
original garden nor the general area to which it gave its name but the
fruit and vegetable market or the opera house). It can refer to the great
cemetery, in Pausanias and other late writers to the agora itself (a somewhat confusing usage), and in certain authors to a quarter notorious for
prostitution and gambling. The broad street which led from the Dipylon
inwards to the agora and outwards, lined with tombs, to the Academy,
was defined by marker stones of the fourth century, of which several

[4] See Kurtz and Boardman, *Greek Burial Customs*, 56ff, 79ff, 105ff; cf. D. W.
Bradeen, *Agora* XVII, *Inscriptions, the Funerary Monuments*, Princeton 1974, 1–2,
for a summary with reference to agora material.
[5] For further finds here see *Deltion* 25, 1972, B1, 79, 84, 87, 90.
[6] *Agora* III 221–24; cf. E. Vanderpool, *Hesperia* 43, 1974, 308 (on Pausanias).

have been found *in situ*, bearing the inscription HOROS KERAMEIKOU (see Fig. 59.3).[7] This is apparently a special or sacral usage, much more restricted than in popular parlance. It was not within these bounds that a character of Alexis (4th century B.C.), wishing to learn the soft voluptuous life, "walking around in Kerameikos found thirty teachers."[8]

The Eridanos stream flows right across northern Athens, approximately east to west; issuing by the Sacred Gate, it eventually joins the Kephisos. An area adjacent to it in the Kerameikos became an important burial ground in sub-Mycenean times, i.e. the twelfth century B.C., and remained so throughout antiquity.

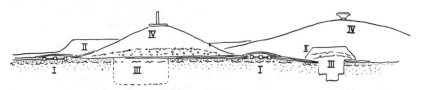

73. Section through part of Kerameikos Cemetery, ca. 650 B.C., I. Scheibler, *Kerameikos 2, The Archaic Cemetery*, 17 fig. 17

    I. Offering ditch. II. Rectangular earthen monument. III. Burial pits.
    IV. Mound with grave marker.

The geometric period in its later phase, the eighth century, was the great age of the monumental funerary amphora, when it was particularly appropriate that the potters' quarter and the principal cemetery should be closely interrelated. Large funerary vases continued to be produced in the seventh century and to be set up on the mounds of various sizes which covered individual graves or family plots. These mounds were sometimes given retaining walls of unbaked brick, and in the latter part of the century by the use of the same material the more compact, rectangular "built tomb" was developed. In the sixth century stone masonry was sometimes used; at the same time the stone-carvers took over from the potters, and developed the funeral stele, a sophisticated form of the old stone marker, besides making figures in the round for grave monuments. Through most of the fifth century funerary sculpture was surprisingly modest, perhaps because of some legal restriction. In the late fifth and fourth centuries the funeral stele reached its greatest artistic heights, and first-rate sculptors, working for wealthy clients, produced reliefs of highly effective and varied composition carved on broad stelai

[7] *IG* II², 2617–2619; *Agora* III 223; XIV 118, 228.

[8] Frag. 203, J. M. Edmonds, *Fragments of Attic Comedy* II 472.

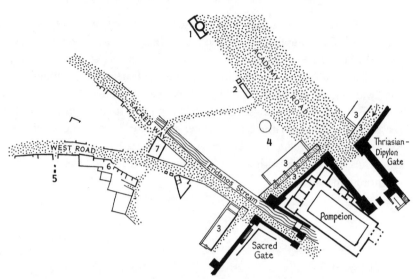

74. Kerameikos and Dipylon (Kurtz and Boardman, *Greek Burial Customs*, Map 5)

1. Large Tomb
2. Tomb of Lacedaemonians
3. Moat
4. Circular bath
5. Shrine of Hekate
6. Dexileos monument
7. Shrine of Tritopatreis

crowned with simple pediments. Set in groups on walled terraces along the streets of the Kerameikos, these monuments made an impressive array. A sumptuary law passed under Demetrios of Phaleron about 310 B.C. put a stop to this luxury, and for a couple of centuries (after which there was a modest revival) funeral monuments took a very simple form, usually a *kioniskos* or small column.

The graves bordered several main roads and several cross streets. The great *dromos* to the Academy left the city by the Dipylon Gate. About two thirds of the way to the Academy, just west of the Church of St. George, a short section of tomb-lined road has been excavated, but this is not in the line of the *dromos* itself, and is only 4.8m wide; apparently it was a kind of duplicate or service road, used by wheel traffic.[9] The Sacred Way to Eleusis, marked by boundary stones, left by the Sacred Gate, immediately southwest of the Dipylon. After about 70m this road divided, the right fork continuing the Sacred Way, still tomb-lined,[10] and the left linking with the road to Peiraeus, which emerged from the Peiraeus Gate some distance to the south. One may also note a fourth

[9] For recent finds on this road note *Deltion* 22, 1967, B1, 88; 25, 1970, B1, 73.
[10] *AAA* 6, 1973, 277–81, gives recent discoveries along the road; in *AA* 1973, 172–93, Kübler discusses the area in front of the Sacred Gate; note also U. Knigge, *AA* 1972, 584–602 and forthcoming Kerameikos volume.

road which left by the gate called Eriai, about 150m northeast of the Dipylon, in the direction of the Kolonos Hippios (Sophokles' Kolonos).[11] There was an important cemetery on this road too; whether one would include it in the Kerameikos in the widest sense of the name is doubtful.

On the road to the Academy was the *demosion sema*, the national cemetery, where the city buried those whom it particularly wished to honor, including those who died in battle; if they could not be buried they were still given a monument, with names inscribed.[12] Pausanias gives us an impressive roll call of famous men, interspersed with groups of unnamed warriors from various battle fields; Thrasyboulos, Perikles, Chabrias, Phormio, Kleisthenes, Apollodoros, Euboulos, Tolmides, Konon and Timotheos, Zeno and Chrysippos, Harmodios and Aristogeiton, Ephialtes and Lycurgus. Two philosophers, one notes, appear in the list, Zeno and Chrysippos; and Plato was buried near the Academy. There does not seem to have been a "poets' corner"; but just one painter is named, Nikias son of Nikomedes. Nikias the famous general, Pausanias tells us, was denied commemoration here, because he had voluntarily submitted to the enemy.

None of the tombs of the great ones has been found, but among those in the thoroughly excavated section just outside the Dipylon are several which are of special interest. One would not expect Spartans to be buried here; but in fact one of the most impressive monuments, on the southwest side of the road about 80m from the Dipylon, a long rectangular walled terrace with marble slabs inscribed with the names of the dead, was the tomb of the Lacedaemonians who were killed at Athens during the troubles in the time of the Thirty, 403 B.C.[13] An even more imposing monument has been found about as far again along the same side of the road;[14] this too is a long rectangle, with guardian dogs at either end, but

[11] *Hesperia* 32, 1963, 113ff, a group of graves on this road which, says C. Boulter, gives a cross section of an ordinary Athenian cemetery; note also D. O. Skirlandi, *ArchEph* 1969 (for 1968) 8–52.

[12] I, 29. The date of the institution of the *demosion sema* and the burial of the war dead in it is doubtful; F. Jacoby, *JHS* 64, 1944, 37ff, places it in 465–464 B.C.; A. W. Gomme, *Historical Commentary on Thucydides* II, Oxford, 1956, prefers to place it well before the Persian War; cf. D. W. Bradeen, *CQ* NS 19, 1969, 155.

Just what Pausanias himself saw is doubtful; cf. Jacoby 40, Gomme 96; the area suffered badly in war time, but it was still apparently the national cemetery, where honor was paid in some form to the city's great men; and Bradeen believes there were still monuments there for Pausanias to see.

For the "casualty lists" see now Bradeen, as n. 4 above, 3ff.

[13] *AA* 1965, 314ff.

[14] *AA* 1965, 322ff.

in the middle of the front is a circular structure crowned by a large marble vase; the tomb is dated about the middle of the fourth century, but unfortunately it cannot be given a name. Between this and graves just north of the monument of the Lacedaemonians are traces of potters' workshops. Even in this hallowed place we find the curious mixture so characteristic of Athens; the name Kerameikos is not merely a survival but represents a reality.

To digress from the Kerameikos for a moment—one of the finest of Athenian monuments, of the fourth century b.c., has been investigated in recent years in Kallithea, to the west of the city, north of the northern long wall outside a gate.[15] The fragments show that it consisted of a podium adorned with friezes and surmounted by a naiskos which probably contained three statues. Other fragments seem to belong to a second large monument. Such tombs are minor works of architecture, if not mausolea. About 700m north of the Dipylon, on what appears to be a cross street between the road to the Academy and the road to Kolonos, an impressive group of fourth-century statues—including three women, a little girl, and a lion—has been found in an isolated excavation. They stood on the burial terrace of what must have been a wealthy family.[16]

One is not surprised to find shrines among the tombs. Pausanias (1.29.2) notes a precinct of Artemis, and wooden images of the goddess under the titles of Ariste (Best) and Kalliste (Fairest); and a small temple of Dionysos Eleuthereus, to which the image of the god was brought annually from the theater shrine. The site of the shrine of Artemis is probably fixed by the discovery of inscriptions, and what may be an angle of the precinct wall, on the southwest side of the road about 250m from the Dipylon. Artemis was also worshiped as Soteira (Savior), and the finding places of inscriptions suggest that this cult may have been associated with Ariste-Kalliste, or else with the shrine of Hekate noted below.[17]

Other curious shrines stand among the splendid monuments in the western area on the Eleusis and Peiraeus roads. Not far from the gate, on the left, is a triangular precinct, with a small temple-like structure in-

---

[15] *AAA* 1, 1968, 35-36; 4, 1971, 108-10; *Archaeology* 26, 1973, 54-57. Graves ranging from Mycenean to Byzantine are constantly turning up in odd places; one should keep an eye on *Deltion* and *AAA*.

[16] *AAA* 2, 1969, 257-68; *Deltion* 24, 1970, 56ff.

[17] *IG* ɪɪ², 4665-4668, cf. 788, 789, 1298; Judeich 411-12; Travlos *PDA* 301-2; *Hesperia* 10, 1941, 242; 28, 1959, 278. Soteira—*IG* ɪɪ² 1343, 4631, 4689, 4695; *Hesperia* 10, 1941, 62.

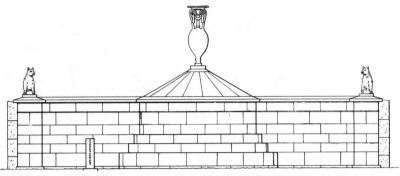

75. Large Tomb (Restoration by D. Ohly, *AA* 1965, 283 taf. 1)

serted in the northwest corner; there is nothing to determine the cult. Just opposite, right in the fork of the two roads, is another shrine which is fortunately identified by boundary stones as belonging to the Tritopatreis, obscure ancient deities associated with ancestor worship, and possibly also with the winds.[18] It has the form of an elongated triangle, with the apex (on the southeast) cut off. The broader northwestern part is enclosed by a solid wall; this no doubt was the *abaton* or inner sanctum, normally inaccessible, the rest of the precinct being an open *temenos*.

Just off the Peiraeus road farther west, on a side street leading south, is an enclosure of irregular shape, kept free from graves. On the south side is a well, in the northern part a curious assemblage of cult objects, a podium or altar base with two steps leading up to it, a marble omphalos (a half-egg-shaped stone with its top cut flat) surrounded by a low rectangular wall of baked brick, and a base with a triangular cutting in it, suggesting that here stood a three-bodied Hekate. The remains are of Roman date, but the shrine may well be earlier.[19]

This area, above the west bank of the Eridanos, adjoining the Sacred Way and the Peiraeus road, was much favored by wealthy and distinguished Athenian families, and here in large numbers stood the fine fourth-century sculptured monuments. The family burial grounds by now commonly took the form of terraced plots with solid stone retaining walls. On these the individual monuments were set up in rows, and we may assume that cypresses and shrubs were planted in between. Besides the stelai there were marble vases (especially the tall graceful *loutropho-*

[18] Judeich 410; D. Ohly, *AA* 1965, 327–28; K. Kübler, *AA* 1973, 172, 302; *AthMitt* 1974, 191ff; cf. A. B. Cook, *Zeus* III, Cambridge 1940, 112ff.
[19] Brückner, *Friedhof am Eridanos* 43–47, 53–55; Travlos *PDA* 302.

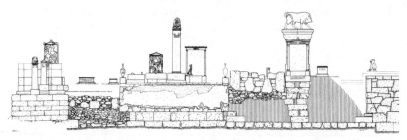

76. Street of Tombs, South Side (Drawing by D. Ohly, *AA* 1965 343 taf. 3)

roi, water-carriers, which distinguished the graves of unmarried girls); and guardian animals. The conspicuous bull of Dionysios may have some reference to his eponymous deity. The stelai with their sculptured reliefs and occasionally painted figures show endless variety in subject, style, and sentiment. Most conspicuous at a corner between the Peiraeus road and a side street, in an unusually elaborate architectonic frame, a quadrant on a square base, was the relief of the heroic cavalryman Dexileos, riding down his enemy. On the opposite side of the road was the gentle Hegeso, wife of Proxenos, selecting a necklace from the box held by her maid. Dexileos' monument was a cenotaph. His body lay with his men on the road to the Academy. One could wish that to match the opulence of the private family piety displayed on the west bank we had more material evidence from the *demosion sema* of the honors paid by the city to her great men and those who died for her.

BIBLIOGRAPHY

A. Brückner, *Der Friedhof am Eridanos*, Berlin 1909

G. Karo, *An Attic Cemetery*, Philadelphia 1943

K. Kübler et al., *Kerameikos, Ergebnisse der Ausgrabungen*, I–IX, 1939–1976 (volumes by Kübler on the cemeteries of the 6th and 5th centuries and by Hoepfner on the Pompeion are announced)

D. Ohly, "Kerameikos-Grabung 1956–1961," *AA* 1965, 277–375 (further reports in *AA*)

D. C. Kurtz and J. Boardman, *Greek Burial Customs*, London 1971; detailed references for the various Athenian cemeteries are given, 345ff

Travlos *PDA* 300ff

I. Scheibler, *The Archaic Cemetery* (Kerameikos Books No. 3) Athens 1973

The Kerameikos Excavation, a comprehensive brochure by D. Ohly, is published by the German Archaeological Institute and available on the site.

CHAPTER XII

Peiraeus

One should not think of the Athenian *polis* as consisting simply of the city itself, the *asty*, together with tiny hamlets and homesteads scattered up and down Attica. Some of the country *demoi* were considerable communities in their own right with their own traditions and institutions, trades and cults, conscious of their identity and peculiar character, each with its local center.[1] Alimous, Zoster, Prospalta, Anagyrous, Prasiai, Lamptrai, Phlya, Myrrhinous, Athmonia—these are singled out by Pausanias (1.31) because they had notable cults. Phlya, northeast of Athens between Pentelikon and Hymettos, had shrines of Apollo Dionysodotos, Artemis Selasphoros, Dionysos Anthios, the Nymphs called Ismenides, Earth, "whom they call the Great Goddess," Demeter Anesidora, Zeus Ktesios, Athena Tithrone, Kore Protogone, and the Semnai. Eleusis of course with its Mysteries was unique in religious importance. Brauron had its famous shrine of Artemis. Acharnai, besides the cult of Ares which we have noted, had cults of Apollo Agyieus, Herakles, Athena Hygieia, Athena Hippia, and Dionysos under the titles of Melpomenos and Kissos. The Acharnians, living north of Athens on the south side of Mt. Parnes, numerically a powerful group, farmers and charcoal-burners, "black and fierce and strange of mouth," are dramatically presented by Aristophanes as something more than so many ordinary Athenians. Some deme centers would be hardly more than little villages; a few possessed, even if in simple form, some of the architectural elements of a small *polis*. Archaeologically, Thorikos in the southeast now provides a specially interesting example.[2] The curious elongated theater, probably also used as an assembly place for the demesmen, and the fine temple of Demeter, built of southern Attic marble, have long been known. This temple stood

[1] See C.W.J. Eliot, *Coastal Demes of Attica*, Toronto 1962; J. S. Traill, *Political Organization of Attica*, Hesperia Suppl. XIV 1975; M. Petropoulakou and E. Pentazos, *Attica*, Athens 1972 (Vol. 23 in series *Ancient Greek Cities*).

[2] H. Mussche et al., *Thorikos, Preliminary Reports of the Excavations*, 1963ff (still in progress); *Thorikos, a Guide to the Excavations*, Brussels 1974; J. E. Jones, "Town and Country Houses in Attica" (see Fig. 69) 120ff. (See Bibliography for Ch. X above.)

somewhat aloof in the plain below, but there is now evidence of small shrines among the houses as at Athens. In recent years Belgian archaeologists have excavated a whole "industrial quarter" comparable with those of Athens, with houses and workshops of the fifth and fourth century B.C., of irregular and variable form, built along narrow streets on the terraced hillside, in which among other things silver from the mines of nearby Laurion was treated. Thorikos had had a history as long as Athens itself, going back to prehistoric times and Mycenean tholos tombs.

Peiraeus was unique in size and importance. Situated on a peninsula (formerly an island) 7 or 8km to the southwest of Athens, developed by Themistokles and his successors in the fifth century as a strong and well-planned port to replace the old open roadstead at Phaleron to the east, it was no mere adjunct or suburb. Of course it was a naval base and a place of transit for the export of Attic products such as pottery and the import of grain from the Euxine and other essentials; but furthermore it was a kind of duplicate *asty*, complete in all its elements, but contrasting with the parent town in both its natural shape and its artificial form. A large and peculiarly important part of the population lived and worked there. "Themistokles thought Peiraeus more useful than the upper city," says Thucydides (1.93.7), "and often advised the Athenians, if they were hard pressed, to go down to it and face all their enemies with the fleet." One can imagine that if this idea had been carried to its conclusion, Peiraeus would have become the main center for political and practical purposes, and the old town around the hill of Athena would then have been left as an impressive appendage, venerable by reason of its historical and religious associations. Athenian conservatism prevailed; but a compromise was achieved, the old town and the new were linked and made into one vast defensive system by the Long Walls; and at the same time the new town received all the elements which constituted a Greek city, powerful fortifications, an agora or indeed two, many notable shrines and temples, and the usual public buildings. In addition it was given something which Old Athens never even began to achieve—a sophisticated and unified overall plan in the contemporary Hippodamian manner.

Remains are pitifully scanty, and highly elusive. Impressive bits of the walls and gates have come to light here and there, enough to make the line of the fortifications fairly clear.[3] It appears that the original wall left

[3] *AJA* 63, 1959, 280, records the discovery of a section built of polygonal limestone in the time of Konon. For inscriptions see pp. 20f.

out a segment of the southern part of the main peninsula of Akte, whereas the wall as restored by Konon after the destruction by the Peloponnesians in 404 B.C. followed the coastline more closely; and that Thucydides' statement that the wall was built of solid stone throughout is true only of certain parts.

Of special interest are a number of *horoi* or boundary stones, demarcating particular areas.[4] One series is concerned with the harbor installations; another, somewhat later, with streets, the agora, the emporion, an anchorage, a propylon, a heroon, and so forth. The latter series may reasonably be associated with the work of Hippodamos, the well-known Milesian architect, who according to Aristotle in the *Politics* (2.5) applied his skills at Peiraeus, presumably in the 460s. The essence of the Hippodamian method was *diairesis*, meticulous division of the area available, and *nemesis*, allocation of particular sites. The archaeological evidence gives no more than hints of Hippodamos' solution of his difficult problem. The lines of streets have been picked up here and there. Vestiges of cross streets near the modern Plateia Korais seem to show that the central part of the ancient city had a rectangular grid with the same orientation as the modern. But in some outlying parts it seems that concessions were made to the contours and the orientation was somewhat different. Slight remains of houses have been noticed here and there; these are similar in general character to the houses of the upper city, as far as one can tell, but conform to the rectangular plan.[5]

The agora of Peiraeus was called Hippodameia after the planner; a likely site is in the center of the town north of the middle harbor Zea and west of the hill Mounychia. Pausanias tells us (1.1.3) that the town had a second agora, near the harbor. This area can perhaps more properly be called the Emporion, and remains of stoas which probably belong to it have been found on the eastern side of the great commercial harbor, Kantharos. It was in this region that a precious find of bronze statues was made several years ago, including a fine archaic Apollo; presumably the figures were awaiting shipment when they became the victims of some local catastrophe.[6]

On the west slope of the hill Mounychia are slight remains of the

---

[4] *IG* i², 887–902; D. K. Hill, *AJA* 36, 1932, 254; R. E. Wycherley, *Historia* 13, 1964, 137–38; A. Burns, *Historia* 25, 1976, 417.

[5] See J. E. Jones (as cited in note 2 above), 98–100; cf. B. C. Rider, *The Greek House*, Cambridge 1916 reprinted 1965, 222–24.

[6] *Arch. Reports (JHS)* 1959, 23.

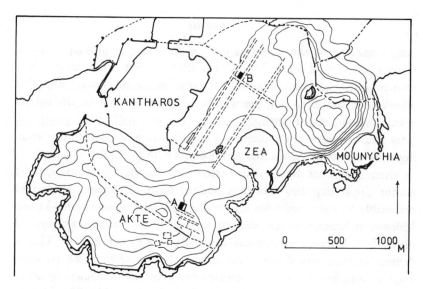

77. Peiraeus (J. E. Jones, after Judeich)

great theater of Peiraeus,[7] used not only for plays but on occasion for meetings of the general assembly of Athenian citizens. Better preserved is a small theater of Hellenistic date a little to the west of Zea.

An inscription tells us of an Old Bouleuterion and an Old Strategion at Peiraeus.[8] Thus it appears that the "usual offices" were duplicated, so that the instruments of government could on occasion function in the harbor town. We also hear of the Boule meeting "on the jetty every day until the fleet sails."

The one major component of a Greek city of which we hear nothing is a great gymnasium; perhaps the ancient gymnasia in the suburbs of the upper town sufficed for all, but we can well believe that some of the numerous palaestras were in Peiraeus.

The shipsheds were reckoned among the glories of the Athenian people.[9] Remains of many have been found, slight but enough to show their form, especially in Zea, the principal base of the war fleet. A typical mode of construction was to build a wall parallel with the sea's edge, and then to set rows of columns at right angles for the support of the roof, with

[7] Thucydides 8.93.1; E. Fiechter, *Das Theater im Piraeus*, 1950; *Deltion* 22, 1967, B1, 143.

[8] *IG* ii², 1035, lines 43 and 44; P. J. Rhodes, *The Athenian Boule*, Oxford 1972, 120.

[9] Demosthenes 22.76; 23.207; there were 94 in Kantharos, 196 in Zea, 82 in Mounychia, *IG* ii², 1627-1631; on 1628 see D. R. Laing, *Hesperia* 37, 1968 244-54.

long stone bases between on which the ships were laid, and which served as slipways.

A great arsenal for the storage of naval equipment, a rectangular building divided into three by internal colonnades, is known in detail from the specifications given in an inscription of the latter half of the fourth century B.C., even though its site has not been precisely located; the architects are named as Philon and Euthydomos.[10]

Peiraeus had many cults and shrines, some of them duplicating those of the upper city. Few can be located. Pausanias was particularly impressed by the shrine of Athena Soteira and Zeus Soter. On Mounychia was a notable shrine of Artemis, and one of Bendis, a foreign importation, natural in Peiraeus. Possible remains are of an Asklepieion, a shrine of Zeus Meilichios, and a healing shrine of a hero called Serangos, all southwest of Mounychia; an enclosure probably sacred to Dionysos in the middle of the city near the Plateia Korais; and a shrine of Aphrodite Euploia (fair sailing), founded by Themistokles, rebuilt by Konon, in the northwest at the base of the peninsula of Eetioneia.[11] Themistokles himself was naturally honored at Peiraeus, and Pausanias saw his grave, possibly at the westernmost tip of the peninsula of Akte.[12]

Thus the general form of a great city, and many curious details, dimly emerge. One could wish for much more. Peiraeus was considered a beautiful city in antiquity. It presented the master planner with a challenging site, more difficult, more complex than Miletos itself or Rhodes, where we see the method more clearly revealed; and we can believe that Hippodamos, and the architects who filled the outlines which he drew, realized its possibilities. Upper city and harbortown must have presented a striking contrast. The plan of Peiraeus was created in a few years, mainly by the genius of one man. Athens itself just grew, accumulating over the centuries, irregular and largely haphazard; and it was never radically replanned. In spite of its exquisite temples and other fine monuments, the city as a whole never attained that state of *kosmos* (orderliness, harmony) which in the Greek view was a constituent of ideal beauty. One need not regret this. In the peculiarity and complexity of its architectural form the city fully reflects the astonishing variety and vigor of Athenian life, and the phases and vicissitudes of Athenian history.

---

[10] *IG* II², 1668; Dinsmoor *Architecture*, 241–42; K. Jeppesen, *Acta Archaeologica*, (Copenhagen) 32, 1961, 221.
[11] Pausanias 1.1.3; *IG* II², 1657; Judeich 446.
[12] P. W. Wallace, *Hesperia* 41, 1972, 451–62.

BIBLIOGRAPHY

Judeich 430–56

A. W. Gomme, *Commentary on Thucydides* 1, Oxford 1945, 261–70

F. G. Maier, *Griechische Mauerbauinschriften* 1, Heidelberg 1959, 17ff

Christos Th. Panagos, *Le Pirée*, Athènes 1968, translated from Greek by P. Gérardat

J. S. Boersma, *Athenian Building Policy from 561 to 405 B.C.*, Groningen 1970 (see Index, "Peiraieus")

R. Martin, *L'Urbanisme dans la Grèce Antique*, 2d edn, Paris 1974, 105–10

R. E. Wycherley, "Peiraeus," in R. Stillwell et al., ed., *The Princeton Encyclopedia of Classical Sites*, Princeton 1976, 683–84

The Stones

"Attica has a plentiful supply of stone," says Xenophon,[1] "from which are made the fairest temples and altars, and the most beautiful statues for the gods." Athens was indeed blessed in its building stones, as in its fine clay. The immensely complicated geophysical processes which created the exquisite landscape of Attica produced a variety of useful and often beautiful materials, nicely distributed about the land. The stones are mostly limestones of different sorts. Marble itself is a limestone miraculously metamorphosed by titanic heat and pressure into its characteristic crystalline structure, thus forming in the body of the earth what M. Aurelius (9.36) aptly calls *poroi*, calluses or nodules. This has happened in many places, but in most the result consists of comparatively small lumps or thin veins; much rarer are the massive beds from which can be extracted the great blocks needed for the major architectural members of temples and other large buildings. In this too Attica is exceptionally favored. More than one huge layer runs through the fabric of both Pentelikon and Hymettos; and other extensive beds lie near the southern tip of Attica.

Yet ancient Athens was not a city of gleaming marble, or even of gray or brown stone. It would be much nearer the truth to say it was a city of mud brick. In sheer bulk this was by far the commonest material. The raw ingredients were ready to hand in inexhaustible quantities, and easily processed and handled. Unbaked or sun-dried brick (sometimes called adobe) on a low stone socle, was used for all houses, even the wealthiest as far as we can tell; for some public buildings and lesser shrines; and for most of the length and the major part of the height of the great fortification walls, even in their later and more sophisticated form, as inscriptions show. This by no means implies that such structures were ill-built. Unbaked brick is a very serviceable material if the bricks are well made and well laid. It is strong and durable, if given protection above from the rain, and a coat of plaster. When fully exposed to the elements it naturally disintegrates, and for this reason very little ancient brickwork has survived. A good example at Athens has been found in

---

[1] *Poroi* 1.4.

the core and upper part of the city wall near the Dipylon gate; in the agora a little brickwork can still be seen in the walls of the South Stoa. On most sites no more than a layer of clay has been left. Baked brick was not used at Athens till Roman methods of construction were introduced, and the same may be said of concrete. Of course terracotta was universally employed for roof tiles and ornamentation. Looking down from the high town on the low town, one must have had a vivid impression of an irregular jumble of red-tile roofs, just as one has looking down the north slope today.

Roof beams and rafters and upper floors, stairs and light pillars were of wood. The supply of timber was none too plentiful at Athens, and large quantities were required for ship-building. Ancient wood has perished almost to the last scrap, but the places where the beams rested can sometimes be seen in stone structures preserved to sufficient height. Even the great standby of the archaeologist, the posthole, is not often found, since posts were normally set on stone bases; but there are some curious examples in the agora, dug for the erection of *ikria*, the wooden stands used by spectators at the festivals. Metal was used in comparatively small quantities for dowels and clamps, door fittings and the like, and occasionally to increase the weight-bearing capacity of large stone beams. Lead was mined along with the silver at Laurion.

Inevitably archaeologists and students of architecture are mainly concerned with stone. This provides almost the whole of their material, with the exception of architectural terracottas, which have their own peculiar importance; and even when the ancient city stood complete, the various stones and the manner in which they were used had a decisive effect on its architectural character. In this synopsis of the stones of Athens, their nature and use, examples will be constantly given from the agora, with supplementation from other sites. Nowhere else can one find in a single archaeological zone such fully representative material, such rich variety, or such good examples of the ingenious combination of different materials in a single building.

The most primitive way of using stone was to gather up what Thucydides (4.4) calls *lithoi logades* from the ground. Such "field stones" occur in the foundations of some early buildings; in the agora we have an example in the archaic apsidal temple of Apollo on the west side.

Good quarried building stone was not only plentiful in Attica but nicely varied. To begin with there was the limestone of the hills on and around which the city of Athens was built. Other very hard limestones were to be found not far away. Then there was the range of less hard and more easily worked stones conventionally known as "poros." A red conglomerate was used for foundations. For the finest work several excellent marbles were available; above all, on Pentelikon a few miles north of the city a large part of a great mountain side consisted of a stone as beautiful as any in the world, admirably suited for both sculptural and architectural work, and incidentally for epigraphical purposes. We saw how a single building in the agora, the Stoa of Zeus Eleutherios, built in the latter part of the fifth century B.C., offers a remarkable conspectus of nearly all these materials; with several grades of limestone, including the brown Aiginetan, and the marble both Pentelic and Hymettian. The building thus produced combined elegance with economy.

On and around the site of Athens, superimposed on the basic schists, are a number of hills, including the Acropolis, whose tops consist of a very hard limestone. This is what one can properly call the *epichorios lithos*, the native, "on-the-spot stone" of Athens, though as far as I know the term does not actually occur in an Athenian context in ancient authors. The stone was a major building material in the Mycenean and archaic periods, and for more limited purposes it continued in use even later, though in general it was replaced in the fifth century by something more tractable. Though it is now usually called "Acropolis limestone," the sacred hill of Athena was not defaced or weakened by quarries, and the stone was extracted from several of the other hills. The man-made chasm northwest of the Hill of the Nymphs, known as the *barathron*, into which certain malefactors were thrown, may be one of the earliest quarries of Athens. The stone has a peculiar beauty, being bluish gray, with a tinge of pale red-brown especially when broken. It is extremely hard, difficult to work into square blocks or other precise shapes, and more suited to "Cyclopean" or rough polygonal masonry. The massive "Pelasgic" wall which protected the Acropolis from Mycenean times down to the sixth century B.C. was of this material; and the stone continued to be employed in the city walls of later times, though less hard limestone and ultimately conglomerate tended to replace it.

The same stone was used for the inner foundations of the archaic temple of Athena on the Acropolis. In the agora it occurs in the foundations and socles of the earliest sixth-century buildings, and the foundations of the first Bouleuterion. In the neighboring temple of the Mother the limestone foundations were set on a bed of field stones; and the leveling course for the great drain in the west side was made of irregular masses of the same rock. After the Persian Wars we still find the stone in use, occasionally in temples and public buildings, frequently in the socles of neighboring houses, sometimes in quite neat polygonal style, sometimes in more careless shape.

The use of the native stone had a special appropriateness, and on the Acropolis itself the walls and foundations seemed almost to grow from the native rock. But it also had its disadvantages and limitations, and from the sixth century the Athenians were going farther afield—to Peiraeus, to the mountains, eventually to Aigina—for different and more tractable material. Transport was laborious and added greatly to the cost, and this factor had to be balanced against convenience in use and aesthetic effect. An alternative hard stone, a "tertiary" fresh-water limestone, was found in the district of Kara, in the foothills of Hymettos, about 3.5 km southeast of Athens. This yellowish gray and somewhat more porous stone is still very hard and resistant but less difficult to shape accurately and capable of a finer surface treatment. The architects of the Peisistratids made good use of it, in the stylobate of the colonnade of the old temple of Athena on the Acropolis and in the foundations of the temple of Olympian Zeus. In the early fifth-century Parthenon, it was used in the lowest of the three steps, the two above being of Pentelic marble, and the foundations below of "poros." In the agora, as we have seen, Kara stone is found in the walls of the fourth-century temple of Apollo. In later times it was not much used.

Kara stone was a fine material; but for most purposes softer stones, less expensive and laborious to quarry and to shape, were quite satisfactory. For such material the Athenians drew on the local limestones, mainly from Peiraeus. Stones of this kind are now commonly called "poros," but only in works on Greek archaeology and architecture. If one takes all its oddly varied ancient uses into account the word should be allowed to include a wide range of stones, medium hard to medium soft, grayish or yellowish, essentially limestones, with different admixtures of other elements (argillaceous, occasionally arenaceous, i.e. clayey or sandy). The color varies with the composition—whitish, grayish, yellowish, brownish; more poetically it is sometimes called "creamy" or "honey-colored" (whatever that means). The word is imprecise and unscientific—it is not recognized by petrographers; in fact it embraces the greater part of the ordinary, work-a-day building stones of the Greeks, which were not specially fine and not excessively difficult to handle. Poros does *not* of course mean "porous," even if some of the stones have this quality in varying degrees. In ancient usage, one should also note that "poros" sometimes means a hard lump or a block; and that for its other sense, a type of stone, *porinos lithos* is an alternative expression.

The virtues of "poros" were workability and adaptability. These stones played a great part in the transmutation of the Greek temple from flimsier and rougher materials into solid well-shaped stone, in the art which Lawrence calls "petrified carpentry,"[2] in the development of the orders of architecture. They were suitable not merely for cutting well-fitted blocks but for architectural detail and ornament and for sculpture, as we see in the archaic buildings on the Acropolis. They prepared the way for finer work in marble. The softer types, unless the blocks were safely buried in foundations, might require a protective coating of stucco, and this might also be applied as a ground for painting or in imitation of marble. Finally one should note that some poros, comparatively soft and easily worked as it emerged from the quarry, acquired a higher degree of hardness after a period of exposure.

Again the Athenians were fortunate. Several grades of poros could be quarried at Peiraeus. Inscriptions speak of Aktites stone, quarried on the peninsula of Akte; and, since it is specified for such important structures as the walls of the great arsenal of Philon near the harbor, perhaps one should assume that the term does not mean Peiraeus stone in general, but stone of the better quality, quite hard and durable, gray or yellowish gray. The builders supplemented local resources with the stone of Aigina, which though geologically similar had its own peculiar characteristics.

"Poros" was in use at Athens from early archaic times, throughout antiquity and even later. Because of its variety and versatility the uses of this stone were almost limitless. It is found in all parts of buildings of all kinds, including great fortification and terrace walls. In substructures both the hard and the soft types were used. Material from the agora covers the whole range and in particular offers a number of nice examples of the ingenious and economical combination of several kinds in a single structure. We have already noted this in the Stoa of Zeus. Turning to the neighboring Stoa Basileios, one first notices a large roughly shaped block of hard tan-colored poros, 3m long, lying in front—it is probably the "archons' stone," on which these officials took their oath. The wall socles are a curious mixture, with polygonal limestone in the

[2] *Greek Architecture*, 3d edn, Penguin 1973, 99.

rear (west) wall, a soft yellowish poros from Peiraeus in the north; the columns were of this latter material, and coated with a fine stucco. For the step and the stylobate a harder gray stone was used.

By contrast, the manner of the use of these stones in the foundations of a major temple can be studied in the Hephaisteion. The foundations of the peristyle are of a brown granular poros; the euthynteria is of a harder gray-veined type, and so is the lowest step, the other two being of Pentelic marble. The cella foundations are of a soft gray poros, except for the top course, which was of the brown stone. Thus though the temple was well-founded, economy of effort and expense was achieved in the working of the stone.

Peiraeus stone was used in bulk in the substructures of the great buildings on the Acropolis, the Parthenon, the Propylaia, and the Erechtheion. As one ascends to the Propylaia, strong well-cut stone of this type can be seen displayed to good advantage in the great terrace walls.

Although they had adequate materials available no farther away than Peiraeus, some discriminating fifth-century architects, in spite of the added expense of shipment, showed a preference for brown stone from Aigina, lighter and easier to work, finer and more uniform in texture than the gray stone of Peiraeus, but not so strong. We have already seen it in the walls of the Stoa of Zeus. Early in the fifth century it was used, above foundations of rough limestone, for the very well-built walls of the large square enclosure at the west end of the south side of the agora, which was probably a law court, perhaps the Heliaia. Most of the bits and pieces which can be safely assigned to the Stoa Poikile are of Aiginetan poros; but certain elements are of the harder stone of Peiraeus. The workmanship again is excellent.

The most conspicuous example of the use of Aiginetan stone in the agora is in the vast Hellenistic Middle Stoa, in steps, columns, screen walls, and entablature, in fact most of the building except the foundations; marble was confined to the metopes and a gutter which ran along the south side.

Peiraeus stone continued in use in the Hellenistic period, and was brought up in great quantity for the walls of the Stoa of Attalos, as for its modern rebuilding, but the foundations of both the Stoa of Attalos and of the Middle Stoa are of a coarse reddish-brown pebbly conglomerate. This stone, not unattractive in appearance but incapable of taking a fine finish, was extremely useful for foundations, underpinning, substructures, and cores. It is in fact a kind of natural concrete. The pebbles consist of limestone, marble, schist, quartz—anything which the streams brought down from Hymettos and the other hills; the red color is due to the mineral content of the cementing medium. This stone too is apt to gain something in hardness through exposure and drying. It was at hand in large quantities, for example at the foot of Hymettos near the Kara beds in the deme Agryle; it may well be what inscriptions call *lithos Agryleikos*, and it is undoubtedly what they call *lithoi arouraioi*, a term which does not mean "field" stones in our sense. In spite of its abundance and accessibility it was not in general use until the fourth century, when we find it in the agora in the foundations of the temple of Apollo Patroos and its tiny neighbor the temple of Zeus Phratrios and Athena Phratria. Its earliest use may be in the latter part of the fifth century. We see it in the retaining wall behind the Stoa of Zeus, alongside poros, but this wall may be somewhat later than the Stoa itself. About conglomerate foundations and retaining walls in the theater of Dionysos there is still some doubt; though they have been commonly dated in the latter part of the fifth century, fresh examination of the archaeological evidence is now said to bring them down into the fourth. Conglomerate was henceforth used on a big scale, in fortifications and in the foundations of the great Hellenistic buildings. As one surveys the southern part of the agora today it dominates and colors the scene more than any other element. This gives a misleading impression since it was all originally intended to be hidden. In the greatly extended Hellenistic Metroon, it is curious to note how the new conglomerate foundations, besides overlying their ancient predecessors at various points, incorporate many re-used blocks of poros and Acropolis limestone. One has to bear in mind that as time goes on the incorporation of material from older buildings, now destroyed or dismantled, produces complications and odd mixtures.

In handbooks of architecture, marble and the buildings made of it naturally receive by far the greatest share of attention; in the present context one can deal with it more cursorily, giving a synopsis and dealing with a few particular points. Marble need not be placed in an entirely different category from all the rest; in fact it is the finest and most beautiful of limestones. Its supremacy as a material for sculpture is obvious. In architecture it can be carved into exquisite moldings and other decorative details which retain their precision of form with remarkable permanence. In plain walls the blocks can be given a perfect finish and knife-edge joints, so that the unity of the whole wall surface is maintained and emphasized; whereas in some stones the joints and the character of the individual blocks are more or less obvious and sometimes even accentuated in various ways.

At Athens in the sixth century marble was used in comparatively small quantities, for sculpture and architectural detail. Island marbles were imported, including the white, pure, large grained, translucent Parian; at the same time the local quarries were being developed, on Pentelikon and Hymettos, on a small scale at first. Early in the fifth century they were greatly extended on Pentelikon; quarrying became a major industry, and marble took its place as a principal construction material, used for whole buildings, mainly temples, and not merely for embellishment in detail.

Either Pentelikon or Hymettos alone could have supplied the needs of a great city. The Athenians preferred Pentelikon, even though the distance was somewhat greater, and they made it their principal source; Hymettos was essentially supplementary. Both mountains had a massive marble core, "the lower marble," i.e. lower in geological stratification, the "crystalline mountain-base" ("das krystalline Grundgebirge," Lepsius) and other layers major and minor. On both mountains the typical product of the main "lower marble" was white and medium in grain size, of the "upper" bluish gray (through the presence of carbonaceous matter) and somewhat finer in grain; but the Athenians came to think of the white marble as characteristically Pentelic, the other as Hymettian; and in spite of objections which have recently been raised, with due caution—recognizing that neither mountain provided one type exclusively—we may continue to use the names as they did. In Periklean Athens stones were known by the place where they were quarried, and the common term for marble was simply *Pentelikos lithos*. The great fifth-century building program was carried out in white stone brought from Pentelikon, as contemporary documents show; and the principal quarries were near the modern quarries which are so conspicuous as one looks toward the northeast from the Acropolis, on the southwestern flank of the mountain above the monastery.

"Tu es vraie, pure, parfaite," says Renan at the end of his *Prière sur l'Acropole*, "ton marbre n'a point de tache." He idealizes, and so mistakes the character of the goddess and of her stone. Sheer whiteness was indeed a virtue in marble in the fifth and fourth centuries. Pliny says "non fuisse tum auctoritatem maculoso marmori."[3] But of course there were

---

[3] *Natural History* 36.44; hardly translatable; "mottled or variegated marble did not have a high reputation then."

Postscript. The Stones

variations major and minor, in color as in texture, even in Pentelic marble, even in stone from the same quarry, impurities and discolorations, "banding," faults and blemishes. Even so an architect could specify "stones sound, white, unspotted," and expect to have his demands satisfied, within reason, by the contractors from the vast resources of Pentelikon. Marble is not a homogeneous substance—"dead" whiteness could be more fully realized in a stucco imitation. The reddish-brown tinge which *we* nowadays admire so much in Pentelic stone is the result of oxydization of the ferrous content in course of time. One must bear in mind that paint was applied not only to common limestones but also to fine white marble, to pick out in contrast the sculptural and architectural ornamentation; it is difficult to visualize the effect, since only faint traces survive, but one should probably imagine that the texture and quality of the stone was not wholly obliterated.

The inscriptions leave no doubt about the provenance of the material of the great buildings on the Acropolis, and of the Parthenon sculptures. For the temple which dominated the agora, the Hephaisteion, we have no such documentary evidence, but recent sophisticated scientific tests have supplied proof, if proof was needed. Above its lowest step the whole of the main structure was of true Pentelic; but at the highest level some elements—cornice, sima, tiles—were of Parian; and so were the sculptured elements, metopes and frieze. Parian was perhaps still regarded as the sculptor's marble par excellence. For the much more ambitious decorative scheme of the Parthenon it would have been enormously difficult and expensive to import Parian stone; Pentelikon supplied the sculptors' needs, and one hardly thinks of the material it provided as a substitute or "second-best."

The base of the two cult statues in the Hephaisteion was made of slabs of hard blue-black limestone from Eleusis (sometimes inaccurately called marble). For a short period in the fifth century elements in this material were incorporated in marble buildings at Athens for the sake of diversification, emphasis, and contrast. It can be seen in steps and other elements in the Propylaia, and most conspicuously in the background blocks of the frieze of the Erechtheion. From the late fifth century onwards the blue-gray "Hymettian" marble was increasingly used for the same purpose. We have noted an early example in the Stoa of Zeus.

The great Hellenistic buildings continue to show this combination; Hymettian is by now established as an important building material. The steps of the Hellenistic Metroon were Hymettian, but the columns and

(275)

the rest of the front of the building were Pentelic; behind this facade, Hymettian was used for the toichobate (base) of the front wall of the rooms, and for the stylobate of the courtyard and the columns which stood on it. A similar combination of materials was used on a vast scale in the Stoa of Attalos. The steps were of Hymettian marble, the rest of the facade of Pentelic; in the rear part of the building though, as we have seen, poros was the principal material, Hymettian marble was used for certain elements such as door jambs and orthostates.

When the builders had all they needed, including blocks of several tons, plenty of smaller stuff was left over for innumerable minor monuments in great profusion and variety. In the agora one finds in particular the *horoi* or boundary markers, and the *perirrhanteria* or lustral basins which served the same purpose of demarcation. Of marble altars a nicely representative set is on display on the west side of the agora—the altar of Zeus Phratrios and Athena Phratria, a simple block of Hymettian on a poros base; the cylindrical altar of Pentelic which has been placed on a base in the center of the Tholos, though it might just as well have belonged to the Bouleuterion; and the much larger and more elaborate structure in Pentelic which may have been the altar of Zeus Agoraios. As curiosities one may note the two half-egg-shaped bits of Hymettian marble in front of the temple of Apollo Patroos, probably *omphaloi* of Delphic type; and the upright Pentelic slabs on the south side of the square which clearly served as standards for the size and shape of large roof tiles. Above all, stelai inscribed with all kinds of official documents stood in appropriate places in their hundreds. These were mostly of white Pentelic marble, on which the lettering would show to best advantage; but Hymettian too was sometimes used.

In Hellenistic and Roman times increasing use was made of marble slabs for the revetment of poros walls, and for the floors and the pavement of open areas. Hymettian was favored for this purpose, but both types were used. In general, in the Roman period marble was used more freely for the embellishment of buildings other than temples.

In the Athens of Perikles the wealth of Pentelikon had been devoted entirely and directly to the glory of Athena and the other gods. It is in every way appropriate that the marble mountain stands up above the central Attic plain, in full view of the city, like a great temple gable. The very existence of Pentelikon, with Hymettos beside it, had a decisive effect on the form and character of the city of Athens, and on the course of the history of art and civilization.

78. Southeast Slope of Acropolis (Photo: German Archaeological Institute)
This photograph, taken many years ago, shows the substructure of the older temple
of Dionysos in the foreground, built of limestone from the Acropolis and Kara; the
conglomerate backing of the wall of the stoa, originally covered with Hymettian
marble and poros of Peiraeus; the auditorium, with remains of seats of Peiraeus
stone; the cave of Panagia Speliotissa in the Acropolis rock, with choregic monuments
adjacent; the Acropolis wall with post-classical facing and buttresses; the southeast
corner of the Parthenon (Pentelic marble) above. Thus this "quarry of ruins"
nicely illustrates the variety of the stones of Athens.

General Bibliography

Geology

G. R. Lepsius, *Geologie von Attica*, Berlin, 1893

N. Herz, "Geology of the Building Stones of Greece," *Transactions of the New York Academy of Sciences* 17, 1955, 499–505. (An unpublished article by Professor Herz, "Stones of the Athenian Agora," of which I received a copy from the agora authorities, has also been very helpful.)

Building stones

A. K. Orlandos, *Building Materials of the Ancient Greeks* II, Athens 1958 (in Greek)

R. Martin, *Manuel d'architecture grecque* I. Matériaux et Techniques, Paris 1965

E. Caley and J.F.C. Richards, *Theophrastos on Stones*, Columbus (Ohio) 1956

R. E. Wycherley, "The Stones of Athens," *Greece and Rome* 2d series 21, 1974, 54–67 (the Postscript is a shortened version of this)

Athenian stones

G. R. Lepsius, "Marmorstudien," 114–23 (see below)
Judeich 1–4
J. Travlos *PEA* 13–16

Marble

G. R. Lepsius, "Griechische Marmorstudien" *Abhandlungen der Königlichen Akademie der Wissenschaften zu Berlin* 1890, Berlin, 1891

N. Herz and W. K. Pritchett, "Marble in Attic Epigraphy," *AJA* 57, 1953, 71–83

C. Renfrew and J. Springer, "Aegean Marble: a Petrological Study," *BSA* 63, 1968, 47–64

B. Ashmole, "Aegean Marble: Science and Common Sense," *BSA* 65, 1970, 1–2

H. and V. Craig, "Greek Marbles, Determination of Provenance by Isotopic Analysis," *Science* 176 (28.4.1972) 401–3

R. E. Wycherley, "Pentelethen," *BSA* 68, 1973, 349–53

Poros

Frazer on Pausanias 5.10.2

General Bibliography

H. S. Washington, *AJA* 27, 1923, 445–46

R. E. Wycherley, "Poros: Notes on Greek Building Stones," in *Phoros, Tribute to Benjamin Dean Meritt*, New York 1974

General Works on the Monuments and Topography

Curt Wachsmuth, *Die Stadt Athen im Altertum*, I Leipzig 1874; II Leipzig 1890

U. von Wilamowitz Moellendorf, *Aus Kydathen*, Berlin 1880

Jane Harrison, *Mythology and Monuments of Ancient Athens*, London 1890

E. Curtius, *Die Stadtgeschichte von Athen*, Berlin 1891 (with ancient texts edited by A. Milchoeffer, now re-edited by A. L. Oikonomides, Ares Press Chicago; see p. 140)

J. G. Frazer, Pausanias' *Description of Greece*, London 1898

Ernest Gardner, *Ancient Athens*, London 1902

W. Judeich, *Topographie von Athen*, 2d edn, München 1931

W. Dörpfeld, *Alt-Athen und seine Agora*, Berlin 1937–1939

I. T. Hill, *The Ancient City of Athens*, London 1953

J. Travlos, *Poleodomike Exelixis ton Athenon* (in Greek; *Architectural Development of Athens*), Athens 1960

J. S. Boersma, *Athenian Building Policy from 561/0 to 405/4 B.C.*, Groningen 1970

J. Travlos, *Pictorial Dictionary of Ancient Athens*, New York 1971; German version also published, Tübingen 1971

J. Travlos, M. Petropoulakou, P. Pentazos, *Ancient Greek Cities* 17: *Athens* (in Greek), Athens Center of Ekistics, 1972

J. Travlos, "Athens," in R. Stillwell et al., ed., *The Princeton Encyclopedia of Classical Sites*, Princeton 1976, 106–10

J. J. Coulton, *The Architectural Development of the Greek Stoa*, Oxford 1976

J. J. Coulton, *Greek Architects at Work*, London 1977

ADDENDA TO BIBLIOGRAPHY

Agora (see p. 90 above)

A. Delivorrias, *Attische Giebelskulpturen und Akroteria des Fünften Jahrhunderts*, Tübingen 1974 (Hephaistos and Ares)

U. Kron, *Die Zehn Attische Phylenheroen* (pp. 199f Leokorion), *AthMitt* Beiheft 5, Berlin 1976

Parthenon (see pp. 140f above)

E. Berger, *Die Geburt der Athena im Ostgiebel des Parthenon*, Basel 1974

E. Berger et al., "Parthenon-Studien, Erster Zwischenbericht," *Antike Kunst* 19, 1976

Theaters (see p. 218 above)

C. W. Dearden, *The Stage of Aristophanes*, London 1976

Index

If a Greek term is defined in the text, the page on which the definition appears is italicized in the index.

Index

Bendis, 265

Blaute, 179

Bluebeard, 145

Boreas, 169, 171, 199

Boukoleion, 45

Boule, four hundred, *28*; five hundred, 20, 33, 48, 51, 52, 168, 215; at Peiraeus, 264

Bouleuterion, old, *28*, 30, 33, 36, 50f, 52, 54, 82, 92, 204, 269; new, 50ff, 204; at Peiraeus, 264

boundary stones, of agora, 33, 35, 62, 91, 237, 276; of fountain, 181; of garden of Muses, 228; of Hekademeia, 224; of Kerameikos, 255, 256; of Kodros, 168; of *lesche*, 194; of Nymphe, 197, 198; of Palladion, 168; at Peiraeus, 263; of pool of Athena, 21; of sacred way, 256; of triangular shrine, 192, 193; of Tritopatreis, 259; of Zeus on Hill of Nymphs, 188; of Zeus Olympios, 159; of Zeus Xenios, 194

Boutes, 150

bricks, unbaked, 9, 11, 14, 19, 20, 21, 28, 44, 48, 58, 197, 224, 238, 255, 267f; baked, 259, 268

bronze casting pits, 30, 70, 180

bronze workers, 50, 69, 92, 97, 238

Bryaxis, 38

building accounts, Parthenon, 113; Erechtheion, 146f, 149; walls, 19ff

Building F, 28, 30, 33

burials, on way to Academy, 3, 219, 222, 256ff; on road to Acharnai, 254; in agora area, 27, 62, 193; west of Areopagus, 194, 237, 253; in Hephaisteion, 71; southeast of Kolonos Agoraios, 253; east of city, 254; west of city, 258; within walls, 253. *See also* Kerameikos, Mycenean Athens

Byron, 71

Byzantine Athens, 24, 90, 143

Caesar, C., adopted son of Augustus, 85

Caesar, C. Julius, 102

Carrey, Jacques, 115, 121, 122

Caryatids, 118, 143, 145ff, 152

cavalry, 36, 38, 43, 46, 118, 204, 228f, 260

caves, 176, 178; of Aglauros, 152, 176f; of Apollo, 177; of Asklepieion, 182; of Pan, 177; above theater, 184

cemeteries, *see* burials

Centaurs, 69, 70, 115, 124

cesspools, 237, 240, 251

Chabrias, 75, 257

Chaironeia, 19

chalkotheke, *134*

chariot group, 63, 135

Charites, 73, 131f

Charon, pipe-maker, 248

choregic monuments, 4, 169, 184, 230

chryselephantine work, 112, 113, 114, 123f, 162, 170, 184, 210

Chrysippos, 231, 233, 257

churches, 24, 71, 88, 126, 171, 180, 185, 188, 222, 224, 229, 232, 256

Cicero, walks to Academy, 3, 221, 233, 234; burial of Marcellus, 253; on statue of Vulcan, 70

cisterns, 40, 127, 150, 177, 180, 197, 248

civic offices, 89

concrete, 89, 238

Corinth, 100

Corinthian order, 146, 155, 160, 161, 164, 184

corn distribution, 73

Cossutius, 160

Council, *see* Boule

Cyclopean masonry, 9, 269

Cynics, 41, 44, 230

Cyriacus of Ancona, 24, 164

Daidalos, 150

Deceleans, 97

deisidaimonia, 175, 200

Delphi, 225

Delphinion, 167

Dema wall, 16, 246

Index

Euripides, on peace, 75; Aphrodite for Hippolytos, 180; *Ion*, 177
Eurykleides, 21
Eurysakes, 97
Euthydemos, 92
euthynteria, 59, 67, 272
exedrae, 222, 227, 232, 234

field stones, 268, 269, 273
foreign cults, 185, 265
fountain houses, northeast of agora, 89; southeast of agora, 32, 44, 47, 89, 248; southwest of agora, 250; southwest of Areopagus, 196; at Dipylon, 19; in public buildings, 250. *See also* Nymphaeum
Frankish period, 24, 143
friezes, temple of Ares, 84; temple of Athena Nike, 40, 130; Erechtheion, 147, 148, 275; Hephaisteion, 70, 74, 275; temple near Ilissos, 171; Parthenon, 108, 114, 117, 123, 129, 130, 146, 148, 206; on tomb, 258

gardens, Aphrodite in, 172, 176; of Epicurus, 231, 234; of Hephaistos, 71; of Plato, 220, 221, 234; of Theophrastos (Muses), 227f
gates, 9, 10, 12, 17ff, 23, 95, 229, 252, 253, 254, 258; made of column drums, 17, 157; postern, 9, 17, 96, 176
 Acharnian, 12, 254; Beulé, 184; Diomeian, 17, 96; Diochares, 17, 226, 228, 229, 254; Eriai, 17, 257; Hippades, 17; Itonian, 17; to Peiraeus, 12, 17, 189, 238, 240, 252, 256; at Peiraeus, 262; Sacred, 12, 14, 17, 18, 72, 89, 255, 256; to sea, 17. *See also* Dipylon
Gauls, 137
Ge, Karpophoros, 136, Kourotrophos, 131, 179; Olympia, 165; on Areopagus, 179; at Phlya, 261
geometric period, 8, 166, 193, 224, 253, 254, 255

giants, 3, 115, 117, 124, 145, 216
gold, earrings, 193; lamp, 146, 150. *See also* chryselephantine work
Graces, *see* Charites
gymnasia, 5, 88, 160, 219, 264; of Hadrian, 229; of Ptolemy, 3, 5, 231ff; late, 216, 235; at Delphi, 225. *See also* Academy, Kynosarges, Lyceum

Hadji Ali Khasseki, 25, 171
Hadrian, 3, 23, 86, 102, 155, 167; arch, 10, 155, 162; eponymos, 53; gymnasium, 229; library, 4, 23, 86f, 162; at Olympieion, 155, 157, 159, 162f; statue, 43, 53; water supply, 89, 250, 251
Harmodios, 10, 73ff, 257
healing shrines, 133, 181, 265
Hegeso, 260
Hekate, 49, 131, 132, 186, 258, 259
Hekatompedon, 145
Heliaia, 35, 53, 54, 59, 80, 91, 250, 272
Helikon, 170
Helios, 121
Hephaisteion, 3, 37, 68ff, 73, 74, 84, 92, 97, 206, 272, 275; architect, 69, 84; called "Theseion," 68, 97
Hephaistos, at Academy, 219; in Erechtheion, 150; in Parthenon pediment, 121; garden of, 71; statute, 70; treasurers, 114
Hera, 167, 200
Herakleidai, 65
Herakleides Kretikos, 160, 245
Herakles, at Academy, 219; at Acharnai, 261; on Acropolis, 136; in Acropolis pediment, 145; Alexikakos, 187, 195; on Hephaisteion, 69; at Kynosarges, 172, 229f; in Olympia metopes, 139; Pankrates, 169f; on enclosure of Twelve Gods, 65
Herm-carvers, 91, 97
Hermes, 65, 131, 170, 178, 225; at Academy, 219; on Areopagus, 179; at Dipylon, 18; in Erechtheion, 150; in gymnasia, 221; Propylaios, 131

Index

Kleisthenes, 33, 36, 52, 257
Klepsydra, spring, 177; water clock, 54
kleroteria, 54ff, 91
Kodros, 168, 204
Kollytos, 149, 188
Kolonos, Agoraios, 27, 28, 40, 68f, 92, 253; Hippios, 17, 215, 220f, 234, 257, 258
Konon, 43, 74, 136, 257, 262, 263, 265. *See also* walls
korai, 139, *144*, 147, 152, 169
Kore, *see* Demeter
Krates, 41
Kreousa, 177, 199
Kritias, 51
Kritios, 74
Kriton, 225
Kronos, 165, 168, 171
Kydathenaion, 187
kykloi, 95, 102
Kylon, 143
Kynosarges, 172, 219, 226, 229
kyrbeis, 31

Lacedaemonians, 11, 19, 40, 43; tomb, 257
lamp, golden, 146, 150
latrines, 251
Laurion, 114, 262
law courts, 53ff, 80f, 97, 210; northeast of agora, 56ff, 60, 80, 101; southwest of agora, 35, 44, 250, 272; Delphinion, 167; near market, 91, 93; New, 60; in Odeion, 54, 60; in Palladion, 168; Parabyston, 60; in south square, 80f; in Stoa Poikile, 41, 60; in stoas, 59; Trigonon, 60; by walls, 60. *See also* Areopagus, Heliaia
lead, curse tablet, 238; pipes, 250; weights, 50; mined at Laurion, 268
Leagros, 33, 75
Lenaion, 205
Leochares, 67, 137
Leokorion, 10, 63f, 98
lesche, 41, 44, 194, 251, 252
leukomata, 52

Libanios, 235
Liberation, War of, 3, 25
libraries, 88; at Academy, 224; of Hadrian, 4, 23, 86f, 162; at Lyceum, 227; of Pantainos, 88, 100; at Pergamon, 82, 88, 227; in Ptolemaion, 233, 234
lions, 51, 258
Lokros, 85
loutrophoros, 200, 259
Lucian, on Athena Lemnia, 124, 138, 139; on Poikile, 41
Lyceum, 204, 219, 222, 226ff, 230, 231, 233
Lycurgus, 3, 58, 77, 182, 257; on oath of Plataia, 106; Lyceum, 219, 226; stadium, 215; theater, 210, 211, 213
Lykabettos, 89, 229
Lykon, 227
Lysikrates, 4, 169, 184, 230
Lysippos, 73
Lyson, 51

magistrates' offices, 45f, 92, 101; at Peiraeus, 264
Mantinea, battle, 43
Marathon, 106; painting, 40f, 118
marble, 273ff
marble workers, 97, 238
Marcellus, M., 253
Mardonios, 150
market, 80, 91ff; buildings, 93, 99, 100. *See also* agora, Roman; *skenai*
Marsyas, 136
masons' marks, 84, 86
Medea, 65, 167
Melite, 98, 149, 178, 187ff
Menon, 241, 248
metopes, Hephaisteion, 69, 275; Olympia, temple of Zeus, 139; Parthenon, 108, 114, 115, 123; Middle Stoa, 272; Stoa of Zeus, 43
metronomoi, *45*
Metroon, 35, 51ff, 269; Hellenistic, 52, 53, 66, 82, 273, 275f; in Agra, 165, 171

(287)

Index

Pandrosos, 150, 152

Panhellenion, 167

Pankrates, 169f

Pantainos, 88

Pantheon, 88

Parabyston, 60

Parian marble, 69, 73, 274, 275

Parnes, 16, 25, 89, 246, 261

Parthenon, 4, 69, 105ff, 127, 130, 133, 134, 136, 139, 143, 146, 148, 160, 200, 272, 275; name, 110 earlier, 105f, 111, 144, 145, 270; Kimonian, 140; church, 126; explosion, 121, 126. *See also* frieze, metopes, pediments

pastas, 240

Patrokles, 128

Paul, Saint, 41, 175, 180

Pausanias, 90; on Athena Lemnia, 124, 138, 139; on Athenian piety, 175; on demes, 261; on Eleos, 66; on Erechtheion, 150f; on Hadrian, 167; on law courts, 167; on segregation of shrines, 200; on tombs of great men, 257

peace, of Kallias, 106, 140; King's, 75; of Nikias, 146

pediments, early, on Acropolis, 144, 145, 271; temple of Athena, gigantomachy, 145; temple of Athena Nike, 129; Hephaisteion, 69; *naiskos*, 194; stelai, 77; Parthenon, 108, 115, 119, 123, 136, 172; temple of Zeus at Olympia, 122, 123

Peiraeus, 12, 16, 40, 49, 100, 124, 139, 181, 244, 246, 256, 258ff, 262ff, 270ff; arsenal, 114; wall, 11, 15, 19, 20, 21, 23, 262f

Peirithoos, 65

Peisianax, 38

Peisias, 51

Peisistratids, 144, 145, 156, 270. *See also* Olympieion

Peisistratos, 3, 11, 36, 64, 219; water supply, 32, 248

Peisistratos, younger, 33, 167

Pelargikon, Pelasgikon, 7, 8, 177, 181, 183, 253, 269

Pentelikon, 25, 114, 261, 267, 269, 274ff

Pergamon, 78, 82, 88, 185

Perikles, 3, 16, 113, 132, 159, 237, 257; building program, 16, 54, 69, 106, 112f, 125, 133, 134, 140, 210, 211, 213, 215, 219, 276

Peripatetics, 227ff

peripatos, in Academy, 221, 225; round Acropolis, 176, 181, 183, 184, 185, 210; in Lyceum, 227f

perirrhanteria, 62, 276

perischoinisma, 58, 59, 60

peristyle courts, northeast of agora, 58f, 60, 80f, 101; southwest of agora, 80; in Academy, 225; in gymnasia, 225, 229, 232; in houses, 243, 245; in Library of Hadrian, 88; in Library of Pantainos, 88; in Metroon, 82; in Panhellenion, 167; in Pompeion, 72. *See also* agora, Roman

Perseus, 136

Persians, 7, 8, 19, 33, 38, 73, 75, 113, 117, 129, 150, 206, 215; war and sack, 11, 36, 42, 48, 54, 64, 69, 100, 105, 106, 108, 126, 135, 138, 139, 144, 145, 159, 177, 206, 240, 270

Phaidra, 180

Phaidros, Epicurean, 72, 234

Phaleron, 165, 215, 230, 262; road to, 17; wall, 16

Pheidias, 51, 70, 73, 75, 108, 112f, 115, 117, 119, 123, 126, 135, 137, 138f, 180, 237; minister of works, 112

Pherrephattion, 98

Philip of Macedon, 19, 99

Philokles, 146

Philon, 114, 265, 271

Philopappus, 171, 194

Phlya, 261

Phorbas, 187

Phormio, 136, 257

Phosphoroi, 49

phratriai, 66, 194

Pinakotheke, 127

Index

triangular shrines, south of agora, 62, 192; southwest of Areopagus, 194; in Kerameikos, 258

tripods, 53, 184, 185

Triton, 145

Tritopatreis, Tritopatores, 192, 259

Trojans, 40f, 115

Turkish period, 3f, 24, 71, 90, 103, 126, 164, 203

Tweddell, John, 71

Twelve Gods, altar, 33, 64ff, 75, 205, 250; cult of Eleos, 65ff; painting, 43

Tyche, 43, 170

Tyrannicides, 73ff. *See also* Harmodios

Valerian, 23

Venetians, 24, 126

violet crown, 175

Vitruvius, on Olympieion, 156, 160; on Parthenon, 112

walls, of city, 3, 4, 7ff, 60, 73, 112, 155, 226, 228, 254, 267, 271, 273; Pelasgic, 7, 8, 9, 134, 144, 269; archaic, pre-Persian, 9ff; Themistoklean, 7, 9, 10, 11ff, 15, 17, 19, 21, 23, 24, 25, 157, 254; Kononian, 14, 19, 262; post-Herulian, 23, 77, 86, 232; Rizokastro, 24; of Hadji Ali Khasseki, 25, 171

covered walk, 20; cross-wall, 12, 21; Dema, 16, 246; of Hipparchos, 219, 224; inscriptions, 19ff; Long, 12, 15, 20, 21, 23, 258, 262; wooden, 7. *See also* Peiraeus

water channels, 57, 58, 89, 210, 248f, 250, 251, 272

water clock, 54, 91, 103

water pipes, 19, 32, 66, 197, 248f, 250

water supply, Peisistratid, 32, 196, 248; Hadrianic, 89, 250, 251

Watson, George, 71

weights and measures, 45, 49f

wells, 49, 196, 197, 248, 257, 259

wheel-shaped city, 10

wine trade, 95, 96, 99, 100

Wolfensberger, 3

workshops, 47, 81, 92, 99, 102, 114, 187, 194, 237ff, 258

Xenokrates, 221, 264

Xenophon, on Bouleuterion, 51; on choruses, 64; on market, 94, 100; on stones, 267

Zea, 181, 263, 264

Zeno, 41, 231, 257

Zenodotos, 233

Zeus, on hill of Nymphs, 178, 188; in Parthenon pediment, 121f; on relief, 178, 200

Agoraios, 66, 83, 137; Astrapaios, 18, 167, 177; Boulaios, 51; Eleutherios, 30, 42, 43, 159; Exopsios (?) 188; Herkeios, 18, 152, 245; Hypatos, 150; Hypsistos, 164, 181, 197; Kataibates (thunderbolt), 152, 159, 219; Meilichios, 189, 199, 265; Morios, 219; Olympios at Athens, *see* Olympieion; Olympios at Olympia, 112, 122, 123, 124, 164, 180; at Palladion, 168; Panhellenios, 167; Phratrios, 66, 273, 276; Polieus, 137; Soter, 42, 159, 265; Xenios, 194

Zeuxis, 96